AFRICA AND THE EUROPEAN CHALLENGE

I dedicate this book to Mr. Paul Kofi Kwarteng and his wife Abena Serwaa of Ghana, and my mother, Ama Addei, without whose sweat and toil my education would have been impossible.

Africa and the European Challenge

Survival in a Changing World

CHARLES O. KWARTENG

Avebury

Aldershot • Brookfield USA • Hong Kong • Singapore • Sydney

Published by
Avebury
Ashgate Publishing Limited
Gower House
Croft Road
Aldershot
Hants GU11 3HR
England

Ashgate Publishing Company
Old Post Road
Brookfield
Vermont 05036
USA

British Library Cataloguing in Publication Data

Kwarteng, Charles
Africa and the European challenge : survival in a changing world
1.Africa - Foreign relations - Europe - 1960- 2.Europe - Foreign relations - Africa - 1989-
I. Title
327.6'04

ISBN 1 85972 550 3

Library of Congress Catalog Card Number: 96-086687

Printed in Great Britain by the Ipswich Book Company, Suffolk

Contents

Figures and Tables

Preface

I developed an interest in international affairs early days in my academic career. I have become more interested in international interactions, particularly supra-national integration. I completed my doctoral dissertation on the Economic Community of West African States (ECOWAS).

Many changes that have taken place in the global system, since the fall of the Berlin Wall, have major implications for Africa. Perhaps, the greatest challenge for Africa in the twenty-first century remains how Africa can cope with the disintegration and integration of Europe. I believe that European unity offers both opportunities and challenges for Africa.

At the time that the late President Kwame Nkrumah of Ghana was dreaming about African unity, some of his colleagues went to sleep. Three decades after his death, Nkrumah's dream of African unity has inspired a new generation of African leaders who are desirous of building an African bloc as a counterweight to a world of competing blocs. On the verge of being pushed out of the global political economy, Africa's only viable option for survival is regional integration and collective self-reliance.

In writing about Africa and the European Challenge, I benefitted from the insight of many people. I had the opportunity to interview numerous European diplomats, businessmen and citizens, as well as African officials and intellectuals about their views on European unity. I hope that this study will rekindle Africa's interest in seriously assessing the implications of European unification for Africa, so as to prepare for any shocks.

C. Owusu Kwarteng
Morgan State University

Acknowledgements

The research that resulted in the publication of this book would not have been possible, without the help of some important people. I would like to thank Dr. Richard L. White of Myers Inc., Pittsburgh, and his wife, Dr. Joann White, and Duquesne University, Pittsburgh, for their support in making my trip to the European Union in Brussels possible.

My sincere thanks also go to Dr. Rudolphe Gachot, formerly of the European Commission, for his assistance concerning this research. While at the Commission, Dr. Francisco Battaller was very sincere, helpful, and inspiring to me. I also acknowledge the accommodation that I was offered by Mr. Guillermo Parodi of Dupont Co. in Brussels. This kind gesture made my stay in Brussels to be enjoyable.

Morgan State University provided the institutional base that helped this academic exercise. Dr Burney J. Hollis, the Dean of the College of Arts and Sciences, inspired my work, when I came to Morgan. Professor Michael Kamara of Morgan State University, also deserves special thanks for sharing with me his intellectual insights. All my colleagues and students are remembered.

Other friends and well-wishers encouraged me to write, and to complete this book. I thank Raquel, Lora, Alhaji Buhari, Dr. Misawa, Dr. Okezie, Tim, Bob Peprah, Dr. Etuk, and my reliable and cherished family friends, the Adebimpes. Also, I extend thanks to the editorial staff at Avebury for their support. Finally, thanks to my family who helped me to overcome all challenges.

1 The crossroad of change: Introduction

After several centuries of political, economic and cultural ties, Africa and Europe stand at an important historic juncture. While Europe has united its economies and is poised to become the largest trading bloc in the world, Africa is slipping backwards, and is on the brink of being "pushed-out" of the global economy. Consequently, it is time to reappraise the relationship between Europe and Africa.

The year 1992 will remain as a dramatic one in the history of Europe. It is closely connected with the efforts at European unification. Some people refer to this process of integration as a movement toward a "Super Europe", and others call it "the United States of Europe". A more ominous epithet might be the "Fortress Europe". By the end of 1992, Western Europe was expected to remove the various barriers to intra-Community trade and investment, as a prelude to an unified Europe. The "1992" program has generated thousands of articles, seminars reports, studies and memoranda. It has also given rise to a new breed of lawyers, consultants, and lobbyists.

Attempts at European integration date back to the early 1950s. In 1957, the Treaty of Rome established the European Economic Community (EEC) that was designed to promote regional cooperation among the original six members.[1] In the 1980s, following suggestions by business people and European politicians, Western Europe began to rethink its policy of integration. In December 1991, following the boost in morale generated by the "1992" Single Market initiative, the EU nations agreed to expand the scope of integration to include a single monetary policy, a single currency, and more integrated policies in environment, immigration, and foreign relations. Furthermore, the twelve members of the European Community (EC) expanded its political horizon, with the signing of Association Agreements with Poland, Hungary, and Czechoslovakia. It was expected that by the mid-1990s, most of the member countries of the European Free Trade Association (EFTA) would have become members of the European Community.

A greater part of the literature dealing with the European Single Market [the "1992"process] has focused largely on the EU itself, and has virtually ignored its external ramifications. The European Single Market program has unfolded a number of economic, social, legal, and political issues in the relationship between the EU and developing countries. The year "1992" connotes both hopes and fears.[2]

Even though the single market was designed as an "internal" deregulation process - with the idea of achieving the original objectives enshrined in the Treaty of Rome (1957) - there has been an increasing concern among developing countries in general, and Africa in particular, that an advance towards European integration means new protectionism. [3]

A detailed and analytical research on the external repercussions of the Single Market must take a closer look at some of the mechanisms that have been deployed to achieve European unification. Such a task is difficult, because all the measures concerned have not yet been implemented.

Europe's global preeminence

The EU includes four of the current G-7 members (France, Germany, Italy and UK), and some of the world's most competitive industries such as Philips, Siemens and Acaltel. France and UK are among the five declared nuclear powers in the world. Largely as a result of the Western Alliance's military strategy towards the former Soviet Union, a large proportion of the world's conventional armaments are located in Western Europe.

EU's global influence is second only to that of the US. The Community has links with nations at every nook and corner of the world. The large size and importance of the EU market translates into a bigger role for the EU in the setting of global commercial standards and regulations.

Despite the international pressure, today's gloomy economic outlook, and recessionary situation, the EU has by all measures (economic, political and social) made enormous strides, particularly compared to its predicament when Jacques Delors, EU's President, first addressed the European Parliament in 1985 about EU integration program. As the EU has noted, the EU "is now a magnet for the newly democratic countries of Central and Eastern Europe who seek a new identity as part of the Community. Brussels has replaced Moscow as the center of their world".[4]

The EU is the world's largest trading partner, and has become a vital partner for developing nations. The developing world would have to improve their negotiation leverage in dealing with the European bloc.

The challenges that the EU pose for Africa's future have not escaped the attention of African leaders, policy-makers, and analysts. Speaking at an international conference in Brussels in 1989, the former President of Nigeria, Olesegun Obasango, reiterated the common concerns that African leaders and policy makers share: that European integration could spell disaster for the continent of Africa. This sentiment has consistently been echoed in speeches delivered at local and international fora by many African scholars and policy makers.

The "African stake" in European unity is high. More than half of sub-Saharan Africa's trade is with Europe-the main destination for 70 percent of West Africa's principal export of cacao, timber, cotton, coffee, groundnuts, gold and diamonds. In 1987, France, Germany, Italy, UK, Belgium, Netherlands, Spain and Portugal accounted for 70 percent of the import-export trade with Africa. Japan and the US took 20 percent, while other nations took 10 percent. Apart from trade and commerce, the significance of Europe unification for Africa appears in the domain of foreign aid: For the year 1987, the EU was the largest source of foreign aid for all but two of the 16 members of the Economic Community of West African States (ECOWAS).[5]

The European Commission in Brussels has tried to assuage the fears that African leaders harbor, by offering a "political guarantee" that the "aims [of 1992] must not be achieved at the expense of third countries".[6] Africa's anxieties about European unity are by no means groundless because:

> In preparing to move towards a single market the European Community now looms as a superpower of staggering economic productivity, its 320 million people capable of producing an overall gross European product of $4.1 trillion, 140% greater than Japan's and only slightly less than America's in 1987. With the added growth and productivity provided by the new markets of Eastern Europe, the European Community's economic weight may soon carry it to the top of the world table.[7]

The European Commission has stated that "1992" will not usher in a "fortress Europe". The Commission's assurance that Europe beyond 1992 will be a "Partnership Europe" is a tactical rebuff of the "fortress Europe" notion that has come to be associated with the EU. The Commission's position is buttressed by its argument that as the foremost trading bloc in the world, the EU has a fundamental stake in a "free and open" international trading system. Accordingly, the Commission has noted that the development of the EU's external trading policy in the run-up of 1992, will be in harmony with the objectives of GATT, and bilateral relations such as the Lome Conventions. Second, the Single Market will benefit both EU and non-EU members because, it would boost the EU's economy, a boost that would allegedly have favorable repercussions on the outside world.

It is quite ironic that African nations have shown little collective alertness to the challenges that EU integration entails. It is equally true that the EU has yet to take any major initiative to address the fundamental issues that underlay Africa's concerns and vulnerability.

As much as Africa and the developing world need the European market, the EU also cannot afford to completely turn away from the South. The EU relies on developing countries as the largest source of its imports - in 1987 one-third of them ($450 billion) came from developing nations, while European imports from the US amounted to $66 billion and those from Japan $42 billion.[8]

The historical origins of "1992"

The origins of the European Single Market can be traced back as far as the signing of the Treaty of Rome (1957), although the impetus for the current efforts at unification was born in the early 1980s.

On May 9, 1950, Robert Schuman, then the French Foreign Minister, proposed to pool European Coal and Steel industry as a first step in the direction of unity-a goal that the use of force even could not achieve in the past. The Six original member countries signed the European Coal and Steel Community Treaty of April 18, 1951. Six years later, the "Six" further signed the European Atomic Energy Community (EURATOM) and the European Economic Community (EEC) in Rome. The EEC Treaty rests on a vision that is determined to lay the foundation of an ever closer union among the peoples of Europe.

In 1973, the first *enlargement* brought Denmark, Ireland, and the United Kingdom into the EEC. In 1981, Greece was included. The last major enlargement in the 1980s was that of 1986, when Spain and Portugal were admitted into the EU. The latest enlargement occurred when Austria, Finland and Sweden were admitted as full members of the EU in 1995.

In 1985, Lord Cockfield, then the EU Commissioner for the Internal Market issued the EU White Paper - "Completing the Internal Market" (1985). The White Paper set forth the necessary program to identify existing physical, fiscal and technical barriers that pose as a barrier to complete European unification.

The resolve to remove these barriers was strengthened by the Single European Act (SEA). Signed in February 1986, the Single European Act was ratified by each EU member states and entered into force on July 1, 1987. Before this Act was promulgated, each decision at the Community level required unanimity. Now, as a result of the SEA, only qualified majority will be required. Decisions on taxation and other sensitive issues, such as foreign policy still require unanimity, though. There are some political dimensions of the Single Act. The Act cemented the political linkages among the EU countries, and pushed the EU further on the rung of the ladder of integration. Article 8A of the Act states that the EU shall adopt measures with the aim of progressively establishing the internal market over a period expiring on 31 December 1992.

In 1988, the Commission issued the Cecchini Report that analyzed the costs to European consumers of the various barriers to intra-EU trade and relations (what some people mockingly called the costs of "non-Europe").

The Single Market program consists of over 279 pieces of legislation aimed at facilitating the movement of goods, services, people, and capital among the then 12 member countries of the EU. The program is expected to give the European economy a major boost—in terms of gains in GDP growth, less inflation, and the creation of a unified market of over 340 million consumers.

Few illustrations about the potential impact of the Single Market can be made here. Trucks carrying goods across Western Europe no longer have to go through cumbersome administrative routines at the borders. The UK electronic giant, Phillips, for example, could produce just one or two television models for all EU countries. In the past, Phillips had to turn out different models at its plants to conform to different national standards in Europe. The advantages for the business community is tremendous. The doctrine of the "right of establishment" means that a Portuguese company, for example, can expand into France without much problem.

The EU "1992" process is a strategic initiative, in the sense that it addresses the basic weaknesses of the EU that existed in the late 1970s and early 1980s: slow growth, high inflation, high unemployment, and decline in high-tech.

Even though the unification program purports to be an "internal deregulation" exercise, it raises serious implications for Africa. EU leaders have speculated that European unity would improve the world economy - a process that could indirectly improve the African economy, too. [9] At the same time, European unity would mean intense competition for Africa. Frances Wurtz, the EEC-ACP Rapporteur on the EU Single market, captured the feelings of Africa:

> The feeling that they [Africa] cannot cope with a further structural shock or further upset is unanimous, and so they are very worried about the idea of the upheavals atten-

dant on the completion of the Internal Market. The liberalization of international trade is exactly the source of disequilibrium that they fear so much. They are particularly worried about disequilibrium in three fields-in trade relations, of course in finance, monetary affairs, divestment and in human relations.[10]

In addition to the economic challenge of European unity, the political implications for Africa are real. The EU has noted that:

> The time when Europe was divided into three distinct regions-the Community, EFTA and COMECON-is now changing. The map [of Europe] is being redrawn with the Community firmly at the heart of the new Europe. This Europe is set to emerge as a new force in the balance of world power.[11]

As Europe prepares its political unification, African nations remain apprehensive about the global orientation of EU's foreign policy. The EU has used its core power, at times, against the weak developing nations. For example, the EU supported the British position (against Argentina's) on the Falkland Island crisis, in exchange for the softening of UK's criticism of EU's Common Agricultural Policy (CAP).[12]

Changing relations

The Macmillian winds of change that blew across the African continent in the period of 1950s and 1960s did not erode all the vestiges of Europe's imperial ambitions. After granting political independence to Africa, European powers would still maintain economic and political ties with their former colonies. The signing of the Yaounde Conventions (in 1964 and 1969)-between France and former Francophone countries - further institutionalized Euro-African relations in the post-independence era. The Convention provided an "associate" status for the former French colonies. Then in 1975, few years after Britain's admission into the EEC, a broader framework for Euro-African cooperation emerged under the aegis of the Lome Convention.[13] Map 1.1 shows the area covered by Lome Convention.

Map 1.1 **Countries belonging to the ACP (Lome) Convention**

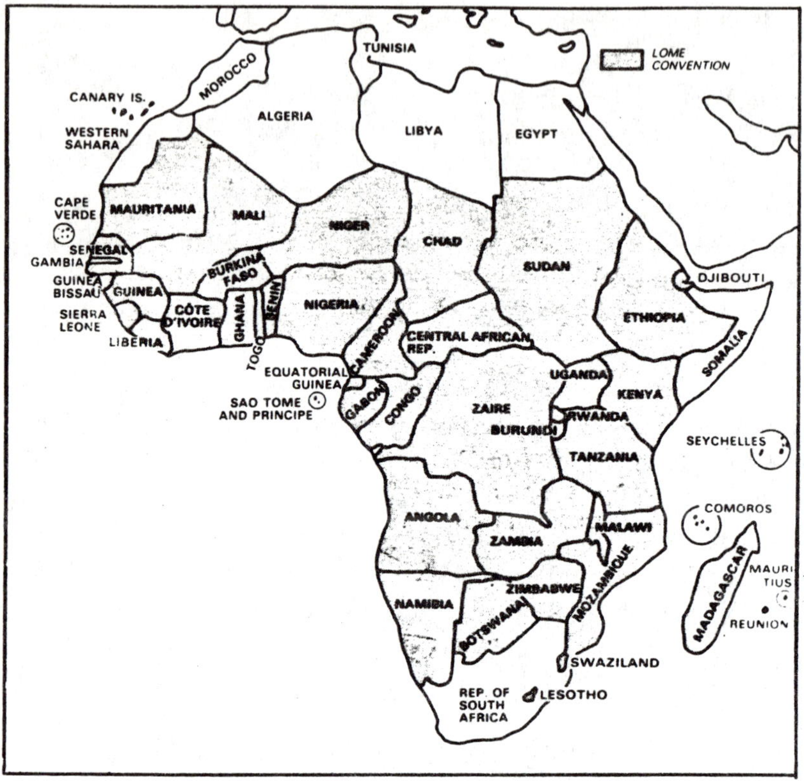

One of the casualties of European unification (the "1992" process) is the historic Euro-African linkages that Metropolitan Europe forged with Africa centuries ago. Since the different colonial ties differ in terms of intensity, it is realistic to expect that European unification would have varied impact on different colonial relations (such as Lusophone vs Francophone Africa).

As an EU member, France has relatively been very much interested in development issues, particularly when they pertain to France's former colonies. Before 1973 (when Britain officially became a member of the EEC), France's influence was greater in the EU's Directorate General for Development-the department at the EU Commission in Brussels that oversees development aid to former European colonies in Africa, the Caribbean and the Pacific[14]

Future enlargement of the EU and the possibility that Eastern European nations might be admitted into the EU in the near future, rekindles the fears about power imbalances in Euro-African relations. That there is an inherent asymmetries in Euro-African relations is evidenced by the fact that as a result of the Lome Convention, 70 peripheral countries in Africa, the Caribbean, and the Pacific bargain with the World's industrial, core nations, albeit, from a position of weakness.

There is an old adage that says that "in unity lies strength". However, the case of Africa's association with the EU 12 symbolizes a major paradox-the "paradox of numbers without strength". In dealing with Africa or the developing world, the EU is advantaged by its relative cohesiveness. This is not to say that there exist no dissensions among EU countries regarding how to deal with third parties.

African nations calculate "the European challenge" in political, military, economic and cultural terms. The completion of the European Economic Area (EEA) - encompassing the 15 members of the European Union and member of EFTA - would further enlarge the European bloc. The reunification of Germany has strengthened Europe. This was capped by the signing of the Maastricht Treaty in 1991.[15] This historic treaty has given the EU a guided optimism at the end of the Cold War.

The relations between the EU and US (and to extent Japan) shows a new trend of Euro-confidence. If the emerging European power is a source of concern for Washington and Tokyo, then it should be more so for Africa.

Another major source of concern that African nations harbor about European unification is the issue of consultation. EU partners, including the US, have often complained about being denied access to major EU decision-making fora, including the controversial exercise of technical harmonization. African countries are rarely consulted on the major issues related to the EU. Should the EU have to consult its partners? An official of the EU informed this author that the US, for example, never informed the EU about the Omnibus Trade Act (1988) - a retaliatory tool wielded by the US President to compel foreign nations to preserve American trade interests.

Before the bell of European unity started ringing, African nations had already sounded an alarm about the erosion of Africa's share of the European market, despite the historic preferences they enjoy. About 95 percent of products that African nations export to the EU are duty-free. Euro-African ideology - that provided a legitimization for closer Europe's ties with African - is losing its symbolism.[16] European politicians and bureaucrats are now looking inward-toward Europe. Even in France, politicians have slowly abandoned *Gaullist* politics that largely influenced Paris' paternalistic attitude towards their former African colonies. Economic recession at home has created a sense of apathy about French grandeur over the Atlantic.

In Africa, too, staunch supporters of closer ties with Europe have left the political scene. The death of President Houphouet-Boigny of the Cote d'Ivoire in 1993 marked a new chapter in Euro-African relations. The end of the Cold War has meant that Europe has redefined its strategic interest, and Africa has lost a greater part of this interest. In order to be able to court Europe, Africa will have to pass the new "test of friendship". No longer is Africa needed as a pawn in East-West confrontation, thanks to the demise of Communism. This change in the strategic relationship has resulted in the dwindling of the support base of traditional Western allies, including Mobutu Sese Sekou of Zaire.

Reactions from Africa

Africa has not remained totally passive to events occurring in Europe and other parts of the world. From North to South, and from East to West, African leaders have proposed solutions to address the "European challenge". Theorists and advocates of Pan-Africanism maintain that an answer to Africa's *marginalization* lies in African regional integration. Despite the awareness of the limitations of small markets and efforts to restructure inter-African economic and political relations, the continent has still not been able to overcome the colonial legacy of *balkanisation*.[17]

During a workshop that was convened on the theme of African Economic Community in Abidjan, in June 1992, Ismail Serageldin, the Director of the African Technical Department of the World Bank, noted that even though over 200 regional organizations have been established to deal with fragmentation, African economies still operate behind arbitrary borders, unnecessary bureaucratic structures, and frustrating tariff systems (see Chapter 8).

European unification, alongside the newly liberalizing trends in the global political economy, has ignited fundamental changes in the world economy. This trend has compelled closed-economy countries (e.g. China and the former Soviet Union)[18] to open up to the world market, or risk isolation. Consequently, this global phenomenon has brought democratic ideas into the political life of many countries.

Africa's major challenge in the face of European unification efforts and the proliferation of other economic blocs-is to build an Africa's alternative market: an African common market. Despite the limited progress in Africa's efforts at regional integration, optimists agree that Africa will still be able to realize its dream of unity. After all, it took Europe half of a century to get to where they are now in regional unification. Ironically, both Europe's own failures and achievements provide hope and encouragement for African integration strategists. The rejuvenation of integration activities in Europe has already served as a catalyst to rekindle Africa's "lost dream" of unity.

By the year 2000, the EU would be more cohesive, and will possess a greater sense of identity than what prevails at the moment. The EU Single Market has the potential to touch on nearly every aspect of Europe's relations with Africa. These include, but are not limited, to: (1) stringent immigration controls; (2) reduced flows of private capital to Africa (as opportunities created by internal liberalization in the EU divert investments from Africa), and (3) lower levels of EU aid to Africa (as the costs of adjustment in the EU increase the demand for social and structural funds in the EU).

The fear that Europe will be a fortress has not only been entertained by African observers, but some EU officials themselves. For example, at the European Council Meeting in Dublin in June 1990, the Council adopted a declaration condemning anti-semitism, racism, and xenophobia that have risen in European capitals.[19]

Significance of the research

The purpose of this book is to examine the EU's unification plan, and its implications for African countries. The major focus of the book is on the future of Africa's relations with Europe in the areas of trade, investments, development aid, and human relations. The timing of the book is important. January 1, 1993, marked a dramatic epoch in European unification. Even though Europe cannot be united in a day, the torch of unity has already been lit. Africa and Africans need to start looking at what European unification bodes for them.

The book's importance are numerous. The EU has virtually shied away from discussing the negative external implications of the EU market. The EU's reluctance in emphasizing the external implications of European unification may not be accidental. Any research that is negative in its findings is contrary to the EU's own public relations objectives, and may be considered inimical to the EU's good standing in the developing world.

An understanding of the major ways in which EU unification may affect non-EU nations is important for policy considerations. Both the EU and African nations could plan on how to ameliorate the negative external consequences of EU integration.

The choice of Africa as the focus of analysis is important. Africa lies in the uppermost tier of EU's preferential schemes with the developing world. Unfortunately, the existing literature on the subject of EU integration, and its implications for Africa, is sporadic, parochial, and basically written, without a focus on African perspectives on the major issues. After reading some of these works, this author has attempted to address some of these shortcomings.

The author had the opportunity to interview African and European diplomats, consultants, and experts on EU integration from the period of 1989-90 in Brussels. Using both theoretical and empirical methodology, the author hopes to improve the quality of research on EU integration and implications for Africa.

In writing this book, the author was deeply motivated by his concern about the shortcomings of the existing literature on the subject of Africa and European unification (the "1992" process). The existing works are either too general in terms of their analyses, or too narrow in scope to be able to depict Africa's vulnerability as a result of European unification. For example, chapter five of William Zartman's book, *Europe and Africa: The New Phase* [20] deals with trade implications of "1992", but in the context of the larger ACP bloc. This situation is not improved by Olesegun Obasango's and Hans d'Orville's book, *The Impact of Europe of 1992 on West Africa.*[21] that principally concerns itself with a mere sub-region of Africa.

Africa and the European Challenge contradicts the findings of the existing literature that has normally reflected the neo-classical deification of the international order that is assumed to benefit all its participants. This book draws on an African perspective of European Unity, and highlights on the conflicts and contradictions, inherent in the Euro-Africa international division of labor, that are likely to be accentuated by the forces of European unification.

African perspectives on the single market

There must be caution in assessing the claims made by the EU in the context of "1992". There are several myths perpetuated by EU officials about the external ramifications of the Single Market that need careful analysis. One of the prevailing myths about the Single Market is that employment opportunities would be created for African immigrants in Europe. Consequently, there would be improved prospects for salary remittances which is an important source of income for many African countries. There is a strong counter-argument against this assertion. For example, EU's tightening of immigration policies in the run-up to "1992" has affected the opportunities hitherto available to African immigrants in Europe.

European officials assume that European unity will be beneficial to

Africa, and that Africa's "Road to Damascus" veers around Brussels. On the other hand, African leaders see the continent's future in closer intra-African relations. Ironically, both sides seem to conclude that interdependence is essential, and cooperation unavoidable.

Europe of "1992" was born in a cradle of strategic coincidence. The end of the cold war has complicated Europe's global policy. The island of prosperity in Europe, North America and Eastern Asia are no longer afraid of communism, as much as they are of the new mass migration from (Third World) poverty.

The EU is worried about mass unemployment in an era of European integration. About 10 percent of the labor force in EU have been excluded from the benefits of the Single Market. Despite its potential strength, united Europe is still worried about the competitive threat posed by the low-cost producers in South-East Asia and other developing nations.[22] As a result of internal strains and external threats, Europe will be prone to look inward - a situation that will be detrimental to the outside world.

Market liberalization in Europe poses political challenges for Africa's own unification. In the first place, Africa must remove the last vestiges of neo-colonialism which still hamper free trade on the continent. These include the existence of linguistic cleavages patterned on colonial divisions, transportation difficulties, varying customs and excise duties, and the absence of uniform banking procedures.

As Chapter 2 suggests, Africa must learn from the positive aspects of the European unification experience. Some African leaders have even suggested that ECOWAS establishes a Regional Parliament (based on the EU model) to help harmonize trade policies across the sub-region.

The route to Africa's own unity is not a smooth one. Afro-pessimists argue that Africa cannot replicate the European experience. According to Ernst Haas and Philippe Schmitter, the favorable background factors for integration depends on size-power homogeneity, the rate of transaction among the nations; the extent to which each state has established a pluralistic socio-political structures, and the degree of complementarity among the elites.[23]

In Africa, there are divergent elite values. While some leaders are pro-capitalist, others are socialist-inclined, and to the extent that they are guided by Pan-Africanist thought, it is minimal. Also, disparities in economic power make Africa prone to the syndrome of polarization that often results from integration among unequal partners. Despite the lack of conventional background factors that are deemed as essential for successful integration, Africa and the developing world see regional integration as a viable strategy of economic development.[24]

A theoretical analysis of the effects of economic blocs

Two primary implications of an economic bloc that are important for non-bloc members are the bloc's effect on (I) the relationship between bloc members and countries outside the bloc (the *bloc effect*), and (II) the relationship among non-bloc members (*counter-bloc effect*). In regards to the bloc effect, the formation of a bloc could be a boom for outside parties, if there is a potential for non-bloc members to gain access to bloc benefits (a *pull-in* scenario). On the other hand, the bloc could seal the doom of third parties, because of the potential that they may be deprived of access to bloc benefits and other privileges associated with the bloc's formation (the "push-out" scenario).

(I) **Bloc Effect**

i) *pull-in scenario*

By pull-in scenario, this author refers to the potential that parties outside the economic bloc might benefit from the bloc's formation, either because they would still retain existing ties with the bloc, or may be able to forge new ties with the members of the bloc.

ii) *push-out scenario*

The author sees an alternative scenario, the push-out scenario, which refers to the tendency for third parties to lose existing or potentially useful ties with unifying groups. Normally, both the pull-in and push-out scenarios occur largely from direct and indirect consequences of enlargement, or deepening of the integrating area.

Propagating mechanisms

Country A may benefit, or lose, as a result of a bloc formed by Country B and Country C, because of the presence or absence of some favorable factors. The first set of factors, I would call *proximity factors*. This refers to the closeness of country A to either country B or Country C (or both), prior to the union between B and C. Such factors can be political ties, geographical propinquity, and cultural similarities or heritage that A shares with the union member (s). For Country A, the absence of favorable proximity factors is likely to reinforce the push-out potential of the union.

The second set of factors relate to *intra-bloc politics*, and the ensuing policies that are designed to regulate the behavior among union members *(internal policy)* and between the bloc and non-bloc members *(external policy)*. The policies of the bloc may be pro-third parties (in this case, a Pull-in scenario) or protectionist (push-out scenario). However, the policy of a bloc must not necessarily result in a push-out scenario because it is protectionist. Also, some policies, while "neutral" in content, may be protectionist to some member nations outside the union, or may have a push-out effect.

The third set of factors relate to *third party characteristics* and *capabilities*. The effect of a bloc may not be uniform in the external environment. Some of the most salient characteristics and capabilities that would determine the extent of gain or loss for non-bloc members include the size of third party economy (hence its share in global economic transactions), the level of technological development (hence the party's ability to penetrate protectionist unions, and political leverage. Where a third party has large economy (or controls a greater share of global resources), technological ability, and political clout, it will be able to negotiate access to the bloc, compete with the bloc in the bloc's own turf, and could initiate a "forced entry" through protective bloc walls. This may be possible because of the use of punitive sanctions or indirect methods of circumventing protectionist mechanisms.

In addition to the above factors, the impact of the bloc on non-bloc members may be shaped by some *externalities*. These include pressures from the international community that result in the bloc making concessions towards "openness" to non-union members. Where there is a prevailing liberalizing trade philosophy in the international environment, the bloc is likely to be more open than when the prevailing ideology is mercantilism.

The Cold War served as a factor in shaping the alignment and realignment of trade blocs after World War II. Consequently, the externalities of trade blocs in the Cold War era were premised on the politics of exclusion and/or inclusion based on ideological leanings and political discretion of nations.

In the case of the EU, the EFTA nations have utilized their proximity factors to gain concession for a push-in into the EU. Of course, GATT regulations and other international commitments have combined to result in some amount of openness in the EU bloc. (II)

(II) Counter-bloc effect

Third parties would be compelled to react to an economic bloc, in order to maximize the pull-in potentials, and minimize the possibilities of a push-out, since the former may represents a gain, and the later a loss. Individual nation's perception of the bloc effect may differ. However, a perception of mutual vulnerability would dictate that third countries unite to counteract the power of the bloc (the counter-bloc effect).

The counter-bloc effect would have been *catalytic*, if it speeds up cooperation among third parties, as a counterweight to, or as a mechanism to bargain with, the existing bloc. On the other hand, the effect of a bloc may be *inhibitive*, if it directly or indirectly prevents the formation of counter-blocs, or neutralizes competing blocs.

Hegemonic and non-hegemonic blocs

Based on the two primary effects of economic blocs (bloc effect and counter-bloc effect), two types of economic blocs may be postulated: (a) *Hegemonic* and (b) *non-Hegemonic* blocs (see Fig. 1.1).

Fig. 1.1 Topology of economic blocs

	Hegemonic	Non-Hegemonic
Pull-In Effect	Low	High
Push-Out Effect	High	Low
Counter-Bloc Effect	Inhibitive	Catalytic

A hegemonic bloc is an economic bloc that has the potential to exert dominating influence in the global system. Such a bloc, while elevating its members onto the sofa of world preeminence, also has a negative repercussion on non-members, because it presents non-union members with a potential low pull-in scenario and a high push-out scenario. Worse still, its effect on non-member nations' alignment is inhibitive. In other words, third parties are in a "double jeopardy" of being pushed out of the world system,while their ability to deploy a counter-bloc strategy to bargain with the hegemonic bloc is inhibited by the Hegemonic Bloc. The overall gains accruing to non-bloc members are likely to be greater with a non-hegemonic union, because in the later case, the push-out scenario is low, and that third parties would be able to unite as a counterweight to the union.

For most less developed nations, economic unions among developed countries (such as the EU) have the tendency to be hegemonic and, hence, negative in their implications.

Assumptions and implications

The following propositions are relevant to the discussions raised above:
1) Regional integration blocs are by their nature restrictive and protectionist to third parties.
2) The benefits of an economic bloc will be greater the net pull-in gains over push-out losses.
3) The more bloc members harmonize their internal and external policies, the greater the likelihood of push-out tendencies, because of substitution of relations with outside parties with those within the bloc. In order to increase their bargaining power, union members will have to close their ranks-politically, economically and geographically-hence limiting the possibilities of pull-in.
4) For developing nations that have non-competitive economies and weak bargaining power, unions among developed countries, such as the EU, generally tend to be hegemonic because of the greater likelihood of low pull-in effect, high push-out effect, and negative counter-bloc effect.

In discussing the external implications of European union for African nations, this book goes beyond the conventional analysis of economic unions. Within the conceptual framework outlined above, the book discusses the possibilities for gains and risks associated with the EU Market. This is done within the contexts of Africa's political, economic and social vulnerabilities. External factors are also considered in the discussion. Such externalities include, but are not limited, to the fall of the Soviet bloc, the impact of GATT negotiations (and preferential erosion), and the changing global arena.

Organization of the book

In Chapter 2, attempts are made to discuss European integration and some theoretical and practical implications for Africa. The author is skeptical about the Vinerian concepts of *trade-creation* and *trade-diversion* in the context of European integration. Viner's theory discusses the welfare implications of customs unions. The theoretical issue raised in Africa's case is what benefits will Africa derive from EU unification?

As an alternative to Viner's approach, the alter adopts an approach that is critical of the historic and contemporary bases of Africa's dependency on the EU, and the implications they pose for Africa's present status in the Europe-influenced global arena. At a time that Europe is on the verge of becoming a major actor on the world scene, Africa is declining as a weak partner - a process that European integration will further accentuate.

Beyond trade, Africa stands to benefit from the lessons of EU's experiences. The EU has been able to promote peace among once-warring neighbors. EU's progress, to date, shows that integration is likely to succeed, if propelled by persuasion and economic cooperation, instead of by force. Formed in 1957, the EEC was galvanized by external catalysts. The need to be self-reliant, and also to ward of possible Soviet intervention, resulted in a conscious effort to terminate Europe's economic and political dependency.

Africa's own marginalization in the world economy, and the need to break its undue dependency on external actors, should serve as a stimulus for regional integration in Africa. Chapter 2 also examines the extent to which European integration serves as a catalyst and also as a hindrance to Africa's own integration.

Chapter 3 looks at the external dimensions of the EU. The chapter adopts an alternative framework for looking at the external implications of European integration. It examines the mechanism for liberalizing the EU economies-physical, fiscal, and technical harmonization - and the extent that they will impact on African countries. The author argues that EU's internal mechanism adopted to liberalize the European economy are as detrimental to Africa's interests as are EU's "protective" policies, such as anti-dumping and rules of origin requirements. The implications of liberalization of public procurement is also discussed.

The major anxiety that third countries harbor about EU's unification is the uncertainty about EU's external policies. It is against this background that Chapter 3 discusses the external dimensions of EU's trade policy. At the political level, the EU will be stronger, if the Maastricht provision are fully implemented. This will have implications for EU's relations with Africa.[25]

An analysis of the enlargement of the EU and the ACP, and how they may impact on Africa is done. While these enlargement possibilities may not be associated with the EU "1992" process, their coincidence with "1992" make them critical issues of concern. Enlargement of the EU furthers Europe's hegemonic credentials in the global system. Worse still, the enlargement of the ACP would not significantly enhance Africa's bargaining position in Europe. What "power" did the admission of Haiti and Eritrea bring to the ACP? By competing for dwindling EU resources, continuing enlargement of the ACP means a diminishing bargaining power for the African periphery. Chapter 3 also analyzes the configuration of "external" factors that have complicated EU's relations with African nations. These factors include: (1) the fall of the Eastern bloc, multilateral trade liberalization via the Uruguay Round, and Africa's marginalization in the international system.

There is a major uncertainty about Africa's position in EU's global policies. Perhaps, such uncertainties pose the greatest threat to Africa than any of the known EU's programs to unify the EC market. Looking at the issue of Africa and EU's global policy, Chapter 4 concludes that EU integration has already affected European policy toward Africa. The assumption underlying this chapter is that as EU moves closer, its attention will shift away from peripheral concerns, including EU's ties with Africa.

Chapter 4 also examines how Africa fits into the whole gamut of EU's external policy. The main pillars of EU's policy toward developing nations are examined. These include the EU Common External Tariff, Common Agricultural Policy, and EU's aid policy. In contrast to other books written on the subject of EU 1992 and Africa, *Africa and the European Challenge* discusses EU's emerging and changing relationship with its partners-including EFTA, Central and Eastern Europe, and Latin America. A critical dilemma remains as to how the EU could still reconcile its ties with Africa with its varied interests and commitments with different regions of the world.

As Table 1.1 suggests, it is best to examine how EU's behavior and policies in the international arena conflict with Africa's quest for collective self-reliance, equitable partnership, and autonomy in the international system. The analysis is consistent with Johan Galtung's theory that the relationship between the core and periphery nations is based on "disharmony of interest".[26]

Table 1.1
Conflicts and contradiction in Europe's policy towards Africa

Issue/Policy	Conflicts/Contradiction
A EU's behavior in the international arena	
-Inward-looking tendency*	-Creates the perception of a Fortress' Europe
-Autonomist tendency*	-Reduces EU's margin of flexibility in dealing with Africa
-Demand for reciprocity*	-Undermines the philosophy of the Lome regime that is based on the principle of " non-reciprocity"
-EU concessions at GATT	-Erodes Lome preferences
B Policy coordination pitfalls	-Europe speaks to Africa with different voices
-Lack of donor coordination	-Duplication of donor activities in Africa
C Lome development policy: STABEX (Stabilizes African raw material exports) STABEX perpetuates Africa's commodity dependency	
E The "1992" process:	Reinforces the asymmetries in Euro-African relations

*See Chapter 4 for elaboration of the "tendencies" in EU's behavior.

A major focus of discussion in Chapter 4 is the Lome Convention that links the EU with its former colonies in Africa, the Caribbean, and the Pacific.

The removal of borders in Europe has meant the tightening of frontier controls and stringent review of asylum applications from non-EU countries-a move that has affected African immigrants in Europe. Chapter 5 devotes its attention to the discussion of EU's immigration policy and implications for Africa. Even though discussions of European immigration policies are done at the EU level, the chapter also looks at specific EU countries-France, Britain, and Germany, in the context of European integration. Particular attention is paid to the social dimension of EU integration, particularly the sensitive issue of EU immigration policy. It is imminent that the harmonization of foreign policies could lead to stricter immigration polices and tension between Europe and Africa. As the *Baltimore Sun* puts it: "Western Europe may be going through an economic recession, but to an impoverished migrant from Eastern Europe or North Africa, its streets still seem paved with gold".[27]

Chapter 6 examines the opportunities and challenges posed by the EU integration. The EU is the destination of major African exports. Three factors are considered as important here: EU's trade measures, multilateral initiatives, and Africa's own structural limitations. The last factor is discussed in details in Chapter 8.

European integration carries potential risks for Africa. Africa faces the possibility of preferential erosion. Furthermore, the EU is becoming self-sufficient in certain commodities. Environmental conditions and regulations are going to be tougher, and possibly trade-diverting.

Despite those real threats, there are some windows of opportunities that could and should be exploited by the African countries. Such opportunities (eg possible increase in demand for African products) may not be equally distributed, because of the element of disparities in terms of the capabilities of African nations to take advantage of the Single Market.

Alongside EU unification, there is a proliferation of trading blocs, such as NAFTA. What do these alignments mean to Africa? Chapter 6 addresses some of the concerns.

Chapter 7 deals with the issues of foreign aid, investment, and development implications for Africa of European Integration. EU's monetary integration, and how it is likely to affect African nations, is also a subject that is treated in this chapter. The myth that EU's growth would potentially benefit the world-hence, Africa's development - is examined critically. In discussing the relative competitiveness of Africa in the realm of investments, Chapter 7 examines alternative scenarios a) the optimist scenario (the argument that Africa may be able to reap benefits from EU-related investments due to favorable conditions and b) the pessimist scenario (the argument that Africa would be at a loss because of the attractiveness of other regions, and Africa's structural weaknesses).

In Chapter 8, the author examines the challenges that most African countries face as a result of EU unification. The chapter looks at issues that are unique to certain countries and sectors of interest to African countries. The working assumption is that certain observations are specific to certain groups of countries or sectors, and should be looked at differently.

The factors that would make a difference in comparing the prospects of African nations in the context of European economic unification include differential resource endowment, relative manufacturing capacities, political and social stability, and overall attractiveness for external, particularly EU-related, investments.

The sectors that are selected for analysis include, but are not limited to: agriculture, the food industry, crude oil, coffee, tea and cocoa. Special attention is focussed on sugar and bananas because of the complexities of the sugar and banana protocols that exist between the EU and some African nations. The service industry provides opportunities, but is also linked to EU's strategy of reciprocity. This chapter examines the prospects of African firms' ability to take advantage of new openings in the service industry. It is argued that both individually and as a group, African nations have structural weaknesses that would potentially reduce their bargaining power in dealing with Europe.

In Chapter 9 (the concluding chapter), the author examines the policy implications of EU integration for Africa. The fate of Third World economies, in the context of "1992", is a topic that has political ramifications in Europe, and the most feasible way of dealing with it has been the politics of non-attention. Africa's strategy in addressing the challenge of EU integration should include concerted initiative at the firm, country, and continental levels. This author believes that the EU also has a responsibility to assist African nations in overcoming some of the difficulties that they are likely to encounter, as a result of EU integration.

Notes

1 The original six members are Belgium, Luxembourg, Netherlands,Germany, France, and Italy.
2 1993 et le Tier-Monde: Qui a Peur du Grand Merchant Marche?", *L'Echo de l'Afrique*, 1 December, 1988.
3. "Europe 1992: Les Craintes de l'Afrique", *Jeune Afrique*, No. 1504 30 October 1989, p. 48.
4 EU, *The European Community in the 1990s*, Brussels, 1989,p. 6.
5 Mary Alexander, "Threats to Developing Countries From EC Integration: 1992 and All That Trade", *West Africa*, 29 June 1992, p. 1091.
6 Manuel Marin, Vice-President of the Commission of the European Communities, "Lome IV—the Scope of a new Convention", *EEC-ACP Courier*, No. 120, March-April 1990, p. 12.
7 *International Management*, June 1990, p. 32.
8 "The Single Market Means New Tests for Third World", *The Wall Street Journal* (Europe), May 9, 1989.
9 See for example, Paolo Cecchini, *The European Challenge: The Benefits of a Single Market*, Brussels: 1988.
10 Francis Wurtz, *EEC-ACP Courier*, November-December 1989, p. 2.
11 EU , *The European Community and its Eastern Neighbors*, Brussels, January, 1991, p. 1.
12 Based on a conversion with an official of the EU in Brussels.
13 The Lome Agreement, signed in 1975, links the EU with 70 countries in Africa, Caribbean and the Pacific.
14 Based on a conversation with an official of the EU in Brussels.
15 The Maastritch Treaty expanded the Scope of pan-European cooperation to include political cooperation among the EU 12 countries.
16 Guy Martin, "The Historical, Political and Economic Bases of France's African Policy", *Journal of Modern African Studies*, Vol. 23, No. 2, 1985.
17 See particularly Kwame Nkrumah, *African Must Unite*, New York: Heinmann, 1963.
18 David Scalise, "Comparative Study on Political Opportunities: China, Eastern Europe and the former Soviet Union", *International Management*, July/August 1993, p. 30.

19 European Council, "Immigration/Security Issues: Presidency Conclusions", European Council, Dublin, 25-26 June 1990.

20 I. William Zartman (ed.), *Europe and Africa: The New Phase*, Boulder, Lynne Rienner, 1993.

21 Olesegun Obasango, Hans d'Orville, *The Impact of Europe on 1992 in West*, New York: Crane Russak, 1990.

22 *Financial Times*, 21 June, 1993.

23 Ernst B. Haas, Philippe Schmitter, "Economic and Differential Patterns of Political Integration: Projection About Unity In Latin America", in *International Political Communities: An Anthology*, Garden City, NY: Doubleday, 1966.

24 W. William Axline, "Underdevelopment, Dependence and Integration: The Politics of Regionalism in the Third World", *International Organization*, Vol. 31, Winter 1977.

25 Walter Goldstein, "EC After Maastricht", *Foreign Affairs*, Winter 1992/93.

26 Johan Galtung, "A Structural Theory of Imperialism", *Journal of Peace Research*, Vol. 8, 1971.

27 "Flood of Immigrants Prompts European Action", *The Baltimore Sun*, 4 July, 1993.

2 European unification: Some theoretical and practical implications for Africa

Writing about the implications of the EU's Single Market for Africa is thought-provoking. A critic asked this author: "Why bother speculate about the implications of the European Single Market for African countries? After all, it is an European affair, and Africa is not in Europe". My answer to the critic is that African nations' concern about European unity must be understood from both theoretical and practical points of view.

The European Union continues to serve as a model for many developing nations that are trying to create regional, and even continental, integrative schemes. Thus, when President Abdou Diouf of Senegal (and former Chairman of the Economic Community of West African States (ECOWAS)[1] made a proposal in Abidjan, Cote d'Ivoire, in 1991, for the establishment of an ECOWAS Parliament, he had the European Parliament at the back of his mind.

Europe 1992: A model of regional unity in Africa?

Countless efforts towards continental unity in Europe failed-from Napoleonic times to later days of Adolf Hitler. For Africa, one important lesson that emanates from the European integration experience is that unity cannot be built solely by force. The late President of Ghana, Kwame Nkrumah, antagonized his fellow statesmen who viewed his proposals for African unity as coercive manipulation. In a 1959 speech, Nkrumah urged the incorporation of neighboring Togo as the seventh province of Ghana. Also, in his Government White Paper of 1960, Nkrumah urged the integration of contiguous and historically related peoples into Ghana.[2]

The EU integration effort-which many developing regions would like to emulate-exemplifies a regionalist approach to economic development. Even though European unity has a political goal, one of its main objectives has been the revival of Western European economies. The Marshall Plan (1948), which was supported by the US, was to help rejuvenate the war-ravaged Europe.

In the 1970s and 1980s, economic decline in Europe added momentum to the drive towards greater economic unity. Beset by economic recession, European nations introduced protective measures that were counterproductive, a situation that earned the European Community the derogatory name "the Uncommon Market". Others referred to EU's lack of progress towards unity as *Eurosclerosis*.[3] The decline in regionalism in Western Europe was exacerbated by the growth in non-tariff barriers in the form of cumbersome administrative, technical and fiscal restrictions.

The EU, however, exhibited some institutional maturity, as it adapted to changes and challenges in its political arena. The current momentum towards a unified market, perhaps, represents a departure from the old days of Eurosclerosis.

While the EU, like Africa, has gone through difficulties in regional integration, the EU - more than Africa - has shown a greater persistence in the strive for continental unity. At a crucial historic juncture, when Europe is on the verge of becoming a truly unified bloc, Africa is still toying with its "dreams of unity".[4] *Africa must learn a lesson from EU's persistence*. Integration is a long process, and entails 'ups' and 'downs'. After all, the "1992" process is the fulfillment of over forty-year-old European dream of unity.

Some African leaders, who have called for African integration, have taken consolation from the European experience. At a Seminar on "Strategic Trade Issues in the Context of Lome IV", the Vice-President of Zimbabwe, Joshua Nkomo, noted that EU unification would be an example to those of us who want to work to create a unified market as part of the Lagos plan of Action.

Comparative perspectives on integration: Africa and Europe

Regional integration in the Third World is largely motivated by the need for mutual economic development. For African nations, economic survival in the global system would be unattainable, without workable regional arrangements of some sort. Most African economies are too weak to stand up to global competition. Even Japan and the US - two nations with large markets, technological prowess, and bargaining power - cannot survive on their own, without cooperating with other countries. American and Japanese firms have, for example, found it expedient to cooperate, in order to be able to compete at the global arena. American and Russian firms are burying their ideological differences for the purpose of cooperation!

Also, individual African economies may be too small to support industrialization. As recent experiences have shown, however, international trade has locked many developing nations in what Cheryl Payer refers to as 'the debt trap'.[5] Thus, to African nations, regional integration provides the middle ground between national isolation and international *marginalization*.

Based largely on the European experience, a large number of authors have concluded that the "background conditions"[6] favorable to successful integration are absent in Africa. These conditions include (1)the presence of "complementarity" in elite values, (2) adequate geographically-based diffusion of power, (3) favorable ethos, (4) a sense of transnational community, and (5) a myth of potential benefit.[7]

To the extent that the "favorable" background conditions are absent in Africa, unification among African nations may be difficult to achieve. Consequently, a large number of writers have written off any possibilities for a successful African integration. Nevertheless, African integration cannot be evaluated solely on existence of the so-called background conditions.[8]

Peace-building has long been the goal of regional cooperative efforts.[9] One of the political lessons that developing nations of Africa must draw from the EU's experience is that progress towards international peace and reconciliation may move faster at the regional than at the global level. For example, Franco-German rivalry was reconciled within the

European Union, in a way that no agreement at the UN, or superpower diplomacy, could have nurtured. When asked about the accomplishments of the EU, Dick Spring, the Deputy Prime Minister of Ireland, boasted that:

> It [the EU] has established a framework for European peace, cooperation, and development of European society. Given the fragmented development of Europe in this century alone, the guarantee of peace is the major significance between countries that have serious differences and difficulties.[10]

Admirers of the European model of integration, and critics of African unity would, perhaps, concede that to an extent, African regional bodies have moved further on the "ladder of integration" than their European counterparts. Several examples could be cited here. The ECOWAS-a regional cooperative organization inspired by the EU, has initiated an unprecedented attempt at security cooperation, by dispatching a regional peace-keeping force to warring Liberia. Map 2.1 describes the area covered by ECOWAS.

Map 2.1 The Economic Community of West African States (ECOWAS)

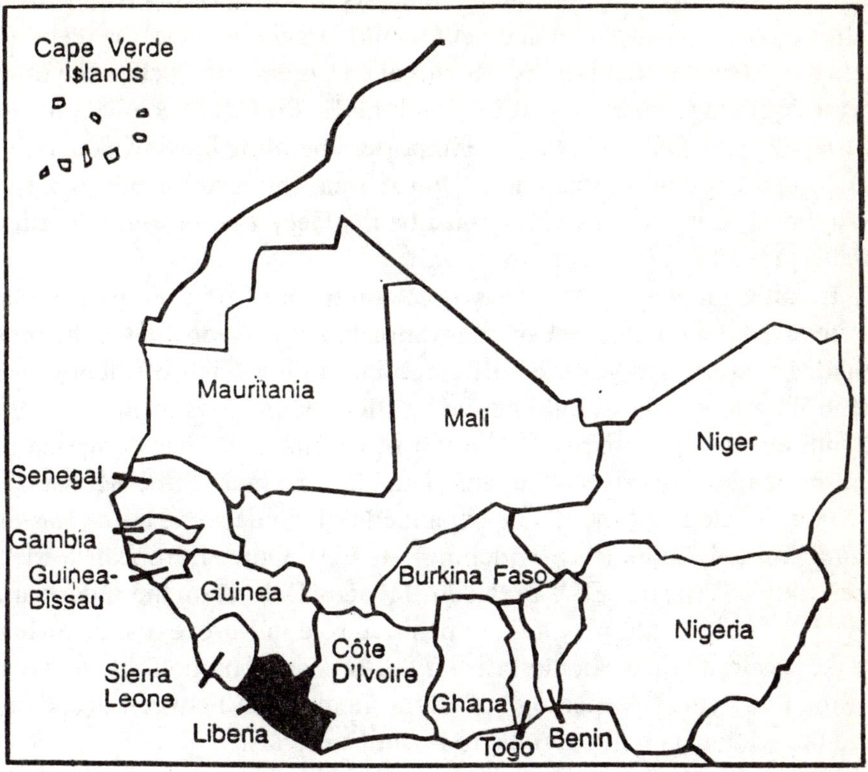

It is ironic that ECOWAS was able to dispatch troops to help stabilize the West African sub-region, when it intervened in the conflict in neighboring Liberia, while the EU hesitated to intervene in the crisis in former Yugoslavia. In the face of a possible widening of the conflict to include other nations in Europe, European leaders dragged their feet, and blamed the United States for not taking the lead in resolving the Bosnian crisis.

As the Cold war recedes, both European and African supra-national institutions will be compelled to assume the burdens of peace building. In the case of Europe, the end of the Cold War and the decline of American hegemony would put the defense of Europe in the hands of Europeans. Similarly, as the geostrategic interests of superpowers recede in relation to Africa, peace management would largely become the responsibility of Africans themselves. Regional arrangements, such as the European Political Cooperation (EPC) and the ECOWAS Peace-Monitoring Group (ECOMOG), will become important building blocks in the political architecture of regional unity. For Africa, and also Europe, it means that the capacity and resources must be in place, if peace and tranquility are to prevail in the integrating area.

African leaders agree that the whole continent of Africa ought to integrate, even though the pace of integration has slowed down. On the other hand, European leaders are still gambling with a crisis of identity: the central issue is what should be the political boundaries of the so-called "common European home". The fall of Communism has compounded Europe's identity crisis. Margaret Thatcher, former Prime Minister of Britain, argued that the EU be expanded to include some to the Eastern European neighbors (the "widening" of EU). Other European leaders, including the former EU's President Jacques Delors, on the other hand, felt that to be able to play a more positive role in Europe and elsewhere in the world, the EU should intensify efforts at its on political and economic unity (the "deepening" of EU). The conflict between deepenists and the widenists will continue to haunt Eurocrats.

On the subject of strategy, however, the EU has an important lesson to offer Africa - a continent where countless efforts at regional co-operation have fallen prey to over-politicization. Unlike their European counterparts such as Jean Monnet and Robert Schuman, the pioneer architects of African unity were divided on the issue of strategy - what should be the starting point of African unity? There were the *minimalists* who preferred an incremental approach to African unity. To them, there must be a step-by-step process of regional unity, as a prelude to eventual continental integration.

On the other hand, the late President Kwame Nkrumah of Ghana, and other more radical critics of neo-colonialism, agitated for a *maximalist* position. Rejecting the gradualism and piecemeal approach of the minimalists, they (the maximalists) were in favor of pulling the bull of African unity by its political horns. To them, any piece-meal effort at unity will be counterproductive, and could even jeopardize Africa's emancipation from neo-colonialism.

European strategists avoided the premature politicization that has bedeviled the debate about African integration. In Europe, integration was to proceed from technical, non-controversial, areas that were to create the basis for a political union. Consequently, political unity in Europe was delayed. Europe, in the end, had to face the consequences of delayed political integration. The fragile political pot of unity was to fall and shatter on the rock of Euro-nationalism, when the Danish people rejected the Maastritch Treaty in a referendum in 1992. To supra-nationalists, the lesson remains that Rome was not built in a day and, thus, the Treaty of Rome that created the EEC cannot be built in a day either.

While the cautious drive towards continental cooperation in Europe is laudable, African strategists, bent on the creation of an African Common Market, would want to avoid the delayed political cooperation that occurred in Europe. If any thing, the European experience vividly has shown that economic cooperation cannot proceed without some form of political cooperation.

Beyond Viner: Evaluating the external effects of economic integration

A premier research work on customs union undertaken by Jacob Viner,[11] distinguishes between two effects of a custom union. Based on Viner's formulations, the establishment of a customs union between two countries, A and B, will cause an expansion of trade between them. The increase in A's imports from its partner, B, may either be at the expense of domestic production in A (*trade-creation* effect), or at the expense of A's trade with a non-member of the customs union, C (*trade-diversion* effect). Viner would conclude that both union members and the world as a whole would be considered worse off, as a result of diversion of production from a more efficient supplier outside the customs union, to a less efficient supplier within the customs union.

Viner's model is useful in understanding the external implications of EU's integration. The "1992" program would affect global trade balance with the EU. EU member countries, at the moment, maintain quantitative restrictions (QRs) for a number of items. Many of the national QRs that exist today were already maintained by EU member states at the time that they acceded to the EU, and were grandfathered following accession. Others are linked directly to agreements concluded by the European Commission, such as the Multifibre Agreement (MFA) and the Generalized System of Preferences (GSP). For non-EU member countries, such as African nations, the abolition or reduction of national quantitative restrictions could facilitate increased exports of the products concerned. The reduction or abolition of internal barriers, as a result of the "1992" program, will also promote trade among EU member countries, at the expense of less efficient producers in the EU, whether they are European or non-European. This, in Viner's parlance, could be trade-creating for third countries if, as a result of trade liberalization, for example, European suppliers could have their monopoly power curtailed, especially if they are dependent on the market power they enjoy, or national protection, rather than on sheer efficiency.

The internal liberalization program, however, may also increase trade among EU countries, at the expense of existing trade with more efficient producers outside the EU. This could be the result of EU's internal or external policy (see Chapter 4). For example, divergent standards among EU member states have held back the competitive potential of non-EU suppliers. If EU's new standards are biased against third-country suppliers - the later could see an erosion of their competitive position.

According to William Axline, although the trade-creating and trade-diverting effects of customs union have been difficult to measure, they have served as the political basis for the establishment of customs union.[12] One of the major objectives of European integration was to promote the mutual trade of its original six member countries. The Treaty of Rome facilitated this process. The Single Market initiative is designed to improve upon this impressive record.

African nations are worried that the net trade-diversion effect of EU's integration may outweigh the trade-creation effects, and that to the extent that African nations may benefit from the Single Market, such benefits may be far limited.

Viner's theory alone cannot predict whether EU's trade with African nations will increase or decrease.[13] Also, while's Viner's conceptualization of the effects of a customs union is helpful, it largely ignores non-trade effects, including the political implications of custom unions. Trade liberalization-as envisaged in the EU White Paper (1985)- is a political act, in that EU nations must cede autonomy over domestic matters such as border controls. Also, it could be said that the "spill-over" [14] effects of internal trade liberalization-such as expanded European cooperation in the social, economic and political spheres. For African nations-as the subsequent chapters of this book suggest-the political, economic, and strategic consequences of European unity are as equally important as the "Vinerian" possibilities of whether the EU process would be more trade-creating or trade-diverting.

Theoretically, African countries may benefit from the trade-creating effects of the Single market, to the extent that the lower-cost producers of given commodities are located in Africa. In practice, however, the limited industrial advancement of most African countries would limit the possibilities that lower-cost, and thus the most efficient, producers of major items would be located in Africa.

According to a study conducted by the Overseas Development Institute (London), the Single Market will initially mean an increase in exports of just 7 billion ECUs, or US $8.6 billion, from developing nations, despite projected boost in European economies.[15] The study noted that an increase in the exports of primary products and manufactured items from developing nations will be offset by losses from trade diversion and trade creation, as the EU becomes more competitive and self-sufficient in goods hitherto imported from developing nations. The accession of Spain and Portugal to the EU in 1986 illustrated the validity of this contention, because the Mediterranean nations, such as Tunisia, lost some of the European pie hitherto enjoyed, because of replacement by exports from the new entrants - Spain and Portugal.

Besides overt protectionism, the increased competitiveness and cost-efficiency in the post-1992 EU will exacerbate the problem of access for African exporters of manufactured goods.

The analyses in the subsequent chapters of this book suggest that the effects of EU's unification on Africa go far beyond Viner's expectations. In addition to possible replacement in trade and investments, there are political, social and psychological implications. Therefore, there is the need for an analytical framework that could help capture the broader impact of EU integration on third countries such as Africa.

Another relevance of EU's initiatives to Africa is its impact on multilateral trade liberalization. Looking at the impact of European unification of global liberalization is an improvement over the Vinerian approach that largely assesses the [trade-creation and trade-diversion] effects of customs union. An assumption underlying this author's method of analysis is based on the recognition that the impact of EU integration cannot be examined without looking at its implications for multilateral trade negotiations. By focusing solely on internal policies of economic blocs, scholars often are unable to put the implications of economic unions in a broader global perspective.

Some observers who have followed recent developments in regionalism have asked important questions: Is regionalism (as exemplified in the EU and NAFTA) a step towards eventual globalization, or does it eventually result in a growing reorganization and regionalization of trade? In other words, is the proportion of trade conducted with neighboring countries increasing at the expense of the share with more distant trade partners?

Answers to these important questions have been given from two major theoretical angles. Optimists, who favor regionalism (and believe in interdependence) argue that to the extent that regional groupings, such as the EU, succeed in increasing the growth rate of its constituent member states, they could increase the demand for imports from outside the group, thereby offsetting any static trade diversion effects. Advocates of regionalism often point to the weaknesses of global negotiations. The realization that GATT negotiations have been unsuccessful in tackling non-tariff barriers (NTBs) to trade has not been lost to critics of multilateralism.

Applauding the EU's initiatives in this regard, Robert Hine noted that "with a more homogenous regional group liberalization of NTBs could progress faster and in deed this is the focus of the EU's single European Market program".[16]

Critics of regionalism, however, are less optimistic. To them, while regional groupings, such as the EU and NAFTA, could be beneficial to the extent that they are "trade liberalizing", there is always the potential for a cost [to non-union members], in terms of deviation from global standards. Solutions adopted by different groupings (eg technical standards) may be mutually incompatible. What is worse, once regional decisions are made, they may be difficult to alter. Thus, the dilemma remains whether Africa must follow EU's technical standards or international ones.

One of the most perplexing theoretical questions is whether or not the EU unification process represents "a step forward" to global liberalization from which African nations could benefit. This question is relevant here, if we are to consider the Vinerian welfare implications of customs union.

What benefits of the European single market?

Paolo Cecchini's book, *The European Challenge: The Benefits of a Single Market*, predicts some benefits in EU unity for members and non-members alike - Africa included.[17] EU Officials have noted that producers in third countries would benefit from the Single Market, because it will boost growth in the EU. This thinking, however, is linked to the theoretical assumption that global welfare will "trickle-down" to all countries equally. In an article titled, "Partners in Progress", Lorenz Schomerus, Head of the Department of Foreign Trade Policy and Development Assistance in the German Ministry of Economy in Bonn, noted that "1992"-related growth in Europe provides excellent opportunities for more competition, growth, and imports from outside the EU.[18] By saying that "we are in the same boat",[19] Schomerus was assuming that there is mutuality of interest in the partnership between Europe and third nations.

Contrary to the Cecchini assumption of "mutuality of benefits" via the EU Single Market, radical scholars, such as Johan Galtung, have repudiated the myth of "mutuality of gains" in international exchange. According to Galtung, to the extent that a harmony of interest exists, it is between the elites of the *center* (advanced) nations and their counterparts in the less developed, *periphery* nations. On the other hand, the masses in the center nations (the "periphery of the center") and their counterparts in underdeveloped nations (the " periphery of the periphery") have little to benefit from growth in the 'center' and 'periphery' nations.[20] The potential for gains from EU's Single Market will be limited, particularly for the peripheral nations that are less competitive.[21]

In order for African nations to gain from EU integration, certain structural reforms will have to take place in the international economy-reforms that will enhance Africa playing more than a subservient role in the international economy, and increase the continent's bargaining position with external actors. European integration has development implications for Africa and the developing world, to the extent that it affects major elements of the relationship between Europe and the developing nations. Among the major issues that are pertinent in North-South relations include the divergent viewpoints regarding non-reciprocal access to markets in the industrialized world, debt relief, technology transfer, and support for sustained development of the Third World.

For African nations, the major question that needs to be asked is: Will a developed and united Europe support Africa's own economic unity or development (i.e., will the counter-bloc factor be positive)? Thus, an alternative way of looking at the (global) welfare implications of the EU integration, as far as Africa is concerned, is to examine whether and how EU's integration would strengthen Africa's own integration.

Students of Euro-African relations have begun to speculate on what the "new" Euro-Africa relationship will be - politically, economically, and socially.[22] Will united Europe support unity among developing nations, such as the current efforts at African Economic Community? To answer this question, we need to apply the concept developed earlier - the catalytic efect of customs union (in this case, the EU). By this way, we could advance beyond the Vinerian typology of trade-creation and trade-diversion effect of customs union.

Since its birth in 1957, the European economic unification has inspired and supported regional cooperation among nations in the Third World.[23] This is not to assume that the policies of the EU in particular, are always supportive of the integration or development of the Third World. As Joseph Nye has observed in an article, "Patterns and Catalysts in Regional Integration",[24] the role of extra-regional actors in integration of the least developed nations could be positive and/or negative.

External interference by European powers, both in the colonial and post colonial periods, has often prevented closer economic and political co-operation among African nations.[25] For example, even though Ghana and the Cote d'Ivoire share the same border, closer economic and political cooperation among these West African nations have been impeded, partly as a result of these nations' exposure to different colonial experiences (Cote d'Ivoire was under French rule and Ghana British). Fearful of Nigeria's geo-political motivations in supporting the formation of ECOWAS (in 1975), President Georges Pompidou (on the occasion of his 1972 visit to Niger) "advised" that while Francophone African nations ought to cooperate with their Anglophone counterparts, there should be an "equilibrium" which, according the French leader, would be achieved if the Francophone nations "... harmonize their efforts so as to counter-balance the heavy weight of Nigeria".[26]

The attempt by France to challenge Nigeria's regionalist ambitions in the West African sub-region provided the politico-strategic arena in which regional economic cooperation was nurtured in the 1970s. Ironically, it is the same fear of superpower interference that makes it critical for African nations to unite today. In other words, European unification might have had a positive catalytic (counter-bloc) impact on Africa.

Among the other contributions of the EU integration for Africa is the practical lessons that Europe offers in the realm of integration to the emerging nations of Africa. There is an African proverb that says that: "He who is behind learns how to walk from the one in front".

EU integration: Some lessons for Africa

The benefits of EU integration for Africa must be assessed beyond the statistical straight-jacket of trade creation and trade diversion, since some of these benefits may not be quantifiable. Perhaps, one of the major relevance of the EU to African nations is its practical, functional, approach to multinational co-operation. The previous efforts at political unity in Europe in the 1950s foundered, amid political animosities, despite the effort to circumvent nationalism in the post-war era. Consequently, European integration strategists, particularly Jean Monnet and Robert Schuman, channelled the energies of (inter-European) reconciliation into much more practical and immediate tasks which pressed on political leaders, such as the joint reconstruction and development of the coal and steel industry.

It would be parochial, however, to assume that the EEC was formed without an ulterior political goal. The creation of the European Council, the direct elections to the European parliament, and the frantic efforts toward the "1992" unification process have propelled Europe to the arena of political cooperation. As the EU propels itself towards ultimate political unity, it must increase its momentum on the political level and move forward politically, or it will stagnate.

The Single Market is, perhaps, the most crucial phase of European union. It extends the logical conclusion of the strategy that was hatched by the founding fathers of the EU: beginning the process of unity through economic cooperation.

Political cooperation, perhaps, the last major phase of [Western] European integration, started much earlier in the life of the EEC. By the early 1970s, during the negotiation for British membership in the EEC, an attempt to add political cooperation to the integration process was relaunched by the six core countries of the EEC, under the aegis of European Political Cooperation (EPC). The negotiations that culminated in the signing of the Maastricht Treaty (1991) is a clear demonstration that regional economic integration cannot proceed smoothly, without some form of political cooperation.

One major reason why African unity has been elusive, so far, is the indecision about where to begin: Should African nations begin with economic cooperation that would eventually lead to political unity, or should they first embark upon political unity? A major proponent of pan-Africanism, Kwame Nkrumah wanted a strong political union as a prerequisite for economic union. He advised his colleagues to "Seek Ye First the Political Kingdom".

The other lesson that Africa can learn from the EU experience is how the EU manipulated the "external cogency" for the purpose of integration. Even though regional (internal) factors serve to promote cooperative consciousness among nations, there are certain extra-regional factors that also act as catalysts for regional unity. The ability of member countries to manipulate these external forces in a more positive way (towards the efforts at integration) will be a prerequisite for successful integration.

In the case of the EEC, Soviet adventurism and the West's fear of Communist domination, provided a source of identity and cohesion among EEC member countries. The US has been a major supporter of European unity. A major reason behind the massive US economic and political support for EEC integration, particularly in early post-War period, was to strengthen Europe's resolve to resist Soviet adventurism. As the EU experience so far has shown, the effective neutralization of hostile external opposition (or the absence of external opposition) is important for regional unity.[27]

Africa has an unique challenge to unite. The continent, for centuries, has been subjected to the manipulations and schemes of foreign powers bent on domination. After granting political independence to their African colonies, European powers still maintain a sway over the continent's development and sovereignty, through a series of contacts that have largely included, but are not limited to: the maintenance of currency zones (France and Francophone Africa), military bases, ideological attachment, religious and intellectual ties, and commercial alliances, such as the Lome Conventions. These ties, which some critics rebuke as "neo colonialist",[28] have reincarnated William Zartman's question as to whether Euro-Africa relations in the post-independence phase constitutes "decolonization" or dependency.[29] Such Euro-African ties serve as an albatross around the neck of Africa that has to decide how much of the existing ties must be retained, as Africa develops its own strategies of survival in the changing global arena.

In addition to external catalysts or "motivators" of unity, there are also internal ones. After World War II, in the midst of destruction and economic collapse, governments appeared ready to develop mechanisms which would bring greater degree of economic cooperation among EU nations.[30] Up to the mid 1980s, perhaps, the major motivation for European integration was the need by EU member countries to redress a major competitive disadvantage-the fact that European nations were falling behind technological giants-such as the US, Japan and the Newly Industrializing Countries (NICs). Individually, European markets proved to be too small, and productivity level too low, for effective competition with Europe's rivals. "1992" is Europe's answer to this challenge.

In 1988, the EU commissioned a study on the benefits of the Single Market. More than a mere academic exercise, the study effectively manipulated "the myth of benefits" of European unity. The study analyzed the "costs of non-Europe" and made projections about the potential gains in employment, competitiveness and income, if Europe removed the barriers to unity.

The exigency of removing the dangers of internal non-viability of the African economies would have to be effectively manipulated, or used by African leaders to mobilize support among their people for Africa's own regional unity.

Though unsuccessful, Kwame Nkrumah of late memory manipulated Africa's vulnerability to both internal and external forces, as he diplomatically attempted to sell his dream of African unity to his fellow African statesmen. He explained to his fellow countrymen and African statesmen that "the independence of Ghana would be meaningless, unless it is linked up with the total liberation of Africa". "Total African liberation", as Nkrumah philosophized, was a *sine qua non* for continental African government. According to Nkrumah, the influence of external powers in Africa's domestic and intra-regional affairs made a mockery of Ghana's independence and political sovereignty. Ghana could not be "free", he said, while the rest of the continent languished under the yoke of colonialism and imperialism.[31]

Nkrumah argued that given individual countries' weaknesses, Africa could enhance its relative power in the global arena through Pan-African unification. Towards this end, the OAU was established in May 1963. Among its objectives was the promotion of peace and security of African nations. Despite the existence of the OAU, regional conflicts in Africa have often been mediated by extra-continental powers. The Somalian crisis, and the UN's intervention in it, has clearly demonstrated the collective vulnerability of African nations, and the need to create African institutions that can provide security for the continent.

Beginning in the late 1980s, there has been a growing consciousness among African leaders about the continent's *marginalization* in the world system - a condition that becomes more critical in view of the changing configurations of the new international order, and Africa's *peripheralization* within it.

The EU could be considered as the living proof of the theory that the existence of core nations that are willing to make sacrifices is a prerequisite for successful regional integration. European integration was also promoted by the political will expressed by EEC leaders and European statesmen. Throughout its existence, the momentum for action has been provided by core catalyst nations that expanded the EU from a membership of 6 (in 1957) to 9, 10, and then to 12 by 1986. The evolution of the Single European Act (SEA)[32] between 1985 and 1987 reflected the determination on the part of the EU Commission, and the resurgence of political will of the EU 12, who were armed with a definite economic agenda. The political muscles of France has been combined with the economic power of Germany to propel forward the wheels of European unity.

In Africa, regional hegemons such as Nigeria and South Africa, could serve as the hub of African integration, in the same way as Germany and France did in Europe. However, the leadership role of Lagos and Pretoria would be limited in the near future. An OPEC power, Nigeria is facing economic recession and political crises. The aborted democratic transition in Nigeria has not only sapped Nigeria of its economic energy, but has painted a tarnishing image of Nigeria as a regional power. South Africa will also have to overcome initial problems associated with transition to non-racial, multi-party rule, and may not be willing or capable of assuming a "God-father" role in Africa.[33] Violence and instability has deterred foreign investment in both nations. Nigeria and South Africa may not effectively cooperate in the spirit of intra-African solidarity, and may even compete for a sub-imperial position in the African subsystem.

As the EU's evolution suggests, non-governmental forces often shape and help regional integration. Social forces have helped the European integration process. Their ranks include the mass media, academicians, and trade unions. It will be important that African leaders encourage social groups, such as journalists, trade unions, marketing and industrial groups, students and non-governmental organizations, to play a role in

Africa's regional integration. It is commendable to state that among the Southern African Development Community (SADC)[34] there is the existence of social groups, including those of accountants, women, etc.

If properly organized, supra-national institutions could further the integration process in Africa. In Europe, the establishment of institutions like the Court, the Council, and the Parliament, enhanced the formulation of policies with EU-wide application.

The pivotal role of business leaders and consumers in the advancement of European unity must also be noted. Like Europe, private sector development should be the linchpin of the strategy to integrate the African economies. The failure of state trading corporations in Africa and elsewhere suggests that the days of government-to-government trade in Africa are changing, and need to change for the better. In an effective regional market, the private sector becomes the principal actor, while the public sector plays the role of formulator and regulator of policies. As one European observer noted, "it [the European market] integrates quietly, while the prime ministers are in bed". [35]

For Africa, another lesson that Europe offers is that *supra national integration entails national responsibilities*. Economic and political integration could not have proceeded up to the present level in Europe, without EU nations carrying out their responsibilities. Multinational program implementation cannot succeed without some sort of burden-sharing. More prosperous nations such as Germany and Italy have been helping their less fortunate partners such as Ireland, Greece, Spain and Portugal.

The record of member nations carrying out their responsibilities is dismal in Africa - a continent where countless protocols are signed, but not ratified. The former Executive Secretary of ECOWAS, Abbas Bundu, noted at the 15th Annual Summit meeting of the ECOWAS in Dakar, Senegal, that a relatively large number of member countries of ECOWAS were in arrears, and that the only member states that were "up-to-date in their payment obligations" were Burkina Faso, Cote d'Ivoire, Nigeria and Togo. One very innovative program that has been established among Africa's regional integration bodies is that of the Preferential Trading Area (PTA) that publishes the names of paying and non-paying member countries, regularly and widely. This discipline that the PTA has imposed on its members could be applied to other regional bodies in Africa. This could be done to enhance the financial viability of African regional organizations.

There has been a growing realization among architects of regional integration schemes that the benefits of integration cannot be realized, if efforts are not taken to combat external dependency. In order to terminate external dependency, the EEC implemented concrete projects, such as the establishment and funding of Customs Union and the European Coal and Steel Community, among others. In particular, the Common Agricultural Policy (CAP) helped Europe to terminate its dependency on external food, by encouraging European food self-sufficiency. Through such initiatives, also, the European Community effectively reduced, if not terminated, American hegemony in Europe. As at now, the efforts to reduce Europe's dependency has been so effective that some observers foresee the end of American hegemony in Europe. In *Europe Without America*, in which he discusses the crises in the Atlantic Alliance after the end of the cold war and the resurgence of Euro-confidence,[36] John Palmer has cast a doubt about America's future hegemonic role in Europe.

The European effort to address the issue of external dependency, however, contrasts with the African experience, where leaders have not seriously debated the need to terminate external dependence. For example, the Lagos Plan of Action was largely expected to be implemented-with foreign assistance-without concrete sequential steps taken to reduce, if not terminate, Africa's excessive external dependency.

One of the major policies that underscores Africa's dependency and subservience to external interests -and which many African scholars condemn - is the so-called structural adjustment polices (SAPs). Supposedly designed to alleviate Africa's structural imbalances, critics maintain that SAPs have meant the virtual surrender of Africa's sovereignty to external actors, principally the Western-dominated Bretton Wood institutions-the World Bank and the IMF.

Ironically, while the Southern African Development Coordination Conference (SADCC) embarked upon a rhetorical repudiation of dependency on South Africa, no major concrete steps were taken to end SADCC's dependence on international agencies and donor countries. The bottom line is that with their weak bargaining power, African nations cannot afford to offend external interests.

The process of integration, like all purposive social actions, entails some discontents. Both Europe and Africa suffer from such crisis of achievement (or lack of it). In the EU, the resurgence of supranationalism since World War II also coincided with the emergence of separatist movements. Some of these movements have expressed a bloody reaction toward cultural homogenization and unity. Unfortunately, the European unification process has unleashed a cloud of xenophobia against foreigners. For example, in the French national elections in 1988, the conservative Jean-Marie Le Pen, and his National Front, won 14 percent of the vote nationwide with the slogan "France for the French". Increased anti-immigrant feelings, even against Europeans from other EU nations, demonstrate the social discontents of European integration.

There is an African parallel. Ghana and Nigeria have fought alien expulsion wars since 1969 - the year when Ghana promulgated an "Alien Compliance Order" that resulted in the expulsion of "illegal" aliens, mostly Nigerians, from Ghana. Largely seen by observers as a retaliatory measure [against the Ghanaian government's decision], the 1983 Nigerian Presidential elections were fought on the emotional issue of illegal aliens. In early 1983, and again in 1985, Nigeria expelled illegal aliens from the country, most of them Ghanaian nationals.

Even though the EU experience offer many lessons for African integration and collective self-reliance, there is a "paradox of relevance". Regions outside Europe must find their own models for regional unity, since the European model has not worked for them. The Maastricht Treaty (1991) established an European Union and committed member nations to work toward closer cooperation in foreign and security issues. It also extended the powers of the European Parliament. Nonetheless, parochial interests and nationalist feelings have negatively affected closer cooperation. To a degree, EU's regional monetary arrangement remains important for developing nations. An African currency union might be supported by an European monetary system. The European monetary union, if it serves as a model for emergent payment unions in other regions, could play a leading role in the construction of a polycentric global monetary system as the basis for eventual world monetary integration. Furthermore, the EU could support core, catalyst powers, eg. Nigeria and Zimbabwe, in the effort at building regional integration in Africa.

Although EU integration is considered as an "internal" matter in Brussels, the external dimensions are important for Africa. The next chapter examines the external aspects of European integration.

Payoffs and pitfalls

Since its birth, the European Community has encouraged the formation of regional groupings in the Third World. These groupings include the Association of South-East Asian Nations (ASEAN), the Lome Group of Countries (the ACP), and the Latin American Free Trade Area (LAFTA) etc.

However, critics of Euro-African relations have often pointed out the deleterious impact that such relations have on Africa's own development. Walter Rodney and other writers using the radical theories of dependency and imperialism, have placed the subject of Africa's *underdevelopment* within the structural context of Africa's dependence on Europe. In his controversial book, *How Europe Underdeveloped Africa*, Rodney contended that Africa helped to develop Western Europe in the same proportion as Western Europe underdeveloped Africa.[37]

Within Africa's structural dependencies lies the continent's own vulnerabilities.[38] To Rodney, Nkrumah, and other neo Marxist writers, underdevelopment was sown in Africa, at the time when European countries were laying the industrial foundation for economic prosperity, which would strengthen their [Europe's] power to compete for secured resources and markets in Africa and elsewhere.

Under colonial rule, Africa was subjected to a special international division of labor that implied that African colonies:

(1) Could only import goods that originated from the metropole.
(2) Could only export to the Metropole on a duty-free basis.
(3) Could not set up their own manufacturing industries.
(4) Had to rely on the carriers of the metropole for the transportation of their exports and imports.
(5) Remained as the suppliers of raw materials and agricultural products while the various European Metropoles reserved to themselves the exclusivity of industrial production and the export of manufactures.

The last point mentioned above conforms to the law of *unequal exchange* as formulated by Arghiri Immanuel. According to Immanuel, unequal exchange occurs since underdeveloped nations are compelled to exchange "a larger amount of their national labor for a smaller amount of foreign labor".[39]

Why should African leaders and sympathizes put the blame for underdevelopment on colonialism, over thirty years since the continent attained political independence? Some critics of African leadership maintain that there is an element of hypocrisy, especially when African leaders blame European powers for Africa's woes, without questioning mismanagement, corruption, and incompetence of the leaders themselves as reasons for Africa's underdevelopment.

George B. N. Ayittey, a Ghanaian social scientist at the American University in Washington, D.C. wrote a book, *Africa Betrayed*, that blames the corrupt African ruling class for the continent's problems.[40] If we take the position advanced by Ayittey and other critics of African leaders, then we would assume that Africa's destiny lies in own her hands.

Taking an opposite theoretical direction, many writers have concluded that the fate of Africa is inextricably linked with Europe, with the later determining to a greater degree, what happens in Africa. In *Neo-Colonialism: The Last Stage of Imperialism*,[41] Kwame Nkrumah contended that Euro-African schemes subvert Africa's pan-African ambitions. Other authors also conclude that certain policies recommended or supported by EU countries and other external donors, such as the World Bank and the IMF, hinder Africa's integration.

In the 1990s, the policy of structural adjustment policies (SAPs) has become a major part of dependency theorists' demonology of external dependency. The EU has supported SAPs in Africa. One of the policy recommendations suggested by SAP sponsors has been the devaluation of African currencies. However, SAPs inhibit regional economic integration in Africa, because at present, some national currencies are either floating or pegged to different foreign currencies or basket of currencies. Consequently, any exchange rate adjustments in one country are likely to frustrate liberalization and payments among member countries of African customs unions. Consequently, the Lome IV Convention, that is tied to structural adjustment, needs urgent reappraisal, so that the aspects that conflict with Africa's regional cooperation could be revised.

The colonial linkage of African economies with Europe facilitated the European-orientation of Africa's external economic relations. This phenomenon was further enhanced by the formation of the EEC in 1957, and eventual association of former European colonies in Africa with this European bloc - through the Yaounde and the Lome Convention in 1969 and 1975 respectively.[42] The European concentration of African exports and imports - directly and indirectly-inhibits intra-African trade, so does Africa's reliance on external financing inhibit Africa's economic development.

Critics of the ideology of interdependence - that is used to justify Euro-African relations - extend their analyses beyond the colonial phase of Africa's development. Their focus of analyses include Euro-African schemes and linkages, particularly the Lome Conventions. To them, the Treaty of Rome (1957), and the Single European Act (1987) are two sides of the same coin: they are part of the historical process of the deepening of European power on one hand, and the marginalization of Africa on the other.

From a dependency theoretical perspective, European unity is a potential threat to Africa to the extent that it could strengthen European power-power that could facilitate the Metropole's ability to capture more of the "global surplus", while Africa, as a periphery, is thrown deeper into underdevelopment.[43]

Walton Brown drew a historical sketch of the relationship between events in Europe and their implications for Africa. He did that by linking the Berlin Conference (1884-85) with the Single European Act (1987). Brown noted:

> One hundred years after the 1885 Treaty of Berlin, in June 1985, the EEC decided to scrap the regional transportation, trade, employment and investment barriers that had separated Europe's national economies for centuries. These traditional boundaries that led to expansion of the individual European national economic and political-military machines in Africa from the 15th century to the present.[44]

Sam Olofin argued that rather than being "complementary", the Lome Convention and the ECOWAS treaty constitute an experiment in conflicting customs union arrangement. [45]

One of the current aspects of Africa's debate on alternative development strategies is the call for *Afrocentricity*. According to this view, instead of the Euro-centric orientation of African development, Africa should be the centerpiece of the continent's development strategy.

Citing specifically some of Africa's established links with Europe that run counter to intra-African links, the former Executive Secretary of the UN Economic Commission for Africa, Adebayo Adedeji, noted that:

> It is odd but typically African that our governments could enter into a ten-year agreement with the EEC at a time of rapid, almost revolutionary, changes in the world and at a time when the treaty to establish an African Economic Community is being negotiated.[46]

According to Afrocentricists, even though EU integration offers useful practical lessons for Africa, the continent cannot afford a blind imitation of European ideals and models. The European integration model has its own flaws, and like Euro-based "democracy", may not be adaptable to Africa's political ecology.

One important thing that Africa must avoid is the delayed financial integration that occurred in the EU. This is because, African currencies are not convertible like those in Europe. Whereas Europe could afford to delay negotiations on a common currency, it will be suicidal, or ill-advised, for African nations to procrastinate on the issue of African common currency. Unlike Africa, Europe has large financial centers to facilitate international financial dealings.

Asymmetrical interdependence

The relationship between Africa and Europe has remained asymmetrical-a reflection of the historic international division of labor and "unequal exchange" that resulted in Africa's exploitation and marginalization. One major consequence of this global division of labor has been captured by Frank Codjoe, who noted that "while Africa was getting poorer, the nations endowed with opportunities for industries and technology were achieving progress and industrial sophistication".[47]

African theorists of neocolonialism, and other observers who are sympathetic to the dependency analysis, maintain that there is a relationship between the internal development of the Metropolitan nations, such as Europe, and peripheral underdeveloped regions. Based on this theoretical assumption, therefore, political and economic changes in Europe not without their implications for dependent nations.

An analysis of the EU Single Market that adopts the dependency approach is theoretically useful. The conventional analysis of the implications of customs union is parochial, to the extent that it ignores the major non-trade effects. Viner's concepts of trade-creation and trade-diversion are quite useful when assessing the implications of EU for Africa. However, our ability to predict the overall balance of trade-creation and trade-diversion is just a tip of the iceberg when assessing the implications of EU unity for Africa. Even if Viner's approach could help us compute all the net trade gains arising from customs union, it is not adequate as a theory for assessing the general development implications for African nations that are at the periphery of the global economy.

In analyzing the implications for Africa of the "1992" unification process, the dependency approach seems more appropriate in that, it considers the nature of Africa's external linkages with Europe, and how they are likely to be affected, either negatively or positively, as a result of the upcoming European unification. Dependency analysis goes beyond Viner's trade creation/trade diversion conceptualization, by examining some of the disparities in Africa's economic relations with the EU.

Africa's vulnerability that emanates from dependence is rooted in a historical phenomenon, not solely in the present structure of Africa's economic relations with Europe. For about five centuries, Africa's trade has been oriented northwards towards Europe. The incorporation of African economies into the global economy, in both the colonial and post-colonial phases of Africa's development was rationalized on the basis of the ideology of "Euro-Africa", which assumes that the benefits of global interdependence are mutual.[48] The "complementary" and "interdependent" nature of Euro-Africa's economic relationship has been mythologized by one observer who noted that:

> The African soil is too poor to be able to do without Europe. The African sub-soil is too rich for Europe to be able to do without Africa. Thus, it must be admitted that Africa is an indispensable complement to Europe.[49]

Such a neo-classical assumption about Africa's relationship with the Metropole takes for granted the partnership, albeit, asymmetrical, between the EU and its weaker associates-Africa.

A notable assumption within the dependency paradigm is that the developmental process of the underdeveloped nations is shaped by their dependent status in the global economy, and is strongly conditioned by it.[50] According to Robert Koehane and Joseph Nye, dependence connotes "a state of being determined or significantly affected by external forces".[51] There is lack of real precision in the particular asymmetric structural or relational properties denoted by the term, "dependence". One of the most frequently cited definitional statements on the terminology of dependence in the context of Metropole-Satellite relations (within which Euro-African relations could best be understood) is the one provided by Theotonio Dos Santos who asserts that:

> By dependence we mean a situation in which the economies of certain countries is conditioned by the development and expansion of another country...the relations of interdependence between two or more economies...assumes the form of dependence when some countries can expand and be self-starting, while other countries can do this only as a reflection of that expansion, which can have either positive or negative effect on their immediate development.[52]

The dependency approach has been adapted and adopted in a variety of ways to discuss the political economy of Africa's external relations and development. Resenting voices within the Latin American school of underdevelopment[53], and African theorists of neocolonialism[54], have questioned the "exploitative" links between the industrialized nations and the post-colonial states. Despite their variety, a fundamental assumption of most dependency theorists remains that Africa's historical incorporation into the global system is an impediment to the continent's development.[55]

When African leaders and policy makers discuss the root causes of underdevelopment, they often point to the existing North-South relations. Critics, using arguments based on the dependence analytic perspective, point to the fact that post-colonial Euro-African links reinforce, rather than reform, the old colonial pattern of exploitation. Like Immanuel Wallerstein, most dependency theorists[56] and African leaders critical of Africa's external economic dependency, have been skeptical about the possibilities of transformation[57] in the present capitalist world order that would be congenial to the development of Africa. Hence, dependency theorists would generally be skeptical about potential gains for Africa as a result of enlarged EU market.

African leaders and their intellectual sympathizers within the dependency school posit that there is a direct linkage between EU's "internal" policy [and for that matter European unification], and Africa's development, or rather, underdevelopment. Julius Nyerere, former President of Tanzania, noted that:

> Europe's Common Agricultural Policy, with such things as subsidized prices for sugar beet production, is not irrelevant to the Third World's export earnings, and nor is the Multi-Fibre Agreement irrelevant to those of Tanzania.[58]

Commenting on the bleak prospects of Africa's economic development via incorporation into the global economy, the former Executive Secretary of the UN Economic Commission for Africa, Adebayo Adedeji, noted that:

> Because of the excessive external dependence of the African economy, development has been substantially affected by cyclical fluctuation in the economies of the industrialized countries...which form the major export market for African countries. This dependence is so pervasive that the upswings and downswings in the industrialized market economies affect the value of African exports, the terms of trade, the cost and value of imports, the level of inflation, and ultimately the trends and levels of (gross domestic products). Indeed, it can be truly said that because of our excessive dependence, each time the European economies sneeze, the African economies catch pneumonia.[59]

Africa's concern about Europe's move toward a gigantic bloc is based on the realization that the EU is her sole trading partner, a hallmark of Africa's dependent position in the world economy. In the 1990s, when an African country devises an export-led economic strategy, the market that would be envisaged is likely to be that of the EU. As Table 2.1 indi cates, in 1987, Africa received 52.8 percent of her total world imports from the EU, while 57.7 percent of Africa's exports were designated for the EU.

Table 2.1
EU trade with major Third World regions (1987) (%)

	Imports from EC	Exports to EC
Latin America	19.7%	20.9%
South-East Asia	15.3%	15.1%
Middle East	37.6%	25.1%
Africa	52.8%	57.7%
All Developing Countries	25.1%	22.5%

* *Source*: European Union, "The European Community and the Developing Countries", Brussels, June 1989, p. 2.

Global implications of European unity

The future evolution of the Single Market also poses a number of implications for EU's global political and economic orientation, not only on East-West issues, but also in Euro-South (Africa) relations. The political leverage of the EU, with its Single Market card, is being felt particularly in international negotiations, such as GATT, and issues related to Africa's external debts. The Organization of African Unity (OAU) earlier pointed out some of the reasons for its concern about the future of Euro-Africa relations in the context of EU integration. The OAU noted increasing protectionism in Europe, Europe's dwindling interest in regional cooperation and human rights in South Africa, Africa's external debt burdens, and the dumping of toxic waste in Africa by European firms.[60]

There will be increasing solidarity among the EU countries, as a result of EU unification. United EU represents a more stronger coalition-a situation that would have been impossible had Western European nations acted separately at international fora. In dealing with global actors, the EU nations always have a "head start" because they benefit from the various rich historical and diplomatic experiences of individual EU member states.

As Europe prepares to put its own economic house together, African leaders are concerned about the dilution of ties with Europe. For example, at the annual Franco-African Summit in Morocco in 1988, the Francophone African leaders were concerned that they see France's slackening ties with Africa, and a growing attachment to Europe, as Europe prepares for unification. France's imports from Africa declined nearly by half between 1984 and 1987 when they accounted for only 5.5 percent of the total French imports.[61] African leaders are worried that even before 1992, there was an imbalance between Europe's economic and political interests in Africa, with the pendulum shifting more and more towards the political. Of course, worsening economic conditions in Africa is also contributing to such an imbalance. Of the 43 least developed countries in the world, 28 are in Africa.[62]

There are also some positive effects of EU's power in the world system. The former EU Director General for Development noted that:

> Experience of past decades has shown that the more united a stand the Community has taken on the international stage, the more firmly it has been able to commit itself compared with other Western industrialized powers, to a constructive balancing of interests in North-South relations.[63]

The EU could point to its more conciliatory stand at the Toronto Economic Summit of the Industrialized Nations on the debt conditions of the developing nations. European officials further contend that the growing economic strength of the EU is expected to give the Community a political weight on which developing nation, including Africa, could lean. The question remains: Would African nations benefit from EU' increased economic and political strength?

Not only is the EU member countries among the richest in the world, but also 4 of them - Britain, France, Italy and Germany - are among the Group of Seven Industrialized Nations (the G7). The EU is the most significant trading bloc in the world: EU's exports accounted for 20 percent of world exports in 1986, compared to 13 percent in the US and 12 percent for Japan. In the same year, EU's imports accounted for 9 percent of EU's GDP, excluding intra-EC trade, as compared with Japan's 6 percent and 9 percent in the U.S.[64]

Within the EU, discussions about the external repercussions of the Single Market on developing countries have increasingly gained attention. It was in reference to the European Single Market in general, and Euro-African "links going back through centuries" in particular, that the EU President, Jacques Delors, welcomed the cooperation between the EU and the Lome Countries (most of which are African), when presenting the Commissions's Program for 1990 to the European Parliament on 17 January 1990.[65] The European Parliament has, on several occasions, raised the issue of "1992" and developing countries. Furthermore, a working group of the ACP/EEC Joint Assembly has prepared a number of reports on the effects of the "1992" Single Market on the ACP countries.[66] In October of 1989, the Dutch Government also organized a public conference on the subject, which was preceded by an expert meeting which discussed a number of papers prepared by experts in the fields of international trade and economic integration.

Even though EU's integration might result in an increase in global welfare, as EU officials have boasted, there would be disparate distribution of such benefits because of asymmetrical interdependence in the world economy. Not only is Africa's share of the EU market threatened by competition from other developing regions, but also leaders of other developing countries have questioned the privileges that African countries enjoy in Europe, especially those which are not extended to non-African countries. In an interview at the Embassy of the Philippines in Brussels, a top official from the Philippines informed this author that the ASEAN leaders are concerned about the Lome benefits that put African countries "at a competitive position" vis-à-vis the ASEAN countries.[67]

The Indian Ambassador to the EU was aware of EU's differential treatment of developing countries (which has been relatively less favorable to South Asia, as compared with Africa) when he noted that:

> On the grounds of past colonial connections or on the grounds of geographical proximity, a kind of pyramid of privilege has been built between the Community and the different regional groups of developing countries—be it the ACP countries or the groupings of countries in the Mediterranean. Unfortunately, South Asia remains in the outermost concentric circles of the external dimensions of the European Community, with South Asian countries ranking as non-associated and enjoying no preferential advantages except the GSP and development assistance.[68]

Increased competition generated by European unification will affect the position of countries that are already less industrially competitive, the situation of most of the African countries. Dieter Frisch, the former EU Commissioner for Development, conceded that African countries are vulnerable to the intense competition when he ironically used two African countries to illustrate the differential impact of "1992" on third countries. The Commissioner noted in a Speech on the effects of the Single Market that Japan for example, would benefit more from the Single Market than a developing country such as Senegal; among developing countries, South Korea would benefit more than Burkina Faso.[69]

In a speech on the occasion of the signing of the Lome IV Convention in December 1989, the Vice President of the European Commission, Manuel Marin, also emphasized that:

> ...As for the advent of the single market in 1992 the Community underlines the new opportunities which are offered to its partners. But it is also aware of the risks which might be involved for certain non-member countries whose structure does not provide a sufficient degree of competitivity.[70]

Regionalism in the global system, such as is occurring in the EU today, has potentially negative effect on Africa. There are several justification for this pessimism:

(1) The preoccupation with regional matters may distract the attention of EU policy-makers from multilateral activities. For example, EU's concerns about the completion of the Single Market, and particularly the

idea of a common currency, redirected EU officials' attention away from the Uruguay Round of GATT negotiations. African leaders also have concluded that as EU gallops for unity, it walks at a snail's pace on the route of Euro-African relations.

(2) Recent regional initiatives are not outward but inward-looking. For example, the US has adopted exclusionary provisions against third parties to the NAFTA, such as strict local content and rules of origin requirements. In the case of the EU, anti-dumping measures, as well as Voluntary Export Restraints, have been deployed against competitive non-EU suppliers.

(3) Regional arrangements also generate some selfish interests opposed to further liberalization. This is primarily due to fears of loss of diverted trade, or of trade creation, in favor of lower-cost suppliers. Competition for concessions and preferences may also erode the traditional ties that Africa enjoys in Europe. For example, Latin American countries lobbied the EU against the concessions that the EU granted to ACP countries, during the Uruguay Round negotiations. The Lome Group also lobbied the EU against the later's tariff cuts in tropical goods.

The Single Market develops at a time that Africa's economic conditions are worsening, even in comparison with other developing countries. As Table 2.2 indicates, the performance of the fast-growing Asian NIEs, China, and India, has contrasted with the deteriorating conditions in Africa.

Table 2. 2

Performance of the less developed countries through the 1980s
Average % Change (1981-88)

	Real GDP	Inflation*
Asian NICs	8.6	3
China & India	8.1	6
Latin America	1.5	120
Sub-Saharan Africa	0.7	23
For Comparison OECD	2.8	5

*Weighted Average of Consumer Price

Source: European Community, "Economic Convergence in the Community: A Great Effort is Needed", 11/159/89, Brussels, Aug. 1989, p. 9.

One needs to consider the inequalities not only within vertical Euro-African relations, but also among African countries themselves. According to dependency theorists, few semiperipheral states or middle powers in Africa may be able to realize some growth possibilities, or even develop, but majority of African states will probably continue to be underdeveloping.[71]

In a comparative assessment of the development progress among other regions of the Third World, the OECD's Report, *Development Co-operation in the 1990s*, noted that for African low-income countries, there has been virtually no progress in per capita income during the past two decades, as a result of deep-seated structural problems, serious policy deficiencies, and adverse external conditions.[72] Africa's linkages with Europe is likely to benefit mostly African states with important strategic minerals (eg. oil-rich Nigeria) rather than resource-poor Sahel Region.

Consistent with the dependency assumption of uneven peripheral development,[73] one could discern the growing domination of ACP's trade with the EU by few African countries. For example, in 1986, the African countries that were among the top ten ACP exporters to the EU were largely those with important strategic materials (in the case of Zaire, Gabon and Nigeria), or favorable investment climate (Mauritius, Kenya, the Cote d'Ivoire). That Nigeria alone accounted for 33.1 percent of ACP's trade with the EU in 1986 provides enough theoretical ammunition for dependency theorists who are skeptical about the possibilities of a more "equitable" world economic order.[74]

Notes

1 The members of ECOWAS are Burkina Faso, Benin, Cape Verde. Cote d'Ivoire, Gambia, Ghana, Guinea, Guinea-Bissau, Liberia, Mali, Mauritania, Niger, Nigeria, Senegal, Sierra Leone, Togo,

2 See Donald Rothchild, "New Trends in African Integration", *Africa Today*, October/November 1968.

3 On the issue of Eurosclerosis, see Loulca T. Katseli, "The Political Economy of European Integration: From Euro-sclerosis to Euro-Corporatism", *International Spectator*, Vol. 24, No. 3&4, July-December, 1989.

4 Claude Welch, *Dream of Unity: Africanism and Political Unification in West Africa*, Ithaca: Cornell University Press, 1966.
5 Cheryl Payer, *The Debt Trap: The International Monetary Fund and the Third World*, New York: Monthly Review, 1974.
6 See for example, Julius Okolo, "Integrative and Cooperative Regionalism in Africa: The Economic Community of West African States", *International Organization*,Vol. 39, No. 1, Winter 1985.
7 Rothchild, *op cit*, reference 2.
8 See for example, Charles Kwarteng, "Difficulties in Regional Economic Integration: The Case of ECOWAS", *TransAfrican Forum*, Vol. 5, No. 2, Winter 1988.
9 David Mitrany. *A Working Peace System*, Chicago, Quadrangle Books, 1966.
10 Quoted in *Europe*, February 1993, p. 13.
11 Jacob Viner, *The Customs Union Issue*, New York: Carnegie Endowment for International Peace, 1950.
12 See for example William Axline, *Caribbean Integration: The Politics of Regionalism*, New York; Nicols, 1979.
13 "The Effects of Greater Economic Integration Within the European Community on the United States", Report to the Committee on Ways and Means of the United States House of Reps. and the Committee on Finance of the United States Senate on Investigation No. 332-267 Under Section 332 of the Tariff Act of 1930, July 1989, p. vi.
14 See, for example, E. B. Haas, *Beyond the Nation State: Functionalism and International Cooperation*, Palo Alto, CA: Stanford University Press, 1964. For a summary of Haas' theory, see his "International Integration: The European and Universal Process", *International Organization*, Vol. 3, Summer 1961, pp. 366-392.
15 "EC Single Market: South Warned of Inertia", *South*, May 1991, p. 14
16 See Robert C. Hine, "Regionalism and the Integration of the World Economy", *Journal of Common Market Studies*, Vol. 20, No. 2, 1992, p. 120.
17 Paolo Cecchini, *The European Challenge: The Benefits of a Single Market*, Brussels, 1988.
18 Lorenz Schomerus, "Partners in Progress", *Development and Cooperation,* 2, 1990.
19 *Ibid* p. 7.

20 Johan Galtung, "A Structural Theory of Imperialism", *Journal of Peace Research*, Vol. 8, 1971.
21 See Charles Kwarteng, "Africa and the European Challenge after 1992", *International Social Science Journal*, Vol. 136, August 1993.
22 See Charles Kwarteng, "Africa and the Changing Global Arena", Department of Political Science & International Studies, Morgan State University, Baltimore, MD, USA, 1993.
23 See for example, European Commission, "European Community Perspectives on Regional Integration among Developing Countries", Brussels, February 10, 1992.
24 See Joseph Nye, "Patterns and Catalysts in Regional Integration", *International Organization*, Vol. 19, Autumn 1965.
25 On this issue, see Charles Kwarteng, "External Influences on Africa's Economic Decolonization", *TransAfrica Forum*, Winter 1989.
26 Quoted in "Nigeria's Shadow at Bamako", *West Africa*, July 1972, p. 867.
27 Nye, *op cit*, reference 24.
28 Kwame Nkrumah, *Neo-Colonialism: The Last State of Imperialism*, London: Heinemann, 1968.
29 I. William Zartman, "The Future of Europe and Africa: Decolonization or Dependency?", in Timothy Shaw, ed., *Alternative Futures of Africa*, Boulder: Westview Press, 1982.
30 Augusto Lopez-Claros, "The European Community: On the Road to Integration", *Journal of Social, Political, and Economic Studies*, Fall 1987.
31 Kwame Nkrumah, *Africa Must Unite*, New York, International Publishers, 1970.
32 The Single European Act stipulated a January 1, 1992 deadline for the removal of the various technical, fiscal and physical barriers to intra-European trade.
33 On the South Africa's leadership role in Africa, see J. E. Spence, "A Post-Apartheid South Africa and the International Community", *Journal of Commonwealth and Comparative Politics*, Vol. 31, No.1, March 1993.
34 The organization has changed its name to Southern African Development Community (SADC).

35 Quoted in Charles Kwarteng, "Difficulties in Regional Integration: The Case of ECOWAS", *TransAfrica Forum*, Winter 1988 .

36 John Palmer, *Europe Without America: The Crisis in Atlantic Relations*, New York, Oxford University Press, 1987.

37 Walter Rodney, *How Europe Underdeveloped Africa*, London and Dar res Salaam, 1972, p. 85.

38 On dependencies and vulnerabilities, see Steve Chan, *International Relations in Perspective: The Pursuit of Security, Welfare, and Justice*, New York: Macmillan, 1984, chap. 7.

39 Arghiri Immanuel, *Unequal Exchange*, New York and London, 1972, p. xxxi.

40 George B.N. Ayittey, *Africa Betrayed*, New York: St. Martins Press, 1991.

41 Nkrumah, *op cit*, reference 28.

42 The Yaounde Convention involved Francophone Africa. The Lome Convention has provided the opportunity for colonies of Britain, France and Portugal to be associated with the EEC.

43 On the impact of European unity on Africa, see Charles Kwarteng, "Africa and the European Challenge after 1992".

44 Walton L. Brown, "The 1992 European Community and Africa", *TransAfrica Forum*, Fall 1992, p. 4.

45 Sam Olofin, "ECOWAS and the Lome Convention: An Experiment in Complementary or Conflicting Customs Union Arrangement?", *Journal of Common Market Studies*, September 1977.

46 Adebayo Adedeji, "The European Integration Process: Lessons for Africa", *EEC-ACP Courier*, No. 125, January-February 1991, p. 53.

47 Frank Codjoe, "Africa's Way Forward", *New African*, October 1990, p. 42.

48 On the ideology of Euro-Africa and implications for Africa's development see for example, Guy Martin, "African and the Idealogy of Euro-Africa: Neo-Colonialism or pan-Africanism?", *Journal of Modern African Studies*, Vol. 20, No. 2, 1982, pp. 221-238.

49 Max Liniger-Goumer, quoted in *Ibid.*, p. 226.

50 See for example, J.S. Valenzuela, A. Valenzuela, "Modernization and Dependence: Alternative Perspectives for the Study of Latin American Development", *Comparative Politics*, Vol. 10, July 1978.

51 Robert Koehane, Joseph Nye, *Power and Interdependence*, Boston: Little, Brown, and Co. 1977, p. 8.

52 Theotonio Dos Santos, "The Structure of Dependence", *American Economic Review*, Vol. 6, No. 2, 1970, p. 231.

53 See for example Andre Gunder Frank, *Latin America: Underdevelopment or Revolution*, New York: Monthly Review, 1969.

54 See Franz Fanon, *The Wretched of the Earth*, Harmondsworth: Penguin, 1967.

55 A good discussion on dependency theory is provided by Timothy Shaw, Malcolm J. Grieve, "Dependence as an Approach to Understanding Continuing Inequalities in Africa", *Journal of Developing Areas*, Vol. 13, No 3, 1979.

56 See for example, Christopher Chase-Dunn, "The Effects of International Economic Dependence on Development and Inequality: A Cross National Study", *American Sociological Review*, Vol. 40, No. 75; Colin Leys, *Underdevelopment in Kenya: The Political Economy of Neo-colonialism*, 1964-71. Berkeley: The University of California Press, 1974.

57 Immanuel Wallerstein, "Dependence in an Interdependent World: The Limited Possibilities of Transformation Within the Capitalist World Economy", *African Studies Review*, Vol. 18, April 1974.

58 Julius Nyerere, "More Poor for the Poor: A Third World View on North-South Relations", *Development and Cooperation*, No. 4, 1985, p. 5.

59 Adebayo Adedeji, "Africa: The Crisis of Development and the Challenge of a New Economic Order", Address delivered at the 4th Meeting of the Conference of Ministers at the 19th Session of the ECA, Kinshasa, Zaire, 28 Feb-3 March 1977, p. 5.

60 Organization of African Unity, *OAU News*, No. 9, Sept-October 1989, OAU Permanent Office, Brussels, pp. 24-25.

61 *Saudi Gazette* (Saudi Arabia), December 20, 1985.

62 OAU, "Africa's Alternative Framework to Structural Adjustment Programmes For Socio-Economic Recovery and Transformation (AAF-SAP)", CM. 15/6/Rev. 3, p. 5.

63 Dieter Frisch, Director-General for External Relations, "1992 and the Developing Countries", Address Delivered in Bonn, 25 October, 1988, p. 9.

64 EU, *European Economy*, No. 39 March 1989, p. 23.
65 "Presenting the Commission's Program for 1990", Address by Jacques Delors, EC President, to the European Parliament, Strasbourg, France, 17 January 1990, p. 15.
66 ACP-EEC Joint Assembly, "Resolution on Fourth Convention of Lome", Adopted in Versailles , 29 September 1989.
67 In a personal interview at Filipino embassy in Brussels.
68 N.P. Jain, "European Community and India", *The Round Table*, No. 320, 1990, p. 20.
69 "Le Grand Marche Interieur de 1992 et les Pays en Developpement", Speech by Dieter Frisch, Director General of Development of the Commission of the European Community, Bonn, 25 Oct., 1988, p. 8.
70 Manuel Marin, Vice-President of the European Commission, Speech on the Occasion of the Signature of the Fourth Lome Convention, Lome, Togo, 15 Dec., 1989.
71 Wallerstein, *op cit*, reference 57.
72 OECD, *Development Co-Operation in the 1990s*, Paris, December 1989, pp. 48-50.
73 See particularly Samir Amin, *Unequal Development*, Hassocks, Sussex: Haverster Press, 1976.
74 See *EEC-ACP Courier*, No. 118, November-December 1989, p. 11.

3 External dimensions of European integration

Europe's influential position in the "New World Order" can only be assessed by looking at some of the changes that have taken place in world politics in general, and in the European political arena in particular. Born in the era of the Cold War, European integration is blossoming under a new world order. Former US Secretary of State, George Kennan, coined the term *containment* as the code word for the conduct of East-West policy. After World War II, Western Europe strived to prevent Soviet-bloc influence in Europe and in European satellite nations in Africa. The EEC remained an ideological bloc separated from its Eastern counterpart, the COMECON.

In 1989 the Berlin Wall - that separated the East from the West - crumbled. Instead of isolationism and containment, the EU is talking about "organized integration" with the East. As the tempo of integration between the East and West increases, so is the increase in the incidence of racism and xenophobia. Immigrants from Africa and other parts of the world's poorest regions have borne the brunt of discontents of European integration and disintegration.

Countries that were in the Soviet camp few years ago, are jockeying for positions in the Western security umbrella, under the aegis of NATO. The fundamental changes (political, economic and social) that are now occurring in Europe will have a major impact on Europe's economic and political relationships with the outside world in the twenty-first century. Largely as a result of the Single Market, Europe has become a major trading bloc in the world, and a stronger actor in international politics. The principal African concern is the possibility that Europe, with a revamped economy and inflated political power, could seek global hegemony.

As European defense industries restructure in a more competitive Single Market, there will be arms export drive to the Third World. There is about 40 percent wastage in the arms industry in Europe, because of duplication. The surplus arm production could be dumped abroad, Africa being one of the targets.[1]

Despite the enormous external consequences of European unification, developing nations in general, and African countries in particular, have been largely ambivalent about the EU's plan. Several reasons account for this ambivalence. In the first place, EU officials have repeatedly assured their African counterparts that Africa has little, if anything, to fear about EU integration. The EU has promised that the privileged relationship that exists between Europe and its former colonies in Africa, the Caribbean and the Pacific, will survive EU's internal changes.

It can be concluded that European officials have tried to downplay the dangerous consequences of the Single Market for the world's poor. In defusing Africa's fears about a *Fortress Europe*, EU officials have contended that the Single Market will "give a major boost to the Community economy, a boost which will have favorable repercussions both inside and outside the Community".[2] The Single Market would mean that there will be only one frontier, instead of 15, that rules, standards, tests and certification procedures will be either uniform or equivalent, and that economies of scale will be possible.

External aspects of internal liberalization

One way of understanding the EU Single Market initiative is to examine the main instruments of internal liberalization and their implications for EU's external relations. The Single European Act (1987) is intended to remove the remaining physical, fiscal, and technical barriers to the free movement of persons, goods, services, and capital within the Community.

The adjustments that would result from deepening integration in the EU will create winners and losers in the European arena. European firms that are on the losing end would seek to deflect competition, via non-tariff barriers, or demand special assistance. Compromises to ensure internal cohesion would mean that the costs of adjustment in the EU might be exported to third parties outside the EU.

Developing nations, particularly those in the ACP camp, would be the principal target of resentment, because they cannot retaliate, and in some cases they are considered as privileged.

Consequently, EU's "political warranty", meant to safeguard Africa's interest post-1992, must be assessed with caution. The EU was founded on a protectionist philosophy. In the first twenty years of its existence, it was based on non-liberal trade policy. In fact, the anticipated benefits of higher growth in the EU market (as a result of "1992") have not been translated into real increases in financial and technical assistance to African nations.

Instruments of liberalization

(A) **Removal of physical barriers**

A major instrument of liberalization in Western Europe has involved the removal of physical barriers to intra-EU trade. According to the "1992" Plan, internal borders are to be dismantled. For African nations, there are external implications of the removal of physical frontiers in Europe. Among other things, it has meant the removal of the existing disparities in import and export arrangements that exist among particular EU member countries and Africa. The completion of the Single Market will mean the removal of these national quantitative restrictions (NQRs), and the imposition of unified import rules in respect of non-EU member countries.

The removal of borders in Europe has immediate repercussions on Africa's trade with Europe. The case of bananas vividly illustrates the realities.

Special case: The banana bandwagon

There has a been a preference in Europe for bananas produced in the EU, or in the ACP countries. This preference is guaranteed through volume limits on banana imports from other developing nations - particularly, the so-called "dollar banana" from Latin America.

Table 3.1
Top world traders in the banana market
(1990 figures in million tonnes)

Top Importers	Volume	Top Exporters	Volume
Germany	1.17	Ecuador	2.19
France	0.495	Costa Rica	1.40
United Kingdom	0.470	Columbia	1.15
Italy	0.429	Philippines	0.847
Spain	0.346	Honduras	0.811

Source: *Development and Cooperation*, (Germany), No. 6, 1992, p. 32.

Europe is set to become the world's largest market for bananas.[3] In a border-free Europe, African countries - which have been exporting bananas to some EU countries under special arrangements - will come under competition from Central America (see Table 3.1) - the main entry being Germany.

The EU banana market is marked by fragmentation. ACP countries (Windward Islands, Cameroon, Cote d'Ivoire, Somalia, Belize, and Jamaica) supply about 20 percent of EU bananas; EU producers (Martinique, Guadeloupe, Canary Islands, Madeira, Crete) 30 percent, and the remaining 50 percent are dollar bananas produced by American Multinational Companies in Latin America. There are about ten different banana regimes that range from tariff-free access in Germany, to almost completely forbidden imports in Greece.[4] The Community would have to replace this variety of banana regimes with a common banana policy.

Liberal EU member countries prefer unlimited imports of the dollar bananas. African bananas will face severe competition from the dollar-bananas, in terms of price and quality. The world's biggest banana exporter - the Cincinnati-based Chiquita Brands International Company which exports from Panama, Costa Rica, and Equador - considered investing $100 million in Panama, in order to meet the increased demand for bananas in the US and in Europe.[5]

The Lome banana regime is intended to help small producers in the Caribbean. Four small islands in the Eastern Caribbean-Dominica, Grenada, St. Lucia, and St. Vincent-are the leading banana producers in the region, and provide about 75 percent of bananas consumed in Britain. Latin American banana exporters, backed by the US, have attacked the legality of the banana regime (under GATT rules), which discriminates against US multinational companies that control the banana market in Latin America. The "banana war" is dividing Latin America and the Caribbean more than any other issue since Argentina challenged Britain over the Malvinas Islands. Caribbean nations have even threatened to withdraw from the Organization of American States (OAS) over the banana issue.[6]

The banana issue illustrates the dynamics of EU's internal politics, where former colonial powers are interested in preserving some advantages for their former colonies. The case of banana also epitomizes the contradictions involving the imperatives of global competition and EU's preferential treatment of ACP bananas. The EU walks on a tight political rope, as it strives to reconcile contradictory and conflicting interests: those of producers (eg. from Latin America, who want "free trade"), consumers in Europe (who prefer better quality and cheaper price, hence competition), and the legitimate interests of African nations with which the EU has special undertakings.

The theory that it is easier to penetrate a (EU) market where the laws are unified, rather than different, is questionable. If the unified laws are more constraining, then the barrier to entry would be harder to clear. An illustration using Caribbean bananas would be relevant here. In the past, Caribbean bananas had been able to gain entry into EU countries with which the ACP partners concerned had preferential treatment. In that case, unified laws will only make the dollar zone banana compete with ACP bananas, to the detriment of the latter, because they (Caribbean bananas) are less competitive.

The ACP countries are asking for the retention of the Banana Protocol, in order to guarantee that the completion of the single market would not reduce or threaten the possibility of access to the EU market.

Security dilemmas: A pandora's box

The removal of borders opens complex security issues that have already affected African interests in the EU. When Europe opened its borders, it also opened a pandora's box containing threats from illegal immigration, drug trafficking, and the export of terrorism. Since the demise of Communism and the dismantling of Europe's internal borders, Chinese and other groups, including Russians, Ukrainians, Amanians, Pakistanis, and Sri Lankans, have used the former Eastern Europe as a transit route to the West. In the past, Budapest was a center for the trading of human cargo, but in the Spring of 1992, the Hungarian police began to round up illegal aliens.

There was a sensational trial involving suspected Ghanaian drug traffickers in Amsterdam in 1992. The trial aroused a national uproar, because of the way it was handled. In the first place, the sentences exceeded the usual: 15 people who were involved were given more than 50 years imprisonment sentences, which exceeded the usual prison terms given to such offenders.[7] In a bid to turn anti-immigrants sentiments against the culprits, the media establishment in Netherlands claimed that there were more than 10,000 Ghanaians living "illegally" in the Netherlands. The Ghanaian Community in Europe and other observers saw the trial as racially motivated.

The *Baltimore Sun* (Jan 9, 1994) reported that 120 pounds of carp and half a carton of marijuana with about $2 million value on the street, were shipped to the US from Nigeria-through Poland.[8] There is increased organized criminal elements from Russia and other Soviet Republics, where law and order has broken down. The Western world is concerned about the threat to its security that is traced to the collapsed Soviet empire, and the Third World "population bomb".

(B) **Tax approximation**

Tax approximation is another major aspect of the European strategy of removing all fiscal barriers to cooperation. Each of the EU member countries has a value-added tax (VAT) that varies considerably between countries. The European Commission in Brussels believes that internal economic frontiers in Europe cannot be removed, without a more uniform VAT rates. This has meant the harmonization, or equalization of VAT rates. This policy has incurred the displeasure of both the high VAT countries (eg Denmark and France) which will lose income, and low tax countries (such as Britain) that could lose their competitive advantage when they raised their rates.

As of January 1, 1993, each of the EU Member States was to apply a standard rate of VAT not lower than 15 percent. Formal border checks were to be abolished by January 1, 1993, but VAT were to continue for a "transitional" period. As part of the integration process, there is also the harmonization of minimum excise duties for three groups of products: manufactured tobacco, alcoholic beverages and mineral oil.[9]

The effect of changes in indirect taxation on African exports would be limited to any changes that occur in the consumption patterns of the products affected. There are consumption taxes in different EU member states (eg. Germany taxes tea, Denmark taxes cocoa). The effect of tax changes on African exports would depend on the price changes (price elasticity) which tend to be lower for products such as tea and coffee.

(C) **Technical harmonization**

The third instrument of liberation involves the removal of technical barriers. The existence of different national standards and regulations for products represents a substantial barrier for European industry. In the past, technical incompatibilities had prevented firms from benefitting from economies of scale offered by the EU market, by compelling them to manufacture different versions of the same product, and subjecting them to different testing and type approval procedures.

The Commission has battled with divergent standards for many years.

Protectionism assumed new forms, at a time that customs barriers had been eliminated. An European lift manufacturing company estimated that the cost associated with the differences in technical standards among EU member countries accounted for almost 10 percent of its manufacturing costs. In the telephones exchanges, the absence of European standards meant that costs were 8 percent higher than they existed in the US.[10]

The "1992" process means the removal of these technical barriers through mutual recognition of standards and limited harmonization. The strategy of mutual recognition means an application of a principle of reciprocal trust. Mutual recognition, as defined by the Commission, means that:

> Any product which is introduced on the Community territory, as long as it satisfies the legislation of the importing country, and is admitted on its markets, will be entitled, as a matter of principle, to the benefit of free circulation throughout the Community.[11]

In addition to mutual recognition, European standards-setting bodies (CEN, CENELEC, etc) operate systematically on the basis of work done at the international level. Wherever necessary, the EU counter argues, European standards will be compatible with international ones. However, in the case of tests and certification, the Community will negotiate mutual recognition agreements where needed.[12]

The standardization of EU product specifications poses a major obstacle to the entry of African products into the EU market, despite the general assumption that they will make marketing in Europe much simpler for third-country exporters. Concerns about public health have meant tougher health standards that have affected African fishery and agricultural products exported to Europe.

African competitors have not been given the opportunity to review and comment on proposed EU standards and directives, particularly during the critical phase of standard development. Usually, when the directives are published in the final form, there is little chance for changes. Compared with advanced nations like Japan, or more technically competitive developing nations like Taiwan, Africa has a relatively greater burden in meeting the financial and technical obligations required in adapting to new European standards or norms.

The "1992" program also provides for the opening-up of sectors where international rules are not well established by the GATT code - water, energy, transportation, and communications. In these sectors, the Community is prepared to negotiate with its partners access to the advantages of the internal market in order to ensure a balance of benefits.[13] For sectors covered by the GATT code, the 1992 program will mean that the European subsidiaries of foreign firms will have the same access to the Single Market as European companies. Suppliers not established in the Community, such as those located in Africa, will still be subject to the GATT code which stipulates that the signatories to GATT accord one another non-discriminatory reciprocal access.

The liberalization in public procurement in the EU provides another example of the external ramifications of EU internal deregulation. Public procurement spending in the EU has been estimated to be about $ 600 billion (about 15 percent of the EU GDP). To the extent that public procurement liberalization affects EU member countries' bilateral aid programs, African countries have a stake in the future of the European public procurement sector.

The EU intends liberalizing Community trade in services, which is marked by restrictive practices, particularly in the areas of road and air transport, as well as financial services. The opening up of services in the Community implies the "right of establishment" and freedom to provide services across borders. There is the fear that EU reciprocity provisions (insisting that third countries provide reciprocal access to Community firms as a condition for entry into the EU market) could imply restrictions to market access for developing countries.

On the positive side, however, African countries may benefit from lower costs for their manufactured imports from the EU. Furthermore, international transport costs may become lower, especially for African countries, that pay up to 20 percent more than other countries for comparable imports from the EU.

Partnership or protectionism?

The initial euphoria that African nations harbored about a "Fortress Europe" must be understood within a context. As the unification process gained momentum in the late 1980s, non-EU member states feared that protectionist pressure would be brought to bear on EU's external policy. Several factors contributed to this initial euphoria. In the first place, many European policy makers invoked the buzz words of protectionists in the US-"reciprocity, "level playing field", and "fair trade".

Some of the official statements made by some EU leaders were often taken out of context. These were often sloganeering statements that later became a source of worry: These included, for example, statements such as: "Europe Neither Fortress nor Sieve" and "Europe Between Liberalization and Protectionism".

Some times, actions speak louder than words. The policies that the EU had adopted towards the developing world in the past, have done little to dispel Africa's fear of the "new" protectionism. These policies include tough anti-dumping actions, the institution of Voluntary Export Restraint Agreements (VRAs), and the imposition of quotas on third-country exports to the EU.

From the perspective of African observers, the razor of protectionism that the EU uses against the Americans and the Japanese could also be turned on Africa. If trade restrictions are enacted by the US Congress, or any major trading partners, it is likely that pressure for protectionism in the EU will also increase.[14] Trade wars among developed nations, such as the EU and the US, could have serious development implications for Africa.

A number of European industries, such as automobiles and financial services, agitated for the prolongation of restrictions, at least, for a transitional period, if they are not to be swallowed by non-EU competitors. While African nations worry about protectionism at the EU, the EU has embarked upon a public relations campaign to create the impression that Europe will play a "fair game". To the charge that the EU will become protectionist, the European Commission counter-argues that the Community has not, and will not be "inward-looking", and maintains that in the past thirty years, EU's trade with the world has trebled.[15]

The Commission, on the defensive, rather describes the "protectionist tendencies" of other trading partners. Referring to other major trading nations, the EU noted that:

> The accusation of protectionism sometimes levelled at it [the EU] by its main rivals on the world scene cannot be taken seriously when we consider the scale of the subsidies granted to American agriculture or the volume of public aid channelled into American research into advanced technologies, or the ingenuity displayed by Japan in adeptly avoiding the effects of competition in sectors in which it is not the world leader.[16]

The European Commission-through its former Director General for Development, Dieter Frisch - emphasized that the Single Market is an "internal" goal, and that "external economic policy is not an instrument that can be used to complete the internal market".[17] The Commission, thus, appears to downplay the external ramifications of the Single Market, particularly regarding its negative repercussions on African nations.

European Officials maintain that preparations for the Internal Market have not distracted the Union from its efforts to help liberalize the global trading system. Officials in Brussels even give the historical evidence that the share of the EU's GNP accounted for by imports of goods and services rose by over 3 per cent between 1960 and 1980, even as the formation of EU substantially enhanced intra-EEC trade.[18]

The Commission also insists that the EU cannot close its market for economic reasons. As the world's leading trading bloc, EU officials explain, the EU has the greatest interest in the liberalization of world trade. In refuting the speculation that the EU will be protectionist, the Commission noted that:

> As the world's biggest exporter accounting for one fifth of world trade (United States: 15%; Japan 9%) as highly dependent on international trade (since exports represent 10 % of its GNP compared with 5% in the case of United States), the Community has a fundamental stake in the existence of free and open international trade.

Despite the assurances that the EU would be a free trading bloc, there is a concern not only in Africa, but also in the US and in Asia, that trade liberalization within the EU will be accompanied by higher protectionist barriers against goods and services from countries outside the EU.

For example, the EU's policy of reciprocity means that a non-EU member country trying to sell in the EU would be subject to the same restrictions that EU firms are subjected to in that particular country. European banks could demand the right to operate in African countries, as the ticket for Africa's participation in banking services in Europe.

In pledging that the EU would abide by liberal trading principles, the European Commission maintains that its external policy in the context of "1992" will be in harmony with international law. According to the European Commission, the closure of the market is "ruled out for legal reasons"[19], since the EU has promised to honor its international contractual obligations in the context of the "1992", including the Lome Convention of which Africa remains a key partner.

A political defence has also been deployed to counter the argument that the EU is becoming protectionist. According to European officials, any protectionist policies would jeopardize the EU's international standing, indeed its credibility.

Pavlos Micheals, a Professor of Business, has argued that "the perception [of Fortress Europe] is dangerous and its purpose is to cover weaknesses [of EU's agitating partners]".[20] It must be noted that while some comments made by EU officials might have been taken out of context-which resulted in allegations that the EU would be protectionist-Africa's concerns about EU's external orientation is justified.

African countries are able to distinguish between reality and rhetoric. Former Nigerian Head of State, Olesegun Obasango, has criticized EU's official assurances about the Single Market. In *The Impact of Europe in 1992 on West Africa*, Obasango counter argues that EU's assurances about the effect of the Single Market "are too general. They apply to all Europe's trading partners and to no one in particular".[21] Likewise, EU's concessions are generalized to many developing regions.

Obasanjo's second criticism about EU's position relates to the fact that the EU has a limited capacity to ameliorate the deleterious impact of the Single Market, because such effects would not be uniformly spread in the EU's trading partners. As Obasango rightly points out, "in the nature of things, 1992 is bound to bestow affluence here and embarrassment there".[22]

It must also be stated that EU's policy of free trade could not be interpreted as benevolence or altruism in EU's behavior as an international actor, but as the only choice that the EU has, if it is to survive in the international economy. Farouk Heiba and Mohammed Khalil have noted that the EU cannot afford to be protectionist, if it has to remain competitive. As Heiba and Khalil put it:

> The [European companies] are aware that a Fortress Europe may protect them from external competitive attack and foreign dumping, but at the same time restrict their competitive advantage outside the Great Market. The strength of Western Europe in world trade would consequently be decreased, which would be devastating to a continent whose world market share has been eroding over the last 20 years.[23]

Confluence of forces

A confluence of events "external" to the EU, but more or less relevant for "1992", compound the problem of assessing the external effects of "1992" on African countries. As if by design, rather than a sheer coincidence, the "1992 euphoria" coincided with the signing of the Lome IV Convention (1989), and the expiry of the Multifibre Agreement (MFA)- which regulates exports of textiles to the EU by developing countries. As the MFA was approaching its end (in 1991), there was increased lobbying activities among European trade associations in Brussels for tougher measures against foreign, especially Third World exports of textiles.[24]

Among the easiest industrial products to manufacture, textiles and clothing from the world's 50 poorest countries saw their market share decline in Britain by 7 percent for the period of 1976 to 1987.[25] UN estimates show that the cost of the MFA to developing countries in lost earnings is a massive 1 billion pounds per year.[26] African countries exporting textiles would be particularly interested in the national quotas stipulated under the MultiFibre Agreement. The retrenchment of national quotas for imports such as textiles will help developing countries in securing better access to the Community's market.

The interaction of these events, and the dynamics of "1992" are of great concern for African countries, especially at a historic time when the world is being marked by increased polarization. According to Edwin Carrington, former Secretary-General of the ACP, "1992" is the most sophisticated example of the general trend towards (bigger) trading units, such as the U.S.-Canada (and Mexico) free trade area, Japan and the Pacific Rim, and the EFTA. In 1988, the U.S. signed a historic free trade agreement with Canada. This now includes Mexico. Since Canada is the largest trading partner of the U.S., and Mexico the third largest, "the emergence of a North American superbloc is certainly in the offing". [27]

In the Far East, Japan evokes the memories of the post-World War II Greater East Asian Co-Prosperity Sphere as Tokyo forges closer economic ties with the Newly Industrializing Economies of Asia.

The dangers of these trends for Africa are real. The Heritage Foundation, a Washington-based conservative group, gave a historical pattern of the relationship between protectionism and global catastrophe. Using the EU as its focus of analysis, the Heritage Foundation noted that:

> In the 1930s, triggered by America's protectionist Smoot-Hawley Act of 1930, the British, French and Japanese each attempted to monopolize trade with their colonies. The economic problem and cost of this caused, to considerable extent, the Great Depression.[28]

The US, Canada, and Mexico have envisioned the elimination of tariffs and many non-tariff barriers to the free movement of goods, services, and capital as a result of the NAFTA agreement. A number of other countries, Japan included, have expressed interest in securing a Free Trade Agreement (FTA) with the US.[29] There is a growing concern among observers that if EU's Single Market initiative turns to be protectionist, and the US also proceeds with new free trade agreements, destructive trading blocs could emerge on the world scene. Inter-bloc politics could undermine the spirit of global trade liberalization. GATT and EU's objectives have, and could conflict, in other sensitive areas-particularly in agriculture.

The type of multilateral system that would be functional for the world system as a whole, and that would also suit the interests of the developing nations of Africa would be the one that expands the world economy, rather than restrict it.

Other external aspects of the Single Market and their implications for African need to be examined, too. In the first place, the EU has renewed, revised, or established different preferential schemes with different categories of non-EU countries (EFTA, Eastern Europe, the Mediterranean countries). In particular, there is the creeping, if not a galloping, alignment with the East - which could be aptly described as the Eastern dimension of the European challenge.[30]

The Eastern dimension of the European challenge

The peaceful revolutions that have engulfed Eastern Europe remain, perhaps, the most significant event, in global terms, in the last half of this century. The unprecedented political and economic changes in the East, as EU officials have admitted, "represents a challenge and an opportunity to which the EU has given an immediate response".[31]

Many observers agree that in response to the unprecedented developments in Eastern Europe, the EU has shifted its agenda in its own regional contexts.[32] Africa's worries about the events in the East is Europe's political dilemma. On one hand, EU does not appear to be seen as sacrificing Euro-African relations on the alter of *Ostpolitic*. On the other hand, Europe cannot afford to neglect the historic events on its borders. As the President of the European Commission noted:

> European public opinion, and indeed world opinion, is focussed on the events in Eastern Europe and this is understandable. These events are of historic significance and Europe must be given time to digest them.[33]

EU's trade deals or concessions extended to the East represent a loss, particularly to African nations that also have trade links with both the

EU and the former Communist countries. The changes in Eastern Europe have affected Africa's position in world politics. The Western world-particularly Western Europe - has been committed to the transformation of the Eastern economies into market economies. The basis of political affinity between the East and the West is the historic ties that bind them together. Jenny Verster made an accurate observation about these ties, when he noted that:

> Development in East Europe have reverberated around the world, but have struck a particular chord with people in Western Europe. Hopes for a more united Europe are not restricted to East and West Germany. Czechoslovakia has close ties with Austria, and the Baltic republics have strong historical links with the Nordic countries. [34]

The emerging "democracies" in the East are an integral part of the new Europe, just as they were of mainstream Europe, until they were drifted offshore by the currents of Communism. Even under Communism, the desire of the peoples of Eastern Europe to return to the Western fold was evident, beginning with the East Berlin uprising in 1953, and culminating in the bloodless revolutions in the Communist nations, three decades later - in the close of the year 1989.

The basis of Africa's anxiety about Western European unity, and its creeping alignment with the East, is that such a process has resulted in a shift in Europe's political interest away from the continent with which Europe has developed economic, political, and cultural ties for centuries. Through a series of colonial and post-colonial schemes, Africa has been tied to the apron strings of dependency on Europe, to the extent that disturbances in such relationships could only lead to disturbances in Africa's own internal development.

Under pressure exerted by Western "political conditionality", Eastern European nations have to demonstrate that they are "democratizing", and are withdrawing support for radical Third World regimes. The former Eastern bloc has reversed its progressive internationalist policies toward the developing world.

Furthermore, the dramatic shift in EU's attention and resources away from Africa towards the East has been detrimental to Africa-from an economic and political point of view. In the short-term, African countries have been negatively affected, to the extent that the EU directs more resources to Eastern countries. Ironically, it was the EU that was designated by the OECD to coordinate Western economic aid to the Eastern European countries. In the long term, too, the Eastern countries are going to compete with developing countries for investment resources coming from the industrialized countries, particularly the EU.

Like Africa, the developing nations in South-East Asia are also concerned about the Eastern orientation of the European Union, although because of differential capabilities, the impact of EU integration should be different on South East Asia, as compared to other developing nations groups such as the ACP.[35] Consequently, Africa and other developing nations may not necessarily express the same concerns about European unity.

From the perspective of the Newly Industrializing Nations (NICs), there is a concern that Europe's preoccupation with assisting the fragile democracies that are emerging in the East will impede the EU's ability to compete with the US and Japan in the burgeoning economies of Asia and the Pacific Rim. This scenario could be detrimental for the Asian nations that rely, for their survival, on open competition in a non-protectionist world market. [36] The benefits that the EU has accorded to Eastern Europe in such sensitive areas as textiles, footwear, agriculture and steel, will reduce the EU's "margin of flexibility"[37] in granting similar concessions to developing nations.

For African nations, an enlargement of the EU is interpreted as part of Europe's quest for a "Superpower" status. The member countries of the European Free Trade Association (EFTA)[38] have secured a position in the European Economic Area (EEA). Swedish firms, particularly, have made strides in cross-border acquisitions, in response to "1992".

There is a possibility that Eastern European nations would be admitted with full membership status into the EU - a few years from now. Immediately after its victory at the polls in April 1990, Hungary's Democratic Forum, which headed the victorious coalition, eyed membership in the EU.

The EEA is expected to further boost economic growth in Western Europe, as it expands EU's populations by 32.6 million people, with a combined purchasing power of over $808 billion.[39] The EU-EFTA alignment, however, is not likely to result in substantial trade diversion against African countries, given the already high level of EU-EFTA trade. Moreover, because EU-EFTA tariffs on industrial products were terminated years ago, the trade diversion effects of the EEA could be minimal.

The EEA will simplify procedures and reduce costs for African firms exporting to Europe-by harmonizing product health and safety requirements throughout Europe. African exporters will be able to take advantage of this continent-wide harmonization.

On the negative side, however, the EEA exacerbates the imbalance that exists in Euro-African relations. New prospective entrants are queuing up for membership in the EU, a process that would definitely increase the bargaining power of the EU. Turkey applied for EU membership in 1988, Austria in 1989, Malta and Cyprus in 1990, Sweden in 1991, and Finland in 1992.[40] Austria, Finland and Sweden have been accepted as members of the EU, increasing the size of this bloc from 12 to 15.

For Africa, EU's enlargement carries major implications that are based on a historic precedent. The enlargement of the Community, particularly to include the two Southern members-Spain and Portugal-complicated the relationship between the EU and its North African partners, by increasing the so-called "sensitive sectors" in the EU, and consequently protectionism against competing products from North African countries, such as Morocco and Tunisia. The EU adopted agricultural restrictions against imports from non-member countries-measures that were aimed at helping Spain and Portugal (two principal agricultural countries) adjust to EU membership.

The Maastricht Agreement, signed in 1991, set up new pan-European structures, and conferred new powers to the European Commission, so that the Community could be more responsive to issues affecting its people. Maastricht deepened the political cohesion in the EU, with far-reaching implications regarding the future of Europe's political union.

The Maastricht Treaty has initiated a "Great Leap Forward" in Europe's march to unity, by deepening the trenches of pan-European cooperation.

The Treaty has also set the groundwork for the enlargement of the EU. After Austria, Finland and Sweden, other nations like Cyprus and Turkey are in the diplomatic queue.
The Maastricht Agreement, alongside the Single European Act (1987) will consequently have a major impact on the changing Europe by the year 2000.

As regards the African continent, the implications of Maastricht are not far to be seen, if we consider the following factors:
(1) The size of the European Community membership may increase from 12 to 19 countries with a population of 400 million people. On the positive side, Europe will constitute a larger market than the original EU 12 arrangement.
(2) The Single Market initiative and the European Monetary Union will accelerate EU's global economic power. This will definitely deepen the already asymmetrical relationship that exits between Africa and Europe.
(3) EU's infrastructure in telecommunication, energy, and transportation will become highly developed, and will link relatively poorer EU countries (Ireland, Spain, Portugal, Greece) closer, economically, with the richer partners in the Union. The EU has been paying closer attention to the poorer regions in Europe. North African countries will particularly lose some of their former ties with the Mediterranean members of the EU.
(4) The EU will move faster on the road to monetary integration, where EU's monetary and economic policies will influence those of its trading partners. This will be more pronounced in Francophone African nations whose currency-the CFA franc-is pegged to the French Franc.

An enlargement of the ACP also bodes some ominous implications for Africa. In 1975, when the Lome Convention was inaugurated, there were only 46 members in the Group. With the ascension of Haiti and the Dominican Republic into the Lome fold in 1989, Namibia's membership in 1990, and Eritrea's in 1993, the Lome rank has now ballooned to seventy-one (as at 1993). There is a possibility that some other countries, including South Africa, may be admitted to the ACP, or be given a special status in EU's external relations in the not too-distant future.

The human dimension of Euro-African relations

A large part of the analyses of the impact of "1992" on African countries have largely focused on economic factors, such as trade and investment. Consequently, the social dimensions of "1992", and their implications for Euro-African relations have largely been ignored. For example, the World Bank-sponsored study (1992) on the implications of the Single Market on Sub-Saharan Africa hardly mentions any social implications.[41]

The removal of internal barriers for the free movement of goods, persons, and services, and the eventual harmonization of immigrations policies of EU member states, have had direct and indirect consequences on African students, tourists, workers, and residents in the Union, in particular, with regard to the conditions of entry, free mobility, and education. For example, if a Rwandan does not need an entry visa for Germany, what happens if once in Germany, s/he moves to another EU country where a visa is needed? The fear of discrimination and harassment, particularly by immigration authorities, have been expressed as member countries in the Union dismantle their internal borders.

EU' s immigration policy, particularly its decision on the right to asylum, presents the real human face of EU integration. (Chapter 5 offers a detailed discussion of this issue). The EU harbors a number of political refugees from African countries. Under a 1982 Belgian law, non-Belgians could be imprisoned and later compulsorily repatriated for committing serious crimes, such as acts of terrorism, drug trafficking, hostage-taking, and armed robbery. This is particularly worrisome for the large North African population in Belgium. For them, there are human costs of "forcing people who may have lived their entire lives in Belgium, and have families or close relatives here, to return to a country they have never known".[42] For Arab North Africa, increasing economic problems, and the upsurge of Islamic fundamentalism are not palatable, as Europe tightens its border checks, and co-ordinates immigration policies in order to combat illegal immigration and terrorism.

GATT, "gattastrophe", and European unification

Because of the deleterious impact of the Uruguay Round of GATT negotiations on African nations, J. Lahai Samboma has argued that African nations "must renegotiate GATT".[43] Samboma's pessimistic assessment of Africa's future within the Uruguay Round is buttressed by studies conducted by the World Bank and the OECD. According to these organizations, Africa would lose $2.6 billion annually as a consequence of the Uruguay Round, while the rich Western nations stand to gain in excess of $270 billion annually. There are certain features of the GATT negotiations (compounded by Africa's own structural limitations) that may render Africa as a net loser.

(1) Africa is not industrialized, so it will not be able to make use of the new opportunities in industrial liberalization.

(2) As a result of structural adjustment policies, African nations have been compelled to divert resources from production in the manufacturing industry, so there will not be an industrial base with which to compete with Europe.

(3) The reluctance of the West to share technological know-how and patents with firms and industries in developing nations culminated in the establishment of an intellectual property regime under GATT, that does not suit Africa's interest. For years, pirated computer programs, record albums, video cassettes and prescription drugs, have been available to developing nations. It is for this reason that Asian nations tried, unsuccessfully, to have intellectual property excluded from GATT negotiations.

(4) In the agricultural sector, the removal of subsidies would increase food prices. Since Africa is a net food importer, she will be a net loser. Also, external competition would continue to destroy local food self-sufficiency in Africa.

(5) Africa's so-called infant industries will be subjected to unbridled competition from capitalist monopolies. Developing nations no longer have infant-industry protection, thanks to the new liberalizing ideology of GATT.

(6) The GATT deal enables non-Lome countries to increase their share of the EU markets, and UNCTAD calculates that Africa would lose 50

percent of its competitive advantage in major markets in the EU, US, and Japan.[44]

As far as multilateral trade negotiations are concerned, the EU intends to frame its own rules in areas which are not covered by GATT rules, and could seek some devices - quotas, ceilings and price-fixing-through bilateral agreements. The Uruguay Round has equally important effect on less developed regions as the effects of the Single Market itself.[45] Unlike Japan and the US, however, developing countries in general, and African countries in particular, are in a weaker position to negotiate with the EU.

European integration raises some thought-provoking questions: Is the process of "1992" going to strengthen or weaken the multilateral trading system? To what extent is GATT going to affect the "1992" process, and how would that, in turn, affect EU's relations with third countries?

There are both negative and positive catalytic effects of "1992". Furthermore, the interaction of GATT negotiations and the European plan of "1992" has implications for the global economy and the level of market access. The government of Hong Kong (one of the so-called "Asian tigers") responded to the threat of anti-dumping to its exports, particularly in the EU, with a campaign in Geneva, at the GATT, for changes in GATT's anti-dumping code.[46]

There has been a divergence of opinion among developed and developing countries, including Africa, on many trade issues. Developing countries see lack of "political will" on the part of developed countries to integrate textiles and farm products into the GATT.

The Uruguay Round of GATT negotiations is of practical significance, in part, because of its interaction with "1992", and its wider scope of negotiation. As the Director-General of GATT noted in a speech at the Wharton Business School in Philadelphia, the Uruguay Round is a departure from the days when GATT was negotiating only tariffs and few selected non-tariff barriers: domestic policies, border measures, and national legislation are now being negotiated.[47]

The efforts mounted by the developed countries to expand the parameters of the GATT to include services, intellectual property, and foreign investments are considered by developing countries as a devastating blow to their development.[48] Developing countries see the initiative on intellectual property rights as attempts by developed countries to maintain a monopoly over patents - a monopoly power which could be used to constrain the technological development of the South.

According to the former US Trade Representative, Carla Hills, foreign piracy of US trade marks, copyrights and patents steals $40 billion a year in American sales.[49] If GATT did not act, the US threatened to use provisions of the Omnibus Trade Act (1988) to retaliate against copyrights pirates. This policy on intellectual property could seriously affect the pharmaceutical companies in Brazil, for example, if they had to pay royalties to American patent-holders.

While in the short-term this problem is a concern mainly for the relatively more industrialized NICs, African countries could eventually face similar problems. It is essential to stress the fact that if the Uruguay Round succeeds in linking trade in goods and services and other matters such as developing countries' policies with regard to foreign direct investments (applies to most LDCs), protection of intellectual property (e.g. Brazil), and fair labor practices (e.g. China), then, trade which could be seen as a means of self-reliant development by developing countries could be threatened.

The patent and intellectual property rights regimes proposed under the TRIPS (trade-related intellectual property rights) agreement, would result in technological monopoly of transnational corporations, massive outflow of royalties from developing nations, and displacement of the South's industries.

The hands of African policy makers are already tight, with economic and financial planning already overseen by the World Bank and the IMF. New GATT initiatives could be seen - from an African perspective-as a new assault on the ability of African countries to chart their own course of development.

The OAU urged developed countries to implement the GATT Ministerial Declaration of 1982 and the Punta del Este Ministerial Declaration of 1986, by which developed countries committed themselves to a standstill and roll-back of their protectionist policies.[50] Such policies include developed nations' subsidies and other farm assistance to domestic producers, and the escalation of tariffs on developing nations' exports in their processed and semi-processed forms. For example, the meat market in the EU is restricted, so is the sugar market in the US. Also, internal taxes on tropical products have put these products at a competitive disadvantage vis a vis alternative products originating from developed countries.

For Africa, one of the disappointing experiences about the multilateral system is the importance of sector or product-specific approach in trade policy. In the evolving EU external trade policy, increasing use has been made of product-specific action. The GATT, however, has traditionally laid emphasis on generalized principles and rules as embodied in 'overall reciprocity' for trade in goods. The developing countries would be better off in relying on such multilateral principles, instead of on bilateral reciprocities.

The "1992" proposals on banking provide for reciprocity of access-a concept that third countries fear could be extended to other areas. If such changes becomes a trend post-1992, developing countries could be affected.

The Uruguay Round is one of America's "best hopes" for improving its balance of payments is export of US services. Foreign governments would be asked to treat American insurance companies, banks, and law firms, for example, the same way they treat domestic firms.

One of the characteristics of the Lome Convention is the absence of a reciprocity clause, and the Commission has assured on numerous occasions that there is no question of it being reintroduced.[51] For Africa countries with membership in the Lome Convention, the inclusion of services provisions in Lome IV raises a number of uncertainties regarding the "1992" liberalization of the service sector in the EU:

(1) ACP's access to the EU market involving such things as the "right of establishment" and the treatment of foreign firms

(2) The nature and extent of reciprocity that the ACP countries could accord the EU member states.

(3) Non-discrimination between the ACP countries and between the Member states.

The main concern for African nations is the phenomenon of ultra-liberalism in international trade negotiations, and its impact on Africa's privileged status in Europe. Speaking at a Symposium on the Impact of 1992 on Africa, in Accra, Ghana, in August 1989, the former Secretary-General of the ACP, Edwin Carrington, noted that non-reciprocal preferences is being sacrificed on the alter of liberalism. He gave a practical example when he noted that EU's concessions to GATT on tropical products would reduce ACP's preferences at a stroke in a single year, to the tune of 75 million ECUs. The fact is, the Lome Convention will have a limited benefit to Africa, despite its duty-free provisions for specified commodities, since the duty applied to most of the commodities from other countries were already low. Also, Africa's relative advantages may decline further as tariffs are cut in the Uruguay Round.[52]

On the European side, too, some concerns have been expressed that ACP (and for that matter African) countries are "caught between the devil of protectionism [at the EU] and the deep blue sea of ultra-liberalism" [a la GATT].[53] For example, farm liberalization under the Uruguay Round could add about $600 million to Africa's foreign exchange needs because world farm prices could rise, and Africa is, on balance, a net food importer.[54] Francis Wurtz, the *Rapporteur* for the ACP-EEC argued that ACP preferences face the risk of erosion under the "double effet de l'Uruguay Round et de l'extension du systeme de preferences generalisees".[55]

The EU has earlier noted that since it (the EU) "is a liberal trading Community and allows market forces to determine trade flows within its trade regime, it is not possible to talk about permanent guarantees for ACP into an indeterminate future".[56] Added to the preference erosion is the diversification of EU's imports.

Speaking on behalf of the ACP group, Francis Wurtz concluded that there is an "obvious correlation"[57] between the Uruguay Round and "1992". The Ambassador of Maurice Island to Brussels, M. Chase asked the EU (during the EEC-ACP Paritaire meeting in Versailles on October 1989) not to forget its preferential relations with the ACP and envisage the necessary complementary measures to ameliorate some of the negative consequences of 1992 on developing countries.

Other spokesmen of the ACP, such as the Guyana Foreign Minister, who served as the ACP representative at the European Parliament-ACP meeting in Barbados, Guyana, in early 1989, urged the EU to compensate the ACP states for the concessions the EU made on tropical products in the negotiations at GATT.

One cannot deny that there is tension between the demand for preferences and the imperatives of liberalized multilateralism. The Spanish Development Minister, Luis Yanez, speaking for the Presidency of the EU Council of Ministers, retorted that the EU would not guarantee any relative level of preference for ACP countries, most of whose products enter the EU duty-free. The ACP states, whose share of the EU market has declined despite their special links with the EU, resent similar advantages being given to other LDCs outside the Lome framework.

Tropical products, which represent about 40 percent of Latin American agricultural exports to the EU, are affected by an existing liberalization compromise within the GATT framework. This has important consequences for the competitiveness of the African countries which enjoy preferential access to the EU under Lome. African countries need to improve their competitivity, if they are to maintain their privileged access to the EU.

Self-interest of developed nations

Sector-specific issues have been important in GATT negotiations. One of the major areas of interest to Africa being trade in agriculture. According to Edward Mayo, "Africa is being treated as no-man's land in a disastrous agricultural trade war with the US".[58]

The US Food Security Act (1985) is of particular interest to agricultural producers in the developing world. For example, under the "Bonus Incentive Commodity Export Program", U.S. exporters of major products received bonuses enabling them to lower their prices in international markets. Also, the enlargement of the European Community (in 1986) to include Spain and Portugal has resulted in the introduction of quotas on oilseeds being imported into Portugal. Portugal was committed to purchase 15.5 percent of its grain imports from the European Union. For Spain, too, there was an alignment of import levies to Community levels.

To the extent that actors' evaluation of their situation depend on relative gains from cooperation as claimed by the realist theorists, it is unlikely that GATT regulations will lead to any comprehensive restructuring of the international political economy in a way that would alter Africa's dependencies. Bargaining between French agricultural and German industrial interests has been politically charged. Comprehensive eradication of EU farm subsidy may weaken France vis-à-vis Germany. It is the realist expectation that France (within the EU) will attempt to block any comprehensive GATT initiative on the reduction of farm subsidies. At international negotiations, advanced nations often "preach water, but drink wine instead". Even though advanced nations have sworn to promote free trade and remove customs and non-tariff barriers, they obstructed the very talks that are striving to achieve this-the GATT negotiations. Between 1980-85, the US and the EU spent $61 billion on agricultural support programs; Japan also spent $ 51 billion for the period 1980-83.[59]

The major source of income for many African nation are the export of raw materials: coffee, cocoa, tea, cotton, rubber and the like. Until there is a fair deal in these sectors, African nations may find it difficult to survive in the international system.

The US government wanted to end all major agricultural subsidies in ten years, a proposal that EU officials find unacceptable.[60] Fair agricultural policies could mean that developed countries could find a truce in their "grain war" in Africa - a development that would benefit African farmers. As Carola Kaps has noted,

> How can poor Sahel farmers with their obsolete, extensive production methods compete without protection against efficient American, Canadian, or European farmers? Who in the developing countries is supposed to buy the expensive local production, if there is cheap rice from Indonesia, subsidized wheat and maize from North American and Europe?[61]

The Common Agricultural Policy (CAP) was established in the 1960s to meet the economic problems of European agriculture. Today, its *raison d'etre* is largely political. Stefan Musto has outlined five main manifestations of the impact of the CAP on LDCs as follows: the CAP (1) imposes restrictions on agricultural imports from LDCs; (2) exerts a downward pressure on world market prices; (3) contributes to a destabilization of food prices on the world market; (4) allows the Community's subsidized exports to compete with exports from LDCs; and (5) introduces distortion in the international division of labor in food production and trade.[62]

A reform of EU's CAP policy depends on the outcome of the GATT multilateral Trade Negotiations. The CAP policy has affected the export positions of third markets of major African producers of beef, cereals, and sugar. The EU's farm surplus has been important in the Community's food aid to Africa. However, this policy could hardly make African countries agriculturally self-sufficient, and globally competitive. African farmers, like their counterparts in other parts of the developing world, could be driven from the land, if they could not match the subsidized exports from the EU and other industrialized nations.

African textiles exports to the EU are affected by Euro-protectionism. The OAU noted in a Declaration it sent to the meeting of UNCTAD VII that the principles of competition, non-discrimination, and the free flow of trade have been conspicuous by their absence when it comes to the export of textiles and clothing from developing countries.[63] African and other developing countries have complained that the continued existence of such protectionist arrangements like the MFA provide justifications that may be used to adopt other protectionist devices in other sectors of importance to developing countries.

The future of the multilateral trading system is also an issue. For Africa, the uncertainties about the effects of multilateral trade liberalization are many. The effects of Lome IV Convention and new GATT regulations put Africa at a competitive disadvantage.

As we enter into the last decade of the century,the credibility of the multilateral system is at stake. For African countries, special treatment or exemptions from GATT rules is less and less attractive when the system is itself decaying, because of frequent violations, circumventions or neglect.

The EU has supported successive rounds of tariff reductions under the auspices of the GATT. Since 1971, the EU has also operated a scheme of generalized preferences to promote developing countries' exports to the EU. The EU is also a party to international commodity agreements and has set up a sizable fund to help stabilize the export earnings of ACP countries.

The European Commission has emphasized that there is a "positive relationship" between European integration and the liberalization of the global trading system. The EU noted that:

> As in previous decades, when each step towards European integration was accompanied by a move toward greater liberalization of the multilateral system, 1992 has been accompanied by EC [now the EU] efforts toward the successful completion of the new round ...In fact, 1992 and the Uruguay Round [of GATT negotiations] are complementary since both aim at opening world markets.[64]

A different picture is, however, drawn by some critical observersof European integration. There is a concern that once the EU trade bloc emerges, competing blocs of nations would also emerge, a process that could undermine the efforts of the GATT in maintaining and improving the international trading system.[65]

Policy uncertainties

African nations are worried about the potential impact of EU integration on their economies. They are also concerned about the confluence of factors that complicate the EU integration, including the fall of the Communist bloc and new GATT initiatives, particularly in sectors of interest to Africa.

The Uruguay Round of GATT negotiations is crucial importance because its failure can adversely affect Africa's medium term growth prospects, and deprive the continent of the potential gains that trade liberalization offers. Africa could also be exposed to the compost heat of trade frictions among industrial nations.

The Uruguay Round is in difficulty because of the protectionist policies in the EU, US and Japan, especially in agriculture. Ironically, pressure is being mounted by international agencies on African governments to open up their domestic markets to the exports of the EU, and other industrialized nations, and also to reduce their trade imbalances and fiscal deficits.

To Africa, there is an uncertainty, if not alarm, about the possible orientation and direction of EU's global policy. Most African leaders fear that as the EU intensifies its efforts at integration, Europe's is shifting from Africa. For example one observer writing in the Ghanaian newspaper, the *People's Daily Graphic*, criticized the West (and Europe in particular) for being overly concerned about deaths in Bosnia, while downplaying the famine in Somalia.[66] This brings into focus the issue of what would be EU's global policy and its implications for Africa.

The question as to whether the EU will be protectionist or a "partner" needs to be seen in the context of EU's external policy. The economies of the EU are now caught in a global recession. When member nations plunge into recession, they become protectionist and look inward. Under such conditions, for example, anti-dumping becomes a matter of political discretion, not 'technical' determination.

Within the liberal institutional theoretical perspective on international relations, an underlying assumption is that states seek to maximize their own absolute gains from international cooperation.[67] Jens Haarh has noted that we need to understand the EU as "the product of a complex political deal".[68] Realists assert that in calculating whether to support a given international cooperative scheme, a state has to consider if other states (actors) will reap more benefits from cooperation than itself, as that could involve a threat to the sovereignty of the state. Realist analysis leads to a more skeptical expectations about European Union, in so far as Africa's welfare is concerned.

The global impact of the EU can be assessed by looking at how unification has widened EU's room of maneuverability in the international political arena. The "Washington-Brussels-Tokyo troika" is hardly a global power structure that would promote Africa's interest.

In the 1980s, the EU came to play a major role in the international political economy - qualitatively, as a direct consequence of EU's absolute growth as the world's largest trading power. The relative importance of the EU, in the last decades, has also been partly due to the decline of US hegemony since the 1970s, and the reduction of tension in East-West relations. Also, in a world of economic blocs, the EU basks in a historical lead and a wealth of experience.

Does the promotion of Africa's development fit in EU's unification agenda? Edward Mayo has concluded that the Single European Act "devotes not a word to cooperation with the Third World".[69] More importantly, Japan has even argued that there should be more donor support for Asia, where majority of the world's poor live. African nations cannot count on Euro-African paternalism to keep them afloat in the changing global political currents. It is against this background that we examine Africa in the context of EU's global policy.

Notes

1 Edward Mayo, "Beyond 1992: The Effects of the European Single Market on the World's Poor", The World Development Movement, 1989, p. 22.

2 EU, "Europe 1992: Europe World Partner", (News Brief),Brussels, 19 October 1988, p. 1.

3 See "Banana Bandwagon", *South*, September/October 1991, p. 49.

4 See Ad Koekkoek, "1992 and the Developing Countries: Fortress Europe or Outward Orientation?", Ministry of Foreign Affairs, Directorate-General for International Co-operation, the Netherlands, and Erasmus University Rotterdam, December 1989, p. 7.

5 "Banana Bandwagon", *South*, September/October 1991, p. 49.

6 Canute James, "The Banana War", *African World*, November-December 1993, p. 23.

7 *Ghana Newsweek*, December 1992.

8 *Baltimore Sun*, January 9, 1994.

9 EU, *Approximation of Taxes: Why?*, Brussels December 1991, p. 6.

10 EU, *Europe, Our Future*, Brussels, June 1987, p. 9.

11 E, *Europe 1992: Europe World Partner*, Brussels, 10 October 1988, p. 3.

12 *Ibid.*

13 EU, "Europe 1992: Europe World Partner", Brussels,19 October 1988, p. 3.

14 The Heritage Foundation (US),"Europe 1992": Ensuring a Fair Deal for the US", *The Backgrounder*, May 5, 1989, p. 2.

15 Commission of the European Communities, *Europe, Our Future*, June 1987, p. 2.

16 *Ibid.*

17 Dieter Frisch, Director-General for Development, "1992 and the Developing Countries", Address given in Bonn, 25 October, 1988, p. 4.

18 *Ibid.* p. 5.

19 *Ibid.*

20 See Pavlos Michaels, "The European Community of 1992" How Can US Firms Cope With It?", Paper Presented at the Conference on 'Europe in Transition, organized by European Research, March 4-7, 1992, p. 17.

21 Olesegun Obasango, Hans d'Orville, (ed.), *The Impact of Europe in 1992 in West Africa.* New York: Crane Russak, 1990, p. 3.

22 *Ibid.*

23 Farouk I. Heiba, Mohammed A. khalil, "Marketing Strategies in Europe 1992: New Challenges to American Executives", Paper Presented at the Academy of International Business, Northeast Conference, Baltimore, MD, 1-3 June 1992, p. 4.

24 Bimal Ghosh, "1992: Third World in the Margin", *European Affairs*, Fall 1989 p, 119.

25 *Ibid.*, p. 11.

26 *Ibid.*

27 "Auf Wiedersehen, USA", *International Management*, June 1990, p. 32.

28 The Heritage Foundation, "Europe 1992": Ensuring a Fair Deal for the U.S." *The Backgrounder*, May 5, 1989, p. 8.

29 *Ibid.*

30 See particularly Charles Kwarteng, "Africa and the Changing Global Arena", Dept. of Political Science, Morgan State Univ., Baltimore, unpublished paper.

31 EU, *The Community and its Eastern Neighbors*, Brussels, 1991, p. 1.

32 Edwin Carrington, former Secretary-General, ACP,Speech in Accra, August 1989 on Conference on the Impact of 1992 on African Unity.

33 Manuel Marin, Vice-President of the European Commission, Speech on the Occasion of the Signature of the Fourth Lome Convention, Lome, Togo, 15 December, 1989, p. 3.

34 Jenny Verster, "Will the Third World Lose to Eastern?", *Development and Cooperation*, No.1, 1990, p. p. 16.

35 See a comparison of ASEAN and the African, Caribbean and Pacific (ACP) countries in Charles Kwarteng, "Confronting the European Single Market: Challenges for ACP and ASEAN Nations", *Journal of Developing Societies*, Vol. III (1992).

36 See Howard Richards, "Developing Relations Between the EC and the Association of Southeast Asian Nations", *European Research*, January 1991, p. 24.

37 "New Europe Promises Little For the South", *South*, December-January 1991, p. 27.

38 The EFTA countries are Austria, Finland, Iceland, Liechtenstein, Norway, Sweden,l and Switzerland.

39 Lori Cooper, Marie Treinen, "The 'New Europe': Europe in Evolution in the 1990s", *Business America*, February 24, 1992, p. 12.

40 EU, *The European Community in the Nineties*, Brussels, 1991, p. 4.

41 Alfred Tovias, *The European Communities' Single Market: the Challenge of 1992 for Sub-Saharan Africa*, Washington: DC, The World Bank, 1992.

42 "Forced Return Vs Human Rights", *The Bulletin*, (Belgium), No. 8 22 February, 1990, p. 19.

43 J. Lahai Samboma, "Africa Must Renegotiate GATT", *New African*, April 1994.

44 "Africa Seeks Redress for GATT Losses", *Africa Recovery*, December 1993-March 1994, p. 9.

45 *Europe*, No. 5102 p. 9.

46 "Anti-dumping Moves Raise Fears of Fortress Europe", *Financial Times*, 1 September, 1989.

47 See his Address to the Wharton Business School at the University of Pennsylvania, Philadelphia, 19 Oct., 1989.

48 See for example, "U.S., EC Prepare to Tackle Talks on Intellectual Property Rights" *Europe*, (Delegation of the Commission of the EC to Washington, D.C.), No. 263, January-February 1987, pp. 16-17.

49 *Business Week*, 22 January, 1990, p. 34.

50 OAU, "Addis Ababa Declaration of African Ministers Responsible for Trade and Development Preparatory to UNCTAD VII", E/ECA/ Trade 79, Addis Ababa, 18 March 1987, p. 40.

51 *L'Echo de l'Afrique*, 1 December, 1, 1988.

52 *Financial Times*, June 7, 1990.

53 Francis Wurtz, EEC-ACP Joint Assembly Rapporteur on the effects of the Single market", interview in *Courier*, No. 118, November-December 1989, p. 2.

54 *Financial Times*, June 7, 1990.

55 Francis Wurtz, Rapport Interimaire, Fait au nom du groupe de travail ACP-CEE sur les effets du marche unique de 1992 dans les pays ACP, 3 Sept., 1989, Doc. ACP-CEE 4/89/B/def., p. 5.

56 L.D.M. Mackenzie, "Export from ACP Countries to EEC under Lome III Regulations", CDI Conference, Nairobi, February 1987, p. 7.

57 See Francis Wurtz, ACP-EEC Rapporteur on the Effects of the Single Market, Interview in *Courier*, November/December 1989.

58 Edward Mayo, "Beyond 1992: The Effect of the Single Market on the World's Poor", p. 12.

59 OAU, "Addis Ababa Declaration of African Ministers Responsible for Trade and Development Preparatory to UNCTAD VII", p. 41.

60 *Business Week*, Jan. 22, 1990, p. 34.

61 Carola Kaps, "Free Market for Africa's Farmers", *Development and Cooperation*, No. 5, 1987, p. 6.

62 See Stefan A. Musto, "The Common Agricultural Policy of the European Community and Its Consequences for Less Developed Countries", *Document Interne*, (EC), No. 15, 1990, p. 285.

63 OAU, "Addis Ababa Declaration of African Ministers Responsible for Trade and Development Preparatory to UNCTAD", p. 40.

64 EU, *European Communities in the Nineties*, p. 12.

65 On this issue, see EU, "Europe 1992": Ensuring a Fair Deal for the U.S", (EU New Brief), no date, p. 2.

66 See *People's Daily Graphic* (Ghana), November 13, 1992, p. 2.

67 On the realist perspective on international relations, see, for example, Hans J. Morgenthau, *Politics Among Nations: The Struggle for Power and Peace* (5th ed) New York: Knopf, 1973.

68 Jens Henrik Haarh, "The Same Old Game? The EC in the International Political Economy:, 1985-1991", *Cooperation and Conflict*, Vol. 28, No. 1, p. 79.

69 Mayo, *op cit*, reference 1.

4 Africa in EU's global policy

Africa is at a historic juncture in its relationship with Europe. The last decade of the 1990s has witnessed dramatic changes in the international system. Amidst all the changes and uncertainties, it is time to question the morality of the so-called "new world order", and to reflect on Africa's relations with the world community. Reflecting on Africa's long experience with external intervention, The *New Federalist* concluded that:

> Africa is the moral test for the Western world. It is the moral test of whether we in the West are finally going to admit the wrongs of post-war policy and post-1957 policy vis-à-vis that continent, and whether we finally admit that a complete reversal of foreign policy of western Europe and North America is necessary and needed, to undo the wrongs that have been done vis-à-vis that continent [Africa].[1]

As former Colonial powers gallop to build a "common European home", African leaders and analysts are worried about the future orientation of Europe's external policy, particularly regarding issues of significance to Africa.

The architects of the European Single Market continue to be haunted by a controversial dilemma: Should the Single Market be "open towards the outside world, or protectionist?".[2] Officials in Brussels have consoled their African partners that European integration would be "beneficial to all", because it would boost the European economy - a boost that would have favorable repercussions on the world as a whole (Africa included).[3]

The argument is that the EU, unlike the US, cannot depend on its own internal growth and development to maintain or increase its [EU's] prosperity. The EU depends on imports of raw materials from developing nations. Therefore, the prosperity of capital-goods industries in Europe will depend on the growth and prosperity of the developing world. Here lies the notion of interdependence.

Whether European integration would be a "boom"[4] or a "doom"[5] to Africa, is often analyzed from different ideological and theoretical angles. Nevertheless, the outcome cannot be neutral: "1992" could just be the beginning of a "Fortress Europe" that could spell disaster for its historical satellite - Africa, or as the Cecchini Report predicted, it would give economies in less buoyant shape a "shot in the arm".

Adebayo Adedeji, the former Executive Secretary of the UN Economic Commission for Africa (ECA), captured this dual scenario when he noted that:

> It [the 1992 process] could further accentuate the socio-economic crisis of Africa and its increasing marginalisation in the international economy, or it could trigger the turn-around process in Africa, a process in which Africa finally cuts the cord that has tied it to the apron string of Europe for nearly five hundred years as an overly dependent neighbor of Europe.[6]

European integration carries with it the added possibility of stringent harmonized policies that could not only close the lucrative EU market to African goods, but also restrict the entry of African immigrants into the EU (the "fortress Europe" scenario). The recent upsurge of racially-motivated anti-immigrants sentiments in Europe (particularly in Germany) has worsened the African's fear of a Fortress Europe. Concern has been growing that tighter immigration controls at the Community's borders would generate large concentration of immigrants - including illegal immigrants and asylum-seekers - in countries bordering the Community, such as Czechoslovakia, Hungary, and Switzerland. The Nordic countries and members of the European Free Trade Association would be compelled to harmonize their visa requirements for nationals from non-OECD countries.

The Eastern corridor of the "common European home"

There is an "Eastern dimension" of the European challenge[7]. Africa had scarcely recovered from the psychological traumas unleashed by the momentum of Western European unity, when the continent was forced to undergo another "political shock therapy" following the dramatic demise of the socialist bloc. Western analysts largely see the [positive] effects of the changes in Eastern Europe in terms of their "democratizing" effects on Africa. One observer chronicles the catalytic effect of *glasnot* in Eastern Europe on Africa's democratization in the following terms:

> In many instances, copycat demonstrations have spread from the capital to regional cities and towns and, in some cases, across frontiers reminiscent of the 'domino theory' infection of communism in South-East Asia during the 1960s.[8]

The Western world has already committed itself to the transformation of the statist economies in the East into market economies. Since the reunification of Germany in 1989, there have been a continuous transfer of funds from Germany to the East. One estimate indicated that the total funds transferred was expected to reach $250 billion by the end of 1992: this is in addition to the $70 billion "transfer" to the former Soviet Union-given by Germany as an incentive for a speedy withdrawal of Soviet troops from German soil.

The basis of political affinity between the East and the West is the historic ties that bind them together. Jenny Verster made an accurate observation about these ties, when he noted that:

> Development in East Europe have reverberated around the world, but have struck a particular chord with people

> in Western Europe. Hopes for a more united Europe are not restricted to East and West Germany. Czechoslovakia has close ties with Austria, and the Baltic republics have strong historical links with the Nordic countries.[9]

The former US Secretary of State, Jim Baker, also described the ties, or rather the "rope" that bind the East and the West, when he emphasized that:

> Held together by a common rope [emphasis mine], a fall toward fascism or anarchy in the former Soviet Union will pull the West down, too. Yet equally as important, a strong and steady pull by the West now can help them to gain their footing so that they, too, can climb above to enduring democracy and freedom.[10]

The former French President, President Mitterrand's message to the opening and closing of the Franco-African summit in Paris (November 19-21, 1991) was about one thing: "democracy". The conference shifted from the traditional focus on French culture and language to issues ranging from human rights to the environment. At this Conference, the first Francophone leaders to be given audience by President Mitterrand were those whose democratic agendas had reached more advanced stages-Benin's Nicephor Soglo, and Ahmadou Toumani Toure of Mali who was, incidentally, making his first official trip to Paris since assuming office in Mali.

EU's crisis of expectation

The EU's immediate concerns remain, among other things, how to stabilize the economies of EU countries, and be able to compete in the world market place. In Washington, Moscow, as well as in Brussels, the EU is also recognized as a crucial element in the process of molding a "new Europe" to replace the old one symbolized by Yalta and the Berlin War. As the political ice of the Cold war thaws, the US would like to see the EU play a major, if not a leading, role in global affairs, whether in the conflict going on in Bosnia or aid to the starving in the Horn of Africa.

The world has varied, and often conflicting, expectations of the EU and its global role. One of the major challenges for Europe is how to reconcile these conflicting expectations. Abel Matutes, EU Commissioner, was confident about the EU's capacity to meet its numerous obligations when he noted that:

> The Community will fulfill both its responsibilities on its own continent and its responsibilities elsewhere in the world. The EC [now the EU] is keenly aware that these are complementary, not exclusive, developments.[11]

It is not only in Europe that the European Community faces high expectations. EU officials acknowledge that:

> It [the EU] also has obligations to the nations bordering the Mediterranean and to the African, Caribbean and Pacific states that are party to the Lome Convention; in Asia, Latin American, indeed throughout the world. It plays a major part in securing the freedom of world trade, acts to mediate in North-South conflict, stands up for human rights, and is bringing pressure to bear world-wide for the protection and conservation of the environment.[12]

Alain Lamassoure, a member of the French national Assembly and also of the European Parliament, defined the scope of Europe's new preoccupation, which include, among other things:

> The definition of new relations with each of the countries of Eastern Europe; tackling the inevitable internal and external crises some of them will experience; the new security in continental Europe after the dissolution of the Warsaw Pact; relations with a Soviet Union in the process of splitting internally; and the dialogue with the countries on the opposite shore of the Mediterranean sea.[13]

This author argues that to regard European unification solely as an "internal" (European) matter is flawed. The EU has a global ambition. The fundamental question remains what policy instruments are available for the EU to meet its complex challenges and also achieve its ambition.

In order to assess the impact of "1992" on Africa, it will be essential to examine Africa's place in the overall parameters of EU's external policy. As the EU moves slowly towards unity, it will be important to map out its broader implications for Africa. This is more than purely an academic exercise. There are practical justification for this complex undertaking. It is not only African nations that must be concerned about the challenge posed by Europe. As the "1992" process gathered momentum, the anxieties in Washington, Tokyo, and in other capitals in the world were premised on the economic and political challenge that a united Europe might pose.

Table 4.1
The Europe of 12

European Union	GNP/GDP ($bil)	Population (million)
Belgium	197.1	9.9
Denmark	125.5	5.1
France	1190.2	56.4
Germany	1648.8	79.5
Greece	67.3	10.0
Ireland	37.1	3.5
Italy	1077.5	57.7
Luxembourg	8.9	0.4
Netherlands	278.0	14.9
Portugal	59.5	10.5
Spain	487.1	40.0
United Kingdom	**979.9**	**57.2**
	$6156.9	345.1

Source: *Business America*, US Dept. of Commerce, Feb. 24, 1992, p. 10

Table 4.1 gives an idea about the enlargement of the EEC from its original 6 members to the 12, as at the year 1992, when the internal market program was to take effect. Looking at the precipitous emergence of the EEC as an international actor, Christopher Hill has noted that:

> From apparently parochial beginnings as a device to prevent the iron and steel industries of the Ruhr from ever again providing the motor force for German militarism, the Community has become the world's largest trading unit, the most significant provider of development aid, and the source of wide-ranging diplomatic initiatives that attract a host of other states keen to be associated with European position.[14]

In the effort to promote freer and fairer competition, only few industries in Europe would be able to maintain protection. For some of Europe's industries, a tougher EU policy towards outsiders (non-EU actors) would help ensure that the benefits of the Single Markets would not be siphoned away by foreigners.

Pillars of EU's external policy

The Community's policy toward the developing nations, and for that matter Africa, has been molded by three principal elements: the Common External Tariff (CET), the Common Agricultural Policy (CAP), and a partial Community aid policy. The CET implies that the bedrock of Europe's external trade policy is established at the EU level. For example, EU member countries adopt a common position at meetings of GATT and UNCTAD. However, CET unity is undermined, since EU member countries adopt national measures that influence trade policies. Even though the Common External Tariff forms the bedrock of a common European trade policy, commitment to this policy has been eroded by national policies that run counter to multilateral cooperation, such as the Voluntary Export Restraint Agreements (VERs) that some EU member countries have concluded with developing countries. The VERs constitute a common defensive response to adjustment pressures that are attendant with EU integration.

Included in the arsenal of EU's external trade policy are tighter EU rules of origin, local content requirements, and the maintenance of quantitative import restrictions. Purely "technical" determination of rules of origin is difficult, since the process is often tinged with politics.

The Lome Convention is the EU's most extensive policy in the context of Euro-South relations. The other broader instrument is the Generalized System of Preferences (GSP) that facilitates access to European markets for developing nation's exports. The third major instrument is bilateral aid from individual EU member countries, and last, EU's multilateral aid.

Europe's commitment to Africa is influenced by trading interests, historical relationships, and humanitarian concerns. It must also be mentioned that Europe is influenced by a guilty conscience, when it comes to responding to development crises in Africa. The EU concedes that "as the former colonizer, it [Europe] has a special responsibility to help the most tragic, poorest continent, Africa".[15]

Perhaps, the major uncertainty that remains on the minds of many African observers is whether the EU will advance Africa's interest, or pursue policies that would further undermine Africa's development. The "Falkland nightmare" (Europe's support of Britain in her war with Argentina) still haunts the EU's relations with the developing world. As weak partners in the world, developing nations often speculate as to what would be the direction of EU policy in a world without a cold war.

One observer provided a more optimist, less scarcely, view about EU's future role in the world arena (that would calm Africa's fears), when he noted that "the fact that Europe no longer seeks to exert hegemony gives it [the EU] an important political and moral advantage [over the US or Russia] in other regions".[16] In projecting an image of "peaceful and benevolent Europe", some European analysts argue that Europe, which has been a pace-setter in pooling of sovereignties within one region, has a "natural mission" to promote international cooperation and regional institutions that are important in establishing peace and a just world order.[17]

We will also have to observe how independent [of the US] the EU will be in world politics, particularly in issues where Africa's interests are paramount. Yves Berthelot, Deputy Secretary-General of UNCTAD, for example, noted that Europe must offer a new model for world order. According to Barthelot, the UNCTAD breakthrough in the North-South dialogue is possible only when Europe has a policy that is independent of that of the US.[18]

The EU reminds her African partners about Europe's political record in Africa, where the European bloc supported the cause of Namibia's independence. The EU draws a great satisfaction from the fact that Namibia has been independent, and has also been admitted into the EU-ACP Convention. In 1977, the EU introduced a code of conduct to govern the operations of EU firms in South Africa. Further, the Community applied selective sanctions against the apartheid regime in Pretoria. The then chairman of the EU Council of Ministers, Danish Foreign Minister, Neils Petersen, said that the EU was ready to help rebuild the economy of South Africa once apartheid was dismantled. Thus, the EU seems to have used a "carrot and stick" diplomacy in dealing with Africa.

Tendencies in EU's behavior

Certain patterns in EU's international behavior can be identified. The EU has been guided by the following priorities. These priorities have resulted in certain evolving patterns, or what this would call "tendencies" in EU's international behavior, particularly in regard to the Single Market. The first major priority is the completion of the internal market. The EU's primary challenge is to adapt to a global economy that is changing rapidly, partly because of EU's own ideas about markets and trade liberalization that are adopted world-wide. The risk remains that the EU may give up the battle of trade liberalization and turn inward ("*inward-looking*" tendency). Even though the EU would like to cooperate with other actors, such cooperation would not be allowed to jeopardize EU's autonomy in international negotiations (the "*autonomist*" tendency). How far would the European powers go in defending African interests at international negotiations without jeopardizing Europe's autonomy? The EU may not sacrifice her prestige and vital interests on the alter of Euro-

African relations. In the presence of other international partners such as the US, Canada, and Japan, African nations cannot always rely on the Community to act firmly and unanimously.

In such cooperation, the EU also insists that it must be based on a "balance of advantages" (the "*reciprocity*" tendency). All these tendencies could negatively impact on EU's policies towards Africa. For example, Europe could not be overly paternalistic to Africa, if it is inward-looking. Also, EU's call for reciprocity undermines the non-reciprocal philosophy that undergirds the Lome Convention.

There is still confusion about how to forge a unified EU trade policy. Such was the case involving the debate as to how to response to China's "toy assault" on the European market. The EU wanted to impose a unified quota on Chinese toys - ranging from stuffed animals to pop-guns, that would have cut EU imports by 74 percent. EU-wide toy quota is part of the Community's proposals to abolish or harmonize some 6,500 national restrictions on imports, many of which have existed since World War II.

The EU Commission trod on the toes of some EU industries, such as toy makers which depend on cheaper imports (and want complete free market), and others such as textiles manufactures, who seek cheaper imports as a threat, and therefore demand greater protection. EU member countries have further complicated the issue by linking the liberalization of quotas to streamlining of the use of EU-wide trade weapons. It was reported that France had been insisting on extensive "technical documentation" before allowing Chinese toys on French soil.

The EU and its partners

European regionalism does not stop at EU's frontiers. With its complex hierarchy of preferences, the EU has fostered closer trade links with its neighbors, including the EFTA.

(A) **EU-EFTA Relations**

The major trading partner of the EU, EFTA was formed in 1960. EFTA takes about 25 percent of the EU exports, and accounts for about 23 percent of EU's imports. Since 1983, the EU and the EFTA countries have gradually established a free trade area for industrial products, by abolishing customs duties and restrictions on trade in manufactured goods. In October 1991, the EU and the EFTA agreed to merge their free trade zones into a single European Economic Area (EEA) for people, capital, goods, and services, by January 1993. On the basis of this political accord, EFTA adopts:

- EU competition rules in the domain of anti-trust mergers, public procurement, and state aids;
- EU rules in company law, consumer protection, environment, R & D, education and social policy.
- EU rules on mutual recognition of professional qualifications, that underlay the principle of freedom of movement of people.

The EU and EFTA act separately, however, in cases concerning anti-dumping, trade sanctions, and participation in international negotiations, such as GATT. For EFTA countries, the EEA is a stepping stone for eventual membership in the EU.

The implication for Africa of the EU-EFTA partnership includes the fact that the EEA will be the world largest trading bloc. At present, the EU and EFTA account for almost half of the world's trade. At the political level, EFTA's close cooperation with the EU could work to South Africa's advantage. For example, the ANC developed good relations with some member nations of EFTA, such as Norway. Sweden's admission to the EU could work to South Africa's advantage, since the ANC developed good relations with Stockholm in the apartheid era. Consequently, the prospect of EFTA joining the EU (particularly those nations with which the ANC of South Africa has good relations) will be beneficial to South Africa. This will facilitate a "pull-in" for Africa.

(B) Central and Eastern Europe

Before the bloodless revolution that blew across the East in 1989, the relationship between the EU and the Council for Mutual Economic Assistance (COMECON) had been slow. By June 1990, the EU signed economic and cooperation agreements with the former Soviet Union, Hungary, Poland, Czechoslovakia, Bulgaria,and the German Democratic

Republic (before reunification). A similar agreement was concluded with Romania in October 1990. To speed up the political and economic reform process in the East, the EU signed a new set of agreements with Poland, Hungary, and Czechoslovakia in December of 1991, known as "Europe Agreements". The agreements encompass:

- Political dialogue and the of coordination of foreign policy positions.
- A free trade area, in which people, capital, goods and services move freely.
- Economic and financial cooperation.
- Cultural cooperation.

The EU has taken steps to promote the exports of the East in the EU market, provide financial aid and technical assistance, and facilitate foreign investment in the former Communist bloc. Further, the EU's efforts in environmental cleaning in the East must be emphasized. In some instances (Poland, the former Soviet Union, Bulgaria, Romania), the EU has sent emergency food and medical supplies. These developments clearly indicate how the EU has been actively involved in the reconstruction in the East. It is doubtful that the EU will continue to increase interactions with the East, without much loss to Africa.

(C) **The European Union and developing countries**

As a regional trading bloc itself, one of the major contributions of the EU is that it has been a supporter of moves towards regional integration and cooperation in the Third World. The EU, perhaps, more than any regional body, would be better able to help African integration since it can "share with its partners its [EU's] own experience in the field".[19] In Latin America, the EU has supported the Andean Pact, of which it is the principal external donor.

As of 1992, there were few developing nations which had not established special ties with the EU, and few that did not receive some form of EU aid (see Table 4.2). In 1990, the Community was actively involved in more than 25 developing nations, ranging from Liberia to South Africa, from Iran to Cambodia, and from Lebanon to countries afflicted by the Gulf War.[20]

Table 4.2
European Union's dialogue with other groups of states

Dialogue Partner	Economic Co-op	Date	Political Coop.	Date
ACP	Yes	1975	Yes	1988
Andean Pact	Yes	1983	Yes	1980
Arab League	Yes	1975	Yes	1974
ASEAN	Yes	1980	Yes	1978/80
Contodora and Central America	No	N/A	Yes	1984
CMEA	Yes	1988	No	N/A
Front Line States	No	N/A	Yes	1986
GCC	Yes	1988	Yes	1986
Mediterranean States	Yes	1975	Yes (Maghreb)	1990
SELA	Yes	1971/5	No	N/A

Source: Adapted from Christopher Hill, "The Foreign Policy of the European Community: Dream or Reality", in Roy C. Macridis (ed.) *Foreign Policy in World Politics* (8th ed) (Englewood Cliff, NJ: Printice-Hall, 1992), p. 127

As one of Latin America's main trading partners, Europe accounts for 20 percent of its exports and 20 percent of its imports. The EU's system of generalized preferences facilitates the access of Latin American products into the EU. The EU takes only about 14 percent of ASEAN total exports which constitutes only 3 percent of EU's own imports. Even though there is a vast increase in the flow of manufactured items from ASEAN, raw materials constitute the main imports of EU from the region.[21]

(D) Euro-Africa relations: The Lome framework

To an extent, the Lome regime respected the doctrine of "political non-alignment", because it emphasized the freedom of each partner to choose its economic system, political regime, and development model. However, this idealism is changing. EU nations have increasingly insisted on political conditionality that ties EU's economic programs in Africa to overly political criteria, such as "democracy" and "good governance".

The main instrument of EU development policy towards Sub-Saharan Africa is the Lome Convention (see Table 4.3). Lome contains some elements that reflect the doctrine of self reliance. During the original negotiations of the Lome Treaty in the early 1970s, the ACP nations called for self reliance - in particular, collective self-reliance and increased intra-ACP co-operation, a greater flow of private investment from the Community, and increased trade promotion between the EU and its former colonies, most of which are African.[22]

Table 4.3
Foreign policy landmarks of the European Union

Apr.18, 1951	Treaty of Paris establishes European Coal and Steel Community; Pleven Plan for a European Defence Community
Mar. 25, 1957	Treaty of Rome establishes the European Economic Community and the European Atomic Energy Community
1963	Yaounde Convention associates 17 African states and the Madagascar with the EC
Jan. 1, 1973	Britain, Denmark, and Ireland join the EC
1975	First Lome Convention is signed between the EC and 46 African Caribbean, and Pacific (ACP) countries
Jan. 1, 1986	Spain and Portugal join the EC
1987	Signing of the Single European Act establishing the EC Single Market by Jan 1, 1992
Feb. 1990	Britain partially and unilaterally withdraws from agreed EC sanctions against South Africa (after consultation as the Single European Act requires)
Nov. 1991	The Maastricht Treaty on Political Union adopted

The Lome Convention was expected to embody the ideals that had been fashionable in North-South agenda over the years: industrialization (both import-substitution, and export-led approaches), trade *not* aid, the stabilization of commodity prices, bridging the infrastructure gap, the provision of basic needs, technology transfer, etc.

The Lome Convention has several features as follows: First, it has resources administered through the European Development Fund (EDF).

Lome I (1975-80) accorded 3.150 billion ECUs to ACP countries; Lome II (1980-85) 5.9 billion ECUs; Lome III (1985-90) 8.5 billion ECUs and Lome IV (1990-95) 12.8 billion ECUs. Second, manufactured and most farm products from the ACP countries enjoy free access to the EU. There is an export stabilization fund, STABEX, financed by the European Fund and designed to offset any value shortfall in ACP's earnings from a list of agricultural commodities.[23] In addition to STABEX, there is another mechanism, SYSMIN-comparable to except that it applies to mineral products such as copper, manganese, etc.

Also, special provisions are made for supporting regional cooperation, including projects for improving maritime and air links in the Caribbean, locust and animal diseases control and the prevention of desert encroachment in Africa. The EU has also offered some large quantities of food aid to African countries affected by famine or other calamities such as drought. The EU-ACP institutional framework provides an arena for political dialogue between the EU and its African associates.

Africa's position in the pyramid of privileges

(A) **Sub-Saharan Africa**

Sub-saharan African lies within the uppermost tier of EU's pyramid of privileges. The Lome Convention provides free access to the EU market for about 95 percent of the exports of the ACP countries. The only major exceptions are the products that come under the Common Agricultural Policy, but at the same time, these products are given better preferential treatment than exports from other developing countries.

Despite this novel treatment, the Lome Convention has been the subject of academic and political debate (see Chapter 2): The main issue is the extent to which Lome has benefitted the African nations. More recently, the debate has been extended to include such issues as whether or not the effects of the Single Market would negate the already shrinking preferences that the African nations enjoy in Europe. Those who have unmasked the Lome schemes as "exploitative" have called for a "new model" of Euro-African relations.

Even though Africa has an abundance of cheap labor, the state of industrialization of the continent can scarcely be counted as a success. Even where economic growth has taken place, a large proportion of the population in Africa has failed to benefit, and still live in absolute poverty.

Of all the ties that exist between Europe and Africa, the one that has been criticized the most by dependency theorists, perhaps, is the Lome Convention. To critics, successive Lome Conventions are "more of the same". S.K. B. Asante considered the Lome Convention as "another machinery for updating dependency",[24] because it guarantees EU's access to raw materials in the ACP countries, and control over investments there, and does not envisage altering the historic unequal trade relationship. Asante noted that:

> The Lome regime as a whole does not seem to give some promise of a release from a state of dependence to a state of mutually balanced set of interest. Instead it deflects attention away from satisfaction of fundamental needs towards increased production, processing and trading, and with the latter, there is no guarantee that the terms of trade will be satisfactory, nor that the spin-off effects from a possible industrialization process will accrue to the developing countries.[25]

Dependency theorists have written extensively about the phenomenon of *unequal exchange* in international relations.[26] Julius Okolo noted that the association of the African countries with the European bloc has increased Africa's dependency [on Europe], in the sense that Africa supplies raw materials in exchange for EU's manufactured items.[27] About 95 percent of the ACP's exports to the EU consists of agricultural commodities and raw minerals, whereas about 80 percent of EU's exports to them consists of manufactured goods.[28] The ideal of European development aid to Africa transcends mere 'humanitarianism'. It is partly an aspect of European paternalism. It is also partly ideological-to symbolize the bond of the ideology of "Euro-Africa".[29] This ideology has been based on two major concepts of *complementarity* and *interdependence*. Euro-Africanism, as an ideology, is a body of thought originating in the colonial period, according to which the fate of Europe and Africa are seen as being naturally and inexorably linked at the political, economic, social, and cultural levels.

As Guy Martin has concluded, this ideological framework provided a justification for colonialism, and also appears to be the basis of the various contractual agreements that have been forged between Europe and Sub-Saharan Africa - from the Yaounde (1964) to the Lome Conventions (1975).[30] Martins acknowledges that Euro-African relations is an unequal relationship, an instrument of exploitation and cultural subjugation.[31] Martin noted that "Europe needed Africa's resources and manpower for its continued growth and development - hence the resort to an ideology to justify Europe's political domination and economic exploitation[of Africa]"[32] .

In "The Future of Europe and Africa: Decolonization or Dependency", William Zartman noted that the association of former European colonies with the EU was not an act of decolonization, but a means of Europe protecting its former colonial markets, and opening the former colonies to European trade and investments.[33] A key evidence of the imbalances in Euro-African relations is the structural content of net EU-ACP trade. Petroleum constitutes the bulk of EU imports from the ACP, while machinery and equipment is the bulk of EU exports to the ACP. The small percentage of manufactured products in Sub-Saharan Africa's exports to the EU originates largely from European firms which have cooperation projects or local branches in ACP countries. A withdrawal of such firms from African countries would worsen Africa's manufactured export capacity.

Because of the importance of agriculture to developing countries, and due to the extensive protection applied under CAP, issues related to agriculture are likely to constitute a major source of EU-Third World tensions in post-1992. For Sub-Saharan African countries belonging to the Lome Convention, the consequences of 1992 must be assessed within the contexts of the nature of economic relations that evolved in the framework of EEC-ACP relations. Although most African countries have preferential access to the EU market, thanks to the Lome Convention, the tendency has been for the EU to limit African exports of agricultural products to commodities (largely unprocessed produce) that do not compete with European products. The accession of Spain and Portugal (two largely agricultural countries) into the EU in 1986, added more political grist to the mill of EU's CAP policy.

(B) **North Africa**

African countries outside the Lome orbit are also concerned about the impact of "1992". The Mediterranean countries, including North Africa (other than Libya), enjoy a preferential trade regime with the EU, second only to Lome. By virtue of their association agreements with the EU, the Mediterranean nations have tariff-free access to the EU for industrial products. However, in the case of "sensitive" goods (in particular textiles and clothing), access to the EU market is restricted by ceiling and quotas. Also, a large proportion of their agricultural exports, including goods that fall under CAP, receive preferential treatment, although this is often subject to reference prices, seasonality, and quotas.[34]

The Southern Mediterranean is an important outlet for the EU, since the region takes over 10 percent of total Community exports, i.e. more than all the ACP countries combined, and half of what the EU exports to the U.S.[35] Because of the importance of the economic and social ties, the EU, shortly after the first Lome Convention was signed in 1975, initiated cooperation agreements in 1976 with Morocco, Algeria, and Tunisia. In 1977, a similar agreement with Egypt was signed. These agreements provided for (a) duty-free access to the Community market for industrial products and highly preferential rates of duty for agricultural products; (b) aid for development (worth 11.6 billion ECUs for the period 1985-91), and common institutions to facilitate dialogue between both sides.

In addition to economic ties, the Southern Mediterranean is of great geo-political importance for Europe. The former EU President, Jacques Delors, told the European Parliament that:

> Down through the ages the Christian, Jewish and Muslim worlds, European and oriental civilization, have met and

> mingled in the Mediterranean. We must make it our concern, firstly because of traditional trade flows and cultural and historic links, and secondly because we cannot ignore the problems in the world around us, the urgent development needs of countries faced with a steep rise in population, the environmental pressures on the sea we share, and the flashpoints of social and religious tension which are a major source of instability.[36]

North Africa presents the European Union with geo-political challenges. There are several millions of North Africans working in Europe. Many of the trade protocols existing between the EU and Morocco, Algeria, Tunisia and Egypt would have to be revised. This happens particularly at a time when these North African countries will be dealing with a more powerful Europe. Particularly because of Algeria's tough price policies, there is the fear that the EU might be looking to Norway and the Soviet Union for its natural gas imports most of which, hitherto, had come from Algeria.[37] This could affect oil prices and, therefore, African oil exporters.

At a forum where participants discussed the effects of the Single Market and the Future of the Mediterranean Countries, Chistiane Scrivener, an EU Commissioner, noted that from 1992 to 1996, Community aid (loans and budget appropriation) to the Mediterranean countries would triple, in relation to the previous five-year period. There will be a number of significant innovations such as a major drive on the environmental front, the support of economic reforms and structural adjustment, and the promotion of venture capital to the region.[38]

According to Scrivener, the purpose of the new EU approach in dealing with the Mediterranean countries is to improve the chances of those countries of benefitting from their proximity to the world's biggest economic bloc. It is also in the EU's best interest "to ensure that its own development takes place in an environment that is-both the East and to the South-as stable and prosperous as possible".[39]

The Commission's proposals to assist the Maghreb countries have excluded Libya - a country that the EU severed ties with, in line with the UN sanctions imposed on Libya, after Tripoli failed to hand over suspects in the 1988 Lockerbie airline bombing.

In dealing with its Mediterranean neighbors in the South, the EU appears to face a challenge from two fronts: (1) how the EU can and will maintain a balance between its interest in Central and Eastern Europe on one hand, and the EU's ties to the South, and (2) how the EU can ensure that this balance of interest is visible to those countries in North Africa.

The EU has proposed new links with the Maghreb countries. European officials concede that they need to improve political and economic links with Morocco, Algeria, and Tunisia, or risk increasing instability in these poor Southern countries. Among other things, Europe is worried about exploding population growth in the Maghreb countries, their debt obligations, and the widening income gap between poor North Africa and wealthy Europe. As Table 4.4 suggests, while the EU will experience 0.7 percent growth in population between 1990 and the year 2000, the Southern Mediterranean would experience as much as 20 percent for the same period.

Table 4.4
Population and work force in 1990 and the expected growth from 1990-2000: EU and Southern Mediterranean

	EU			Southern Mediterranean		
	1990	Increase	%	1990	Increase	%
Population	340.5	2.4	0.7	245.0	49.6	20.2
Work Force	153.3	1.5	1.0	82.4	22.4	27.2

Source: Ritt Bjerregaard, "Population Movements in the 1990s: Challenges of Policy Makers in Europe", *Development*, No. 1, 1993, p. 17.

(C) EU and Post-Apartheid South Africa

The growing influence of the EU has not been lost to officials in Pretoria, particularly the newly elected Mandela Administration. South Africa planned a cooperation agreement with the EU that was to take effect by June 1993.[40] The options for South Africa include (a) most-favored-nations (MFN) status (b) reciprocal or non-reciprocal association with the

EU (c) "associate" Lome Convention status and (d) full membership in Lome.

For South Africa, a MFN status might hurt: it could compel Pretoria to face very high tariffs on its deciduous fruit exports to the EU. The potential benefits of EU trade preferences are also dependent on the outcome of GATT talks. GATT members could also challenge an EU-South African arrangement if they thought that their trade interests are damaged. For South Africa, the EU is the major trading partner - with Germany and the UK being the most important. Since EU nations also benefit from trading with South Africa, they are likely to help South Africa get a better deal at GATT negotiations.

South Africa will need the EU market, though there are some roadblocks in EU-South African relations. All of Pretoria's 15 principal commodities are primary goods or slightly processed metals. In education and health, South Africa ranks seventieth, internationally on the Human Development Index (UNDP 1992). The EU may have to assist South Africa to restructure its economy in a way that would rectify the misdeeds of apartheid.

Some EU member nations might be reluctant about allowing Pretoria's entry into the Lome orbit, since this would mean South Africa's competition in the labor intensive manufacturing sectors. Furthermore, Lome membership would allow South African tenders to bid for European Development Fund's aid contracts to carry out work with the ACP countries.

South Africa's technological know-how will benefit the EU and African countries. Perhaps, South Africa, more than the EU, might be able to find an "African solution" to Africa's problems. Access to the EU market would be very beneficial to South Africa - perhaps, the only African country that has the capacity to sustain a substantial level of industrial production that could benefit from an enlarged EU market. As a member of the Lome Accord, South Africa would benefit from the trade preferences granted to the ACP countries, which are the most substantial, so far, offered by the EU on non-reciprocal basis.

Based on a study conducted by the European Research Office (ERO), the size of South Africa's population will enable that country to benefit from a minimum of 250 million ECUs ($306 million) over five years, under a national indicative programme of EU development aid. This will constitute a *lateral erosion* of Lome preferences.[41] There is another political problem. There could be a possible hostility to South Africa's membership in the Lome Convention, as this would mean that Pretoria will share EU's aid with the ACP nations.

There are some other unpalatable pills that Pretoria will have to swallow. Should South African join the Lome Convention, it may be reclassified from a "semi-developed" to a "developing" nation. Officials in Pretoria fear reclassification of South Africa's status might deliver a psychological blow that could impact negatively on the perception of investors about South Africa. Furthermore, the EU may push some political buttons on Pretoria, by attaching some strings to EU aid offers. For example, aid allocation may be tied to Pretoria's observance of human rights and good governance.

The ties that don't bind

The move towards European unity puts Africa in a delicate strategic dilemma. There is a greater possibility of Africa's marginalization, to the extent that the EU reduces its ties with the continent. In dealing with the West, the "Soviet leverage" can no longer be used to Africa's advantage, as we move towards a unipolar world in which Russia plays a virtual subservient role.

The impact of the Cold-War on Africa's international relations is enormous. President Mobutu has pillaged his country with scarcely a murmur of dissent from his Western sponsors. There are two major reasons for this: Zaire is an important supplier of minerals, including industrial diamonds, copper and cobalt (essential for the defense industry). Second, Mobutu allowed his country to be used as a base for covert American military and diplomatic expedition into Angola and Chad. As his reward, Mobutu (in 1988) became the first African Head of State to meet with President Bush.[42]

European left-wingers should also be blamed for implementing in African the biggest socialist fantasies which they were not able to implement in their own countries in Europe. As the mystique of socialism is shattered, Africa's ties with the East will wane.

Africa should not solely rely on the US, just because Russia is no longer a Superpower. As a strategy, Africa might want to diversify their relations with the EU, perhaps, to include Japan or some of the NICs. A unipolar world headed by the US may not be in Africa's best interest. The US tended to defer to European leadership in Africa during and after the colonial period, and has viewed Africa primarily in strategic terms. For example, it was not until 1958 that the US government established a Bureau of African Affairs in the US State Department. Also, until President Bush's last-minute foray into Somalia in the new year in 1993, Jimmy Carter remained the only American president to visit sub-Saharan Africa whiles in office.[43] Once the strategic threat of Communist-bloc influence in Africa has been neutralized, Africa is likely to remain in the periphery of the Western world's global concerns.

Of all the Euro-African ties, those between the Francophone bloc and France is the deepest. Even when ideological schisms divide France and Africa, economic relations have prevailed as in the case of Benin, Congo, and Madagascar. The more dramatic reversal of ties, perhaps, has been the case of Guinea-the "prodigal son" that decided to return to the French fold, after the death of President Ahmed Sekou Toure in 1984. Paris invested a lot of diplomatic capital in initiating links with Africa as a way of upholding French prestige, influence, and *grandeur* in the global arena. Francophone Africa has been content in receiving French technical assistance, investment, and in particular guarantees in terms of economic balancing of the CFA.

In strategic terms, Paris' role in Africa has involved the provision of military support. In fulfilling her "gendarme role" in Africa, France has, in the past, stationed troops in some African countries, including Central Africa Republic (CAR), Cote d'Ivoire, Djibouti, Gabon, and Senegal. France has also used interventionist forces in Chad, Western Sahara, and Zaire.[44] As the Cold War thaws, and Europe's geo-strategic interests in Africa erodes, African dictators - who have traditionally relied on foreign protection, rather than on their regimes' legitimacy - are left in the cold.

European unification has brought its own discontents: the upsurge of racism and xenophobia. Discussions about the European Single Market have ignored the human (social) dimensions of competition. It is necessary, therefore, to discuss the social dilemmas posed by the issue of immigration in Europe, from the perspective of Africa. The following chapter deals with this issue.

Notes

1 *The New Federalist* (USA), April 13, 1992, p.5.

2 "Europe: Our Sort of Community", Address by the Rt. Hon. Sir Leon Brittan, QC, Vice President of the Commission of the European Communities,London, 7th November 1989, p. 7.

3 See particularly Paolo Cecchini, *The European Challenge: The Benefits of a Single Market*, Brussels: EU, 1988.

4 Numerous working papers and documents prepared by the EU predict that the Single Market will benefit developing nations.

5 On the fears "1992" see, Baffour Ankomah, "Who is not Afraid of 1992?", *New African*, February 1989.

6 Adebayo Adedeji, Excerpts from a paper presented at the Seminar on "European Economic Community after 1992: Consequences for Africa", organized by the Nigerian Ministry of External affairs, reprinted in *The EEC-ACP Courier*, January-February, 1991, p. 50.

7 See particularly, Charles Kwarteng, "Africa and the European Challenge of 1992", *International Social Science Journal*, August 1993.

8 Simon Baynham, "Geopolitics, Glasnost and Africa's Second Liberation: Political and Security Implications for the Continent", *Africa Insight*, Vol. 21, No. 4, 1991, p. 263.

9 Jenny Verster, "Will the Third World Lose to Eastern Europe?", *Development and Cooperation*, No. 1 1990, p. 16.

10 James Baker III, "America and the Collapse of the Soviet Empire", *Vital Speeches*, 1 January, 1992, p. 164.

11 Quoted in *European Report*, No. 1566, p. 7.

12 EU, *The European Community: 1992 and Beyond*, Brussels, 1991, p. 6.

13 Quoted in "Three House, One Home", *European Affairs* (no date), p. 20.

14 Christopher Hill, "The Foreign Policy of the European Community", in Roy C. Macridis (ed.), *Foreign Policy in World Politics* (8th ed.) New York, Printice Hall 1992, p. 108.

15 EU, *Biblio-Flash*, No. 14, 1988, p. 3.

16 *Ibid.*

17 *Ibid.*, p. 4.

18 Remarks Made at a Conference on "Europe and World Order", January 14-16, 1987, London, cited in *Ibid.*, p. 16.

19 EU, *The European Community and Latin America*, Brussels, 1991, p. 5.

20 EU, *European Community and the Third World*, Brussels, 1991., p. 3.

21 For a comparative assessment of the challenges that the EC poses for ASEAN and Africa, see Charles Kwarteng, "Confronting the European Single Market: Challenges for the ACP and ASEAN Countries", *Journal of Developing Societies*, Vol. 8, 199.

22 "The Lome Convention: Practical Aspects Past Experience and Future Prospects", Address to the Committee on Developing Countries, by Dieter Frisch, Director General for Development of the Commission of the European Communities, Berlin, November 30, 1984, p. 5.

23 A similar system has also been approved for several least developed countries which are not signatories to the Lome Convention.

24 S.K.B. Asante, "Lome II: Another Machinery for Updating Dependency?", *Development and Cooperation*, No. 3, 1981.

25 *Ibid.*, p. 19.

26 Arghirri Emmanuel, *Unequal Exchange and the Imperialism of Trade*, New York: Monthly Review, 1972.

27 Julius Emeka Okolo, "Integration and Cooperative Regionalism: The Case of the Economic Community of West African States: *International Organization*, Vol. 39, No. 1, Winter 1985, p. 145.

28 Resolution Sur les effects du marche unique CEE de 1992, adoptee a Versailles par l'Assemblee Paritaire ACP-CEE, 25-29 Sept. 1989.

29 See Guy Martin, "Africa and the Ideology of Eurafrica: Neocolonialism or Pan-Africanism?", *Journal of Modern African Studies*, Vol.20, No. 2, 1992, p. 231.

30 *Ibid.*, p. 231.

31 *Ibid.*, p. 222.

32 *Ibid.*

33 I. William Zartman, "The Future of Europe and Africa: Decolonization or Dependency?", in Timothy Shaw (ed.), *Alternative Futures for Africa*, Boulder: Colorado, Westview Press, 1982, p. 120.

34 Michael Davenport, "Africa and the Unimportance of Being Preferred", *Journal of Common Market Studies*, June 1992, p. 233.

35 EU, *The European Community and the Developing Countries*, Brussels, June 1989, p. 5.

36 "Presenting the Commission's Programme for 1990", Address by Jacques Delors, President of the EU, Brussels, 1989, p. 14.

37 Baffour Ankomah, "Who isn't Afraid of 1992?", *New African*, February, 1989, p. 25.

38 From a press release, EU, Brussels, 9 April 1992.

39 Scrivener's remarks on "the EC and the Mediterranean" were reported in the, EU's *Press Release*, Brussels, 9 April 1992.

40 "South Africa Forges New Trade Links With Europe", *Africa Business*, January 1993, p. 10.

41 *Ibid.*, p. 10.

42 David Aronson, "Why Africa Stays Poor", *The Humanist*, March/April 1993.

43 Stephen Wright, "The Foreign Policy of Africa" in Roy C. Macridis (ed.) *Foreign Policy in World Politics* (8th ed), New York: Prentice Hall, 1992.

44 John Chipman, *French Power in Africa*, Oxford, Basil Blackwell, 1989.

5 Immigration policy and refugee control

The final scene in the movie, "The March" in which European commandos defend a Fortress Europe at the Strait of Gilbratar - against economic and environmental refugees from Africa-can hardly be counted as a fictitious human scene. As a result of revised European immigration policy, marine units from Spain and Italy, and infantry units from Austria, Hungary and Poland were deployed to intercept refugees at sea or the green borders.[1]

The problem of controlling illegal immigration into the EU has been addressed by several bodies. The Trevi Group, consisting of the Ministers of the Interior of the Twelve, added immigration control to its agenda. The so-called "Coordinators' Group chaired by the Vice-President of the European Commission, Martin Bangemann,[2] also discussed the issue of immigration. The countries that were signatories to the Schengen Agreement (Luxembourg) - a document signed secretly for the purpose of establishing a uniform border control and immigration policy among signatory countries - initiated stringent immigrations controls that would form the basis of EU's future immigration policy.

At its meeting in Dublin in June 1990, the European Council asked the Trevi Group to speed up work on the creation of a common information system, and an European program for the training of law enforcement officers from drug producing and transit countries. Among other security issues that were discussed was the necessity of coordinating the member states' program for technical police cooperation, and the establishment of an European Drug Intelligence Unit.

Parameters of the problem

The completion of the Single Market has already had an impact on the movement of people within Europe's borders. It has, and will continue to have an impact on the immigration policies of EU member nations and the rights and privileges of immigrants. As one human rights activist puts it:

> The prospects [for free movement of people] are exciting for Western European tourists, or graduates from member countries seeking to work abroad as passports will no longer need to be shown at internal frontiers. But Western European governments could seize 1993 to tighten further their asylum procedures, making Western Europe virtually impenetrable for fugitives from oppression.[3]

Ironically, as European border-control measures are tightened, and immigration laws revised, the factors that often trigger outward emigration have increased in Africa. Between 1980 and 1987, [4] war and famine forced nearly 8 million people in Africa to free to neighboring states. The *Baltimore Sun* (in the US) noted that:

> In the decade through 1992, an estimated 2.8 people sought asylum in Western Europe, fleeing the breakup of the Soviet Union, civil war in former Yugoslavia, poverty in Somalia and Ghana and bleak economic prospects in Romania and Bulgaria.[5]

According to the OECD, application for asylum in Western Europe rose from 70,000 in 1983 to 700,000 in 1992. This figure excludes those who live in Europe illegally.[6]

There are anti-immigrant, and particularly anti-African, sentiments in a number of European countries, especially France and Germany. Therefore, it is important to review and comment on recent immigration policies in some EU member countries.

After walking through a demolished "iron curtain" in Berlin, immigrants from Eastern European also woke up to find a new "paper curtain" in the West - that is as restrictive to immigration as the old iron curtain imposed in the era of communism.

Many Africans have now been condemned as virtual prisoners in their own native countries, behind the "visa curtain" that has been imposed by EU diplomatic missions abroad. For the prospective African immigrant to Europe, the handwriting of a fortress Europe is now boldly written on the European political wall. All EU countries now tie acquisition of citizenship to "blood relationship" obtained through parents, and not through "the place of birth".

Critics argue that EU's immigration laws are becoming more and more racist, anti-foreigners, and more so anti-African. The decision to abolish entry visas for Eastern Europeans - while at the same time visa applications for Turks and Africans are tightened - is interpreted by some observers as purely "racist".[7] These critics also see an element of hypocrisy in the emerging immigration control policies in Europe. As Kingley Orish noted, "it is so surprising that Westerners worry so much about the presence of Africans on their soil, while for one hundred years their forebears trooped in and out of Africa as *explorers* (emphasis mine)".[8]

Other critics also contend that EU immigration policy is putting more and more emphasis on rules relating to expulsion, family reunion, admission of workers and asylum claims (those issues that strike a sensitive chord in domestic politics in Europe), while at the same time, paying less and less attention to procedural protection of immigrants and their right of appeal.

A growing number of people debunk the myth that immigrants are responsible for Europe's rising crime rate and unemployment. While anti-immigrant activists find it convenient to use immigrants in their "scape goat theory" of socio-economic malaise in Europe, such problems are largely the consequence of the development syndrome that industrial societies have to contend with. The pain of structural change, which has taken place in Western industrial nations, for some time, is being aggravated by economic recession: unemployment in Europe is the most visible sign of these economic malaise. On the eve of European unification, opinion polls reported low popularity ratings for most European governments. Perhaps, this may be one of the reasons for the upsurge in the number of extremist parties that have used immigration as a grist in the mill of nationalist politics.

The EU was increasingly criticized for doing less about the Bosnian crisis. The crises in the East have reduced that region of the world to an active "refugee volcano", whose political larva has already poured on Western Europe. EU's stringent approach to immigration, particularly from the East, must be seen as a "damage control" maneuver that is intended to shield the EU from criticism that it has failed, in the first place, to solve the conflicts in her Eastern corridor, and hence, is "part of the problem" of mass emigration from the Eastern and Southern corridors of the European Union.

Germany is particularly confronted with acute dimensions of these strategic problems. It is located at the most eastern edge of affluent Western Europe. Reunification in 1990 transformed 16 million East Germans into Western Europeans. In 1992, under stressful political situation, United Germany took in about 200,000 Russians of German origin, as well as thousands of Germans in other parts of Eastern Europe. There were also refugees from former Yugoslavia, who were among about 440,000 asylum seekers who flocked to Germany in 1992 - a figure greater than the total number of refugees for the rest of Western Europe.

Germany and the asylum nightmare

In Germany, where asylum laws have hitherto been considered the most liberal, anti-immigrant sentiments exploded in the fury of rightist militants. By the end of 1993, neo-Nazi extremists had singled out foreigners in more than 2,220 attacks that killed scores of Germans and immigrants.

After World War II, in a bid to rebuild the German economy, bilateral labor recruiting agencies were set up to import "guest workers" from the Mediterranean countries (mostly from Turkey and North Africa). Before

1973, the Federal Republic of Germany used alien labor to increase its productive capacity, while supporting an export-oriented economy. With unsatiable consumer demand and cheaper alien labor, restrictions on the influx of immigrant workers was not a big issue. Within a quarter of a century, migration from the Mediterranean areas outstripped what it took a century to attain in the era of the Great trans-oceanic migration.[9] Migrants, that had in the past been complementary to German labor, become competitive, as the German economy went into recession. Thousands of aliens circumvented the legal hurdles of residency, by applying for "political asylum".

The term "foreigners" is now being used as a pejorative one, which has eclipsed the vital role that foreigners play in the German, and for that matter European, economy. Consequently, many Germans perpetuate the dangerous myth that aliens are "welfare parasites".

At the Adam Opel Company in Germany, the words "Made in Germany" means skilled Turkish craftsmanship. About 53,000 people from 48 nations work for the Germany subsidiary of General Motors. One in six of the workforce is a foreigner.[10]

The issue of foreigners and asylum-seekers remain key domestic issues in German politics in the post-unification era. In United Germany, support for reunification could only be bought by protecting workers and labor unions from loss of jobs, and also from foreigners seeking higher salaries and better working conditions.

Africans and other immigrants in Europe have been sacrificed on the alter of German reunification. They have suffered from deportation, torture, and even death. Pollsters after the 1990 reunification indicated strong xenophobic sentiments, particularly in the *Bundeslaender* (federal states) in the East. Right wing activities in Germany have substantially increased during the past years. At the close of 1993, estimates put the number of "hard core members" of neo-Nazi groups at over 40,000.[11] Together with the nationalist potential of the 1990 reunification, the issue of immigration has led to the formation of over a dozen associations that can be classified along a spectrum that spreads from nationalist conservative to neo-fascist.

The bone of legal contention in Germany's immigration debate centers on article 16, section 2, sentence 2, of the German *Grundgesetz* (Basic

Law) which states that "political refugees enjoy the right of asylum". German's liberal asylum law was an attempt to right the wrongs of the past, and must be seen in the context of the country's totalitarian past, where the state weeded out "undesirables", through racist legislation.[12] Despite the tightening of asylum rules by the Bonn government, the breakdown of Communism in the East led to an exploitation of asylum application.

From the reunification year of 1990 through the end of 1992, rightist violence increased 800 percent; nine out of ten incidents were directed against foreigners. Also, non-violent right-wing offenses, such as displaying swastikas or distributing Nazi literature, nearly doubled in 1992 to more than 7,000.[13] About five hundred neo-Nazis "outwitted" the German police, and appeared in the city of Fulda on August 14, 1993, to commemorate the death of Hitler's Deputy, Rudolf Hess.

France changes nationality laws

In France, it doesn't matter whether the government in power is of the left or right-all are the same when it comes to immigration issues, as related to "1992". For example, it was the Socialist government in Paris that adopted the Schengen Accord which refused entry of immigrants onto European soil. Between 1988-92, the French government arrested and deported more than 12,000 "illegal" immigrants annually.[14] Measures were also taken to stop the issuance of resident permits to immigrants.

Automatic citizenship, hitherto conferred on children born of foreigners in France, has been terminated. Now, such children will have to make a formal request for citizenship which will require a "suitability" test.[15] About 25,000 children have been affected by this new law - one-third of whom are of African descent.

Observers point to the fact that Africans are the "main target" of such anti-foreigners laws, even though they account for less of the immigrants.[16] There are random checks on foreigners to "control" identity cards. However, as George Ola-Davies notes, "security officers tend to check the identity of only a particular category of foreigners - blacks, and sometimes Arabs". [17]

After reading the racial barometer in France, Lisa Pilgram-Mandrone concluded that the fear which the French harbor about Africans and Arabs is because these people:

> Are invading their [French] space-taking their jobs, destroying their cities with ghettoes, ruining the Catholic tradition, threatening not only to outnumber and overrun the white race (at their rate of reproduction), but even worse, to bastardize it by breeding babies of mixed race who lay claim to Frenchmanship.[18]

If the predictions by *la Figaro*, the popular French daily are true, then the European population in France will decrease by 5.2 million in the next 30 years,[19] while non-Europeans will increase their numbers in direct proportion, or will eventually make up 17 percent of the French population.

African immigrants have already suffered humiliation, extortion, and even death at the hands of racist and conservative groups in France and other parts of Europe. In France, in 1981, a new refurbished state housing project - the abode of about 320 Malian immigrants - was bulldozed with no warning. In 1983, an Algerian was murdered on a train bound for Bordeaux. Again, in France (in August of 1989), a mosque was "accidentally" bulldozed in Charvieu-Chavagneux. Extremist groups, such as the National Front headed by Jean Marie Le Pen, were believed to be behind the upsurge in racist violence in France and other parts of Europe. The racial underpinning of such acts of violence is clear. A large number of these extremist groups are anti-Black and anti-Arab. Their political agenda is also clear. They chant anti-immigrant slogans, such as: "Two million immigrant workers equals two million unemployed Frenchmen"; "France for the French". Hardline interior Minister, Charles Pasqua, even aims at "zero immigration".[20]

The way in which African immigrants are treated in France is blamed on the "unequal treaties" that France imposed on her ex-colonies in Africa. An African immigration attorney living in France emphasized that some of the Franco-African protocols have been one-sided, to the disadvantage of the African signatories.[21] Since 1960s, there have been a series of accords on cooperation between France and these countries, but Paris has amended certain of their provisions, unilaterally, to suit its own purpose. For example, the accords with Togo and Central African Republic (CAR) state that citizens from France and these nations can live and work in France with their local identity cards. There is reciprocity with French nationals in those countries. In reality, however, citizens from CAR need resident permits to get a job in France. When they go out for resident permits, they are usually told they need work permits, thereby swinging them into a "devil's dilemma". Criticizing this policy that make African immigrants stand in long queues in France for work permits, an African attorney residing in France asked a rhetorical question: "Have you seen a Frenchman standing in a queue in Africa for a resident permit?".

The negative publicity about "illegal immigrants" ignores the positive contribution of immigrants to the economic rejuvenation of Europe. Basile Boli, the Ivorian-born libero of the Olympic Marseilles Football Club scored the only and wining goal of the European League Cup (1993), via a corner kick taken by Ghanaian star, Abedi Pele. Before this "African-made" victory, no French football team had ever won a continental championship.

French anti-racism and civil rights groups are calling the new French immigration law "judicial apartheid".[22] The French police can check the identity card of anyone in a given area, as defined by the judicial warrant. Foreigners whose papers are not in order risk being expelled. The law allows police officers to demand identification from almost anyone they deem suspicious, a policy that has raised fears in the immigrant communities. The law was overwhelmingly approved in June 1993 by the conservative-dominated National Assembly.

A large percent of the French immigrant community are Arabs and Blacks from France's former colonies in Africa and the Middle East, who began arriving in the 1960s to meet demands of French industry and government for cheap labor. These immigrants are more likely to be relegated to the drug-and-crime ridden ghettos of France's major cities, if they are not assimilated in the French culture. [23]

Britain: Should the immigrants go back "home"?

Thanks to the politics of *Pax-Britannica*, a large number of immigrants from ex-British colonies, particularly from Africa and Asia, flocked to the "Mother Country". The British government, particularly during the tenure of office of the conservative Margaret Thatcher, became stern on illegal immigration to Britain. The Thatcher government went on record of positioning the prison ship, *Earl Williams*, off the English Coast, so that detained refugees could not even set foot on British soil. Also, the Thatcher government introduced a fine of 1,000 pounds sterling on any airline for every passenger aboard that airline who did not possess legal immigration documentation.

Under Thatcher's tight immigration control policies, a group of Kurdish refugees were even sent back to possible torture in Ankara, Turkey, without being allowed to leave the aircraft. This practice, the refugees claimed, was in contravention of the 1951 Geneva Convention.

As other EU member countries tighten their immigration policies, all available information indicate that Britain is willing to adopt the strictest immigration policy possible. For example, bilateral negotiations between Britain and the Peoples Republic of China regarding the future of the British colony of Hong Kong has included London's attempt at preventing policy changes that might lead to many outmigration (to Europe) by millions of Hong Kong residents holding British passports.

The Tory government in London sent to the House of Commons a restrictive immigration package that has resulted in tightening of immigration. An African taxi driver, who was living in England illegally, told this author in Brussels that he always had to carry all his money on him all the time, because he did not know "when I will be deported".[24]

As in Germany and France, Britain's domestic politics has been influenced by concerns about immigration. Extremist groups have capitalized on popular public discontent to galvanize support in electoral politics where the "immigration issue" is a major factor. For example, Derek Beackon, an open racist who demands "forced deportation" of all "non-whites", won a Council election in London's East End in September of 1993. There is the fear that anti-foreigner sentiments will rise, especially among low-income segments of the British population.

According to sources published by the Joint Council for the Welfare of Immigrants, 10,000 immigrants are detained in Britain without trial every year, under the detention powers of the Home Office. The British government is making excessive and unfair use of prisons and control as deterrence. What is worse, most detainees are black - a situation that has made many observers to conclude that the control exercises are racist in nature, and anti-African in particular. The granting of political asylum is increasingly seen as a privilege reserved for Christians and White people, not Muslims and Blacks or Brown people. Britain's immigration law include a tight penalty for illegal asylum seekers. The rights of visitors and prospective students (and their dependence) as well as their appeal against the refusal to leave or enter, are not adequately protected. Britain demanded and won an "opt-out" from the Schengen Accord, allowing London to maintain border control for the foreseeable future.[25]

Even though a black middle class is emerging in Britain, inter-racial relations are deteriorating. In response to this phenomenon, Bernie Grant, one of the few black MPs in the UK suggested that if Britain wanted the immigrants to "go home" (to their native countries), London must provide financial assistance.

Some observers contend that in France, Italy and Netherlands, and other European countries, stricter immigration laws are being enacted to appease neo-Nazi and other right-wing activists.

Barbed wire around Europe: Controlling Europe's frontiers

In order to effectively police Europe's external borders, there has been intensive collaboration in Europe involving the exchange of information, control networks, and electronic exchange of data between Community and member states and among member states.[26]

Computer programs, such as the S.I.S. and Euro DAC, were installed at European airports to deal with the issue of illegal immigration. The S.I.S. can track information on immigrants so that the refusal of asylum in one nation will be known to others. EURODAC, which employs finger prints for identification, will assist the police in mounting "controls" on so-called undesirables.

Human rights activists have sounded alarm about a "Fortress Europe", largely because of EU's immigration initiatives. The harmonization of EU immigration policies does not bode well for would-be African immigrants. This is because the "refusal of entry by one country will mean a refusal by all [EU nations], and all information, including passport details and travel routes, will be stored on a computer with terminals at each border".[27]

The politics of "scape-goatism" continues to hurt African immigrants in Europe. These immigrants are held responsible for the failure of capitalism to provide enough jobs. About 50,000 jobs were retrenched in the telecommunication industry in Britain. If local miners in Britain lose their jobs, is it because of (African) immigrants? How many (African) immigrants are coal miners? As European and American corporations try to compete with Asian "Tigers", more jobs will be lost in the Western world, and immigrants would be sacrificed as scape-goats. The Asian nations, compared to European nations, produce cheaper, sell cheaper, and are less politically motivated in choosing trading partners. They are less constrained by the activities of lobbyists in their Parliamentary halls.

In an appeal for a "united front" against racism on May Day in 1993, the European Trade Union Confederation called on European governments and institutions to implement policies that would guarantee equal rights to immigrant workers in the work place, and ensure that their families are integrated into European culture, while respecting their cultural identity. The removal of borders in Europe, as part of EU unification program, poses a challenge to Europe - a challenge to be gentler, kindlier, and more humane to the world's poor and persecuted.

These immigrants would need housing, vocational training, and a recognition of their political rights. Outside of Europe, EU's economic assistance to Africa will be a right policy, if the EU is to be able to stem the tide of African emigration to Europe. For example, the Kissinger Commission Report on Central America recommended an economic package to Central America - that would help reduce poverty and, among other things, stem the tide of illegal immigration into the US.

As the EU moves closer to a unified immigration policy, there is the fear that refugee quotas could be granted that would possibly give preference for those refugees from Eastern Europe on purely racial (because they are white), if not on political (anti-communist), grounds. It is politically more rewarding to grant asylum to people fleeing from "communism" than those in Africa and the Third World who are perceived by the wealthy nations as "economic refugees".

Linda Boateng, Miss Ghana (UK, 1993) won a beauty contest which had, as one of its prizes, a visit to Italy. The Ghanaian woman forfeited the chance to travel, for the mere fact that she held a Ghanaian passport. According to the clearance procedure at the Italian embassy in London, a Ghanaian resident in the UK who intends to visit Italy on a tourist visa, had to submit his application, at least, three weeks before the date of departure. He is also required to submit his recent bank statement, and a letter from his employer confirming his employment status. The fear of the "browning of Europe" [by the people of darker pigmentation] is affecting European public perception of immigrants from Africa.

Critics of EU immigration policies often cite, as the source of their concerns, the secrecy that enshrouds immigration debates and policy-making in Europe. For example, the Trevi Group-originally given the mandate to deal with terrorism and drug trafficking in Europe-was the same organization that was later authorized to recommend immigration policies for the EU, and refused to open its doors to the public.

In fact, a common problem faced by many immigrants from Africa is that the qualifications they obtain in other countries of origin are not recognized in Europe. In some cases, there are stringent policies, too. In Netherlands, the time allowed for processing of asylum application was reduced from one year to 30 days. At present, measures have been considered to identify and expel foreign students and residents who take up jobs without authorization.

Critics of EU's immigration policies concede that there is an abuse of political asylum by immigrants, including those from Africa. At the same time, these critics argue that:

> In adopting tough and repressive measures, EC governments are almost all pandering to the wishes of extremist elements whose political stars are on the ascendancy throughout Europe.[28]

Mass immigration and resentments against foreigners, particularly from Africa and the developing world, have become part of the opposition's rallying point in national politics in Europe. In the 1988 French elections, in which the conservative Le Pen won 14 percent of the national votes, a major issue that was on the political agenda was what was to be done about the huge number of newly-arrived North African residents. As nationalism becomes a defense of the status quo, Africans and other nationalities in Europe will pay a high price for resurgent Euro-nationalism and xenophobia.

Opposition groups in Europe have made a case against the economic and cultural implications of Turkish membership in the EU. For example, Lord Bethel, a British member of the European Parliament, was said to have described the free movement decision [of "1992"] a "great peril to Western Europe's political and economic hopes".[29] Even though the "free movement" of labor within the EEC was one of the main provisions of the Treaty of Rome, (West) Germany made it clear that it could not agree to Muslim Turkey's entry into the EEC, if Turkey insisted on the right of free movement. Like Turkey - that provides a fodder for Le Pen - North African nations are Muslim. They also, like Turkey, have a high birth rate - a source of threat to Europe's racial hegemony.

Part of the xenophobia generated by European unification is based on the resentment that Europeans have traditionally harbored toward foreign job seekers. Italians of the chronically poor southern half of Italy were accorded sometimes violent reception, when they arrived in France and in Belgium. Even when they were welcomed by many employers, the *Gastarbeiter*, or guest workers, who flooded the industrial regions of Northern Europe from Italy, Spain and Portugal in the 1960s, were met with a wave of resentment. Now, it is not being a Catholic that is the issue, as much as being a Muslim or Black.

The wave of anti-immigrant sentiments in a number of European cities goes beyond mere historical intolerance and rigid nationalism. It is a defense of parochial interests. To assess the broader direct and indirect implications of EU immigration policies for African travellers, some factors stand out as very crucial in this author's analyses. They include the fact that:

- Tighter immigration controls at the EU's external frontiers would result in concentration of migrants in states bordering the EU, particularly

Czechoslovakia, Hungary and Switzerland.
- The Nordic and EFTA countries will be compelled to harmonize their visa policies for nationals of non-OECD countries
- The immigration policies of Western nations would compel former Eastern European countries to be tougher on immigration. Several Eastern European countries, such as Hungary and Czechoslovakia, are facing the immigration bing involving asylum seekers and other irregular immigrants, some of them from Africa. Eastern European nations have been compelled to collaborate with Western Europe, as was demonstrated by the Pentagonale group composed of Austria, Czechoslovakia, Hungary, Italy and Yugoslavia.
- Amnesty International, and other human rights groups are concerned that the stringent visa requirements and procedures that deny refugee full hearings, and other regulations, threaten bona-fide asylum seekers in Europe.

Eastern Europe's policy, in the run-up to European unification in the post-Cold war era, contrasts sharply with the East's previous immigration policy toward Africa. Gone are the days when Eastern European nations gave a blind eye to illegal immigrants from Third World countries who used the East as a spring board to enter Western nations.

In the past, Communist nations used collaboration with illegal immigrants as a weapon to hasten "the demise of the capitalist system". The recent political mood in the East suggests that the closer the former Eastern European countries move towards unity with the West, the greater will be the pressure on the East to align their border control policies with those of the EU nations. A continent-wide collaboration among European officials on the issue of immigration and refugee matters is politically justified for one major reason. The EU would want to ensure that third-country nationals do not use Eastern Europe as a spring board for illegal entry into the West. They would, therefore, expect and encourage Eastern Europeans to coordinate their policies regarding the examination of visas and controls at the borders.

This author watches domestic politics in Industrial societies with great concern. Neo-nazi groups and far right parties are now clawing their way into national politics. They are wining seats across Europe. In France, the National Front gained 12.5 percent of the votes in the general elections in March of 1993. In Belgium, the Vlaams Blok (VB) won 12 seats in the Chamber of Representatives and five in the Senate with 6.6 percent of the votes cast in the 1991 general elections. The VB Party stands for the repatriation of all immigrants and an amnesty for all Second World War II "collaborators". In Italy, the Movimento Sociale Italiano-Destra Nationale won 34 seats in the national elections in 1992, and for the first time since 1945, took control of small community councils.

Eminent European scholars, parliamentarians, and the Western press have used their agenda-setting powers to push the issue of refugees to the forefront of national politics. In the US, Californian Republican Governor, Pete Wilson, wrote a letter to President Clinton asking for a constitutional amendment denying US citizenship to children born in the US to illegal immigrants.[30] The Governor also urged Congress to find some ways around a 1982 Supreme Court decision guaranteeing public education to all children, regardless of their immigration status. The Governor is playing the anti-immigrants card in a state whose economy is falling deep into recession.

Considered as one of the most liberal in terms of immigration policy, Canada has changed her policies on immigration. The Conservative party's bid to cut down on immigration was a tactical ploy to cover up the failure of Canada to pull itself from recession. What is more racially-motivated, the Canadian Government allowed 2,600 people in former Yugoslavia to reunite with their families in Canada, but at the same time denied compassion to some Somalis who had fled political persecution at home.

Africans pay high price for gate-crashing

Compared to other developing nations, Africa has been the most harshly affected by tighter EU immigration policy. Racial discrimination in Europe has traditionally targeted blacks and Muslims, a phenomenon that makes the whole of Sub-Saharan and North Africa vulnerable.

African immigrants have already paid a high price for the resurgence of Euro-nationalism, racism and xenophobia. According to one account that appeared in the *West Africa* magazine, more than 50 Africans, including women and children were held under deplorable conditions by immigration officials at the Sofia Airport in Bulgaria, in November 1992. In defending this cruel policy of detention, Bulgarian officials maintained that a number of them [Africans] enter Bulgaria as a "transit route" in the hope of proceeding to Western European countries, without the necessary visas.[31]

An Ukrainian sailor of an Ukrainian vessel, *McRuby*, was charged in France with "piracy, assassination, attempted assassination, extortion, theft, and sequestrating",[32] after allegedly killing and throwing into the Atlantic ocean seven African stowaways. In another incident, police mishandling of "illegal immigrants" was so brutal that Andre Nkala, an African who was residing in France illegally, jumped over a railing and leapt into the Seine River - the first known mortality from Europe's tough anti-immigrant law.[33]

The French Constitutional Council wanted constitutional changes that would enable mayors to block marriages between foreigners and French partners, if they suspect that the only purpose of the marriage is to acquire French residency. The law would prevent foreign students from bringing their family members to France. Critics have described this law as both anti-family and anti-culture.

The racist underpinnings of emerging French immigration law have stirred fear among Blacks and Arabs in France, a country where the police stage surprise raids on housing projects and carry out sweeps of subways and train stations, looking for "clandestine" immigrants. In the summer of 1993, a Togolese woman, who had entered France illegally, jumped from a fifth floor window to elude the police, even though they were seeking for some one else.

This author had a personal experience in Brussels, the political capital of Europe. While conducting the research that formed the basis of this book, the author was confronted by the Belgian police who demanded his identity card. The author did not have one. They became very excited when they found out that he is from Ghana. The police officers asked the author to board a police van so he could take them to his residence to collect "your immigration papers". The author refused to board the police van, because based on his interviews with some African immigrants in Belgium, he suspected that the police would rather take him to the police station, and start preparing documents for jailing him, after which he could be deported to Ghana. The police were very furious because this author was bold and not intimidated.

The police also questioned why the author was holding a French magazine, since he told the police that he did not speak French. This author asserted that he has the right to buy a magazine in any language he chooses. The author walked, escorted by the police, to his residence just a hundred yards away. The police officers were very embarrassed and disappointed, when they finally saw his valid passport with a valid Belgian visa stamped by the Belgian Consulate in New York.

Mass emigration from Africa to Europe poses strategic problems for both European and African governments. EU's crackdown on illegal immigration and political asylum seekers removes, perhaps, the "last safety valve" of outmigration that is important to the stability of some African regimes.

According to the *Ghana Drum* (April 1993), about 15,000 Ghanaians were affected by the post-unification crackdown on illegal immigration. The emergence of democracy in Ghana has compounded the political asylum status of many Ghanaians in Europe. About 98 percent of the Ghanaian refugees claimed repression by the PNDC regime of Flt. Rt. Jerry Rawlings.

The extreme nationalist and anti-immigrant political attitudes that are ravaging Europe is partly in response to the large number of refugees from Eastern Europe and particularly from the former Yugoslavia who are trying to enter the EU.

Writing from an African perspective, one observer noted that after the collapse of the Cold War, and the removal of the iron curtain, European governments re-imposed a "visa curtain" to keep dark-skinned people from the Third World out of Europe.[34]

This situation is ironic, if we look back into the history of European economic revival, and the role that foreigners played in that revival. In the boom years in the 1970s, European nations like Germany, the Netherlands and France, courted foreigners to dig ditches, harvest crops, and collect refuse. One wonders, who is exploiting whom? That Albert Einstein, the world renowned scientist was the son of an immigrant suggests the positive role that immigrants play in international development.

There would be a deep crisis of confidence if the EU did not take a firm decision on (illegal) immigration. EU's forecasts projects an influx of about 25 million immigrants into the EU over the next decade. EU's disparate treatment of asylum seekers create irritations among African regimes and nationals alike. For example, ordinary African citizens fleeing political repression at home may be termed "economic refugees", and may accordingly be refused political asylum in Europe. At the same time, politicians who have embezzled their nation's money and had committed serious political crimes against their people may be granted political asylum in Europe.

The Nigerian government was very disturbed that the British government would grant political asylum to former fugitive Nigerian Transportation Minister, Umaru Dikko, who had reportedly embezzled billions of dollars from Nigeria's public coffers. Dikko was offered a forum on the BBC to criticize the Buhari regime in Nigeria that had overthrown the civilian administration, of which Umari Dikko was a Minister of Transportation.

The EU has been wary of terrorism that increased in the late 1970s and in the 1980s. Revolutionary activities, mounted by Iranian exiles in that period in France, provide a factual example of this problem. Ayatollah Khomeini directed the Islamic Revolution from his suburban Paris villa. The religious leader forged, perhaps, the first mass revolution directed over international telephone circuits by means of cassettes and tapes.

In addition to race, the "Islamic dimension" of the immigration crackdown is evident. The phobia about Islam in Europe is a response to the resurgence of "Islamic fundamentalism" in North Africa. In Algeria, there is an escalating conflict between Islamic militants and an unpopular military-backed junta - a conflict that is spreading across Europe. European strategists are alarmed that Muslim grievances in the Balkans and North Africa can destabilize their own societies, if disgruntled militants launch terror campaigns on the European continent, and ferment radicalism among migrant workers. Already, the EU has faced harsh criticism for failing to come to the rescue of Bosnia Muslims. European leaders are hesitant to choose sides in Algerian civil unrest that was exacerbated by the decision taken by secular authorities to cancel elections in 1991, that the Islamic Salvation Front was poised to win.

There is a dilemma for Europe. If the EU investors were to withdraw from these North African nations, there would be the possibilities that the economies of these nations would collapse under a heavy debt burden ($26 billion in the case of Algeria).[35] Any major crises in Northern Africa could trigger a refugee crisis in Europe, at a time that most European nations are battling with immigrants. There are nearly four million Muslims, including one million from Algeria, that live in France.

The French Interior Minister, Charles Pasqua, ordered a crack-down on Islamic militants in Europe, as three French diplomats were kidnapped in October of 1993. Eighty-eight suspected members of the anti-government Algeria's Islamic Salvation Front (FIS) were rounded up by the police.

To the extent that a successful completion of the Internal Market leads to a more buoyant and dynamic European economy, European countries are less likely to embark upon overly defensive trade policies. After all, the new surge of protectionism in Europe began largely as a result of economic instability and stagnation in the 1970s.

New policy directions

In examining immigration policies of a number of major countries, Michael S. Teitelbaum concluded that there is a linkage between immigration decisions and foreign policies.[36] For example, former US Secretary of State, George Shultz, and his predecessor, Alexander Haig, had in their minds the prevention of mass exodus of Caribbean immigrants into the US, when they spoke in favor of the Caribbean Basin Initiative (CBI).

The increase at the beginning of the 1990s in the numbers (see Table 5.1) of spontaneous asylum - seekers and illegal immigration have prompted OECD nations to take action. They have taken measures to discourage the abuse of political asylum, and have sought to co-ordinate their present and future immigration policies.[37]

Table 5.1
Foreign population in selected EU countries, 1980-1990
% of total population

	1980	1981	1982	1983	1984	1985	1986	1987	1988	1989	1990
Belgium	8.9	9.0	9.0	9.0	9.1	8.6	8.6	8.7	8.8	8.9	9.1
Denmark	2.0	2.0	2.0	2.0	2.1	2.3	2.5	2.7	2.8	2.9	3.1
Germany	7.2	7.5	7.6	7.4	7.1	7.2	7.4	7.6	7.3	7.7	8.2
Italy	0.5	0.6	0.6	0.7	0.7	0.7	0.8	1.0	1.1	0.9	1.4
Lxbg	25.8	26.1	26.2	26.3	26.5	26.7	26.2	26.5	26.9	27.5	—
UK	—	—	—	—	2.8	3.1	3.2	3.2	3.2	3.4	3.3

Source: Jean-Pierre Garson, "International Migration: Facts, Figures, Policies", *The OECD Observer*, No. 176 June/July 1992, p. 19.

Without jeopardizing either the completion of the Single Market or its accessibility, the Community should always see that the measures that are adopted take special account of the interests of the developing countries, especially the weakest amongst them.

The future of Euro-African ties

Compared to other regions, Africa enjoys important proximity factor' with Europe. These factors are political, historical and geographical in nature. The first consideration is the colonial attachment that has catapulted Africa onto a privileged spot in the arena of EU-Third World relations. The paternalistic policies of individual EU country are also a factor. There are also external factors. Basically, the Lome Accord is one of the Cold-war imposed European initiatives designed to steer Africa off the Communist orbit. The question is whether it will survive the demise of the cold war. It could be adulterated, and its economic basis dismantled, leaving only its political trappings of Euro-Africanism. The risk remains that the proximity factors that Africa used to enjoy in Euro-African relations may be eroding.

In order to alleviate this problem, there is the need for an intensified EU's development cooperation policy. The EU, itself, has found three major shortcomings of the present cooperation policy toward Africa: the coordination shortfall (between member states and the EU's development cooperation policy); the linkage or cohesion shortfall (between cooperation policies and other Community polices or other aspects of the EU integration process); lastly, the fact that the Community does not speak with one voice in international fora.[38]

This situation is prejudicial to Africa for several reasons. African nations do not fully benefit from the impact of a coordinated EU policy. On the other hand, African countries could try to play on inter-European rivalries and derive the maximum benefit from Euro-African relations. This situation is also prejudicial to the Member states of the EU. The failure to coordinate policies, speak with as single voice, and take initiatives, contribute to rivalries in the European Union, which sometimes may not be helpful to the Union's own interests.

The crux of the "European threat" is hinged on one major dilemma. Will changes in EU's domestic and external policy undermine Euro-African ties? In the shifting arena European unity, Europe will be compelled to think in terms of a global foreign policy approach that could undermine, if not abrogate, preferential ties that Africa enjoys in Europe.

For Africa, a critical issue remains whether the EU market will be accessible. When the Treaty of Rome was signed in 1957, it was predicated on an Euro-Africanist vision by which Africa's resources would be used to support European industrialization. Euro-African relations, as exemplified in the Lome Accord, did not industrialize Africa, but led to the proliferation of neo-colonial structures in Africa.

In reality, then, this author assesses the argument that the Single European Act (1987) and the Maastricht Treaty (1991) would benefit Africa with caution and skepticism. As the then President of European Union, Jacques Delors, noted, the Single Market is "ni forteresse, ni une possoire" (neither a fortress nor a soft torch).

Globally, the response to the crisis in the Middle East and Eastern Europe has meant that Africa has lost its strategic importance in the West. Three examples are relevant here. In the Somalian crisis, Europe followed American lead and abandoned her "colonial responsibility". Second, in the Liberian crisis, the US dispatched warships to the region, but there were on instructions to rescue Western nationals trapped in the conflict. Furthermore, since the release of Nelson Mandela from jail, attention on the apartheid struggled died down, and refocussed on "black-on black" violence. European powers, the former colonizers of Africa, stood idly and helplessly, and allowed massacres in Rwanda (1994) to occur. This sharply contrasts to France's response to Libya's incursions in Chad, or Belgium's assistance Mobutu when he was threatened with internal opposition.

Notes

1 Franz Nuscheler, "Fight the Causes of Flight, Not the Refugees", *Development and Cooperation*, No. 4, 1993.
2 ACP-EEC Joint Assembly, *Working Documents*, 5 September 1989, p. 9.
3 Hilary Clarke, "Fortress Europe Confronts Third-World Asylum-Seekers", *Gemini*, September 5, 1989.
4 *Ibid.*
5 *The Baltimore Sun*, (USA) February 14, 1993.
6 *Ibid.*
7 See for example, Alfred Tovias, "Migration and the Deepening of the European Community", Paper submitted at the 3rd European Community Studies Association, Washington, DC., 27-29 May 1993, p. 11.
8 *West Africa*, 5 July 1993, p. 1132.
9 See G. W. Yannaopulas, "Mediterranean Labor in an Era of Slow Economic Growth", *World Today*, 35, December 1979, p. 492.
10 "Neighbors With Foreign Passports", *Scala*, (Germany) March-April, 1993.
11 See Manfred Steger, F. Peter Wagner, "Political Asylum, Immigration and Citizenship in the Federal Republic of Germany", *New Political Science*, Nos. 24-25, Spring-Summer, 1993.

12 *Ibid.*
13 *Washington Post*, August 28, 1993.
14 The Stick Against Immigrants", *West Africa*, 31 May 1993, p. 909.
15 *Ibid.*, p. 899.
16 George Ola-Davies, "French Nationality Changes", *West Africa*, 31 May 1993, p. 908.
17 *Ibid.*
18 *Ibid.*
19 Cited in Lisa Zanetta Pilgram-Mandrone, "France: The New European Racial Barometer?", *Urban Profile*, (USA) Spring 1990, p. 12.
20 "Flood of Immigrants Prompts European Action", *The Baltimore Sun*, 4 July, 1993.
21 See *West Africa*, 31 May 1993, p. 908.
22 *The Final Call* (Published by the Nation of Islam, USA), June 30, 1993.
23 *Ibid.*
24 Based on personal conversation.
25 Richard Evans, "Contesting the Euro-Vision", *Geographical Magazine*, January 1993, p. 23.
26 See for example, Commission of the European Communities, *Report of the Commission to the Council and the European Parliament on the Implementation of Measures to the Internal Market*, Brussels, 19 December 1991.
27 Hilary Clarke, "Fortress Europe Confronts Third-World Asylum-Seekers".
28 "The Stick Against Immigrants", *West Africa*, 31 May 1993, p. 899.
29 "The Superpower Sties in A Web of Self-Interest", *Insight*, June 20, 1988, p. 11.
30 *Washington Post*, September 1, 1993.
31 *West Africa*, 23-29 November 1992, p. 2026.
32 *Ibid.*
33 *Washington Post*, 16 August 1993.
34 *West Africa*, 27 September. 1993.
35 *Washington Post*, 17 December, 1993.
36 Michael S. Teitelbaum, "Immigration, Refugees,and Foreign

Policy", *International Organization*, Vol. 38, No. 3, Summer 1984.

37 Jean-Pierre Garson, "International Migration: Facts, Figures, Policies", *The OECD Observer*, No. 176 June/July 1992.

38 Commission of the European Communities, "Communication from the Commission to the Council and Parliament, "Development Co-operation Policy in the Run-up to 2000", Brussels 15 May 1992, p. 9.

6 Securing access to the European single market: Opportunities, challenges and risks

There are *push-out* implications of European unification. The globalization of the world economy, and the emergence of the Single Market, are blowing out the last vestiges of EU's linkages with their former colonies in Africa. The EU is adopting a more globalist approach in trade policy that has already undermined the preferential arrangements that undergird the Lome framework of Euro-Africa relations.

There is conflict between the Industrialized nations and the developing world that have advanced on the ladder of competitiveness. We can cite the dispute involving copyright infringement between the EU and Thailand, or voluntary export restraint agreements (VERs) between the EU and the developing world. Even as the European Commission is bent on removing the various barriers to intra-EU trade, there is still a patchwork of virtual "indemnity" in specific sectors designed to protect European industry from outside competition.

Non-tariff barriers are used as instruments of protecting domestic markets. In 1991, there were 250 of them, mainly in Japan and the new industrialized countries of Asia.[1] Despite their duties that reach 150-200 percent, developing nations do not have a monopoly on high customs tariffs. The developed countries have their well-known tariff peaks, too. The US has heavy 50-56 percent tariffs on goods in sectors that American prices are not competitive (ceramics, glass and textiles), Europe also has 90 percent on tobacco and 300 percent of customs duty equivalent on some agricultural products.[2]

Textiles and clothing exports from developing countries are subject to tight quotas, which are subdivided into member countries' shares. Largely as a result of these restrictions, including the strict application of rules of origin, only about 30 percent of the dutiable exports of the GSP-beneficiary countries receive GSP treatment.[3] This is unfortunate because as Mary Alexander noted, the multifibre Agreement was textile exporters' "springboard into manufacturing",[4] since it guaranteed developing nations some degree of market protection in the EU. The delicate decision of calculating benefits and preferences is tinged with politics.

Even though EU and multilateral policies affect Africa's access to the EU, the policies of individual African nations can also make a difference. For example, the African nation of Mauritius effectively used the MFA to increase her access to the EU market, at a time that the same arrangement inhibited the access of her major developing nation competitors. Pressures to do away with the MFA could erode Africa's textile export competitiveness.

In general, the loss to developing nations, as a result of protectionist tendencies in advanced nations, is about $500 billion a year-ten times more than the international aid they received from advanced nations.[5] According to the UNDP's Human Development Report (1992), global markets are neither efficient nor free, and LDCs are prevented from fully exploiting the potential in the market.

Africa's stake

For the continent of Africa, the implications of European economic unity cannot be understood, without examining what African interests are at stake. The EU is the destination for more than half the exports of Sub-Saharan Africa, 70 percent of cocoa exports from West Africa, and the major import partner of Africa. Africa's close economic relations with Europe were forged through a series of preferential arrangements that began in the colonial era.

In the post-colonial era, as European integration intensified, bilateral preferences were largely subordinated to multilateral schemes, principally through the Lome framework. To the extent that further integration in the EU would preserve the current (trade) preferences that African countries enjoy, European unification will be in the best interest of Africa. However, there is increased competition as other developing nation groups are asking for the extension of the same preferences that are accorded to the African nations.

In addition to EU's internal liberalization program, as Chapter 3 suggested, multilateral initiatives have also eroded Africa's preferences. The architects of GATT intended to create a world trading system based on non-discriminatory practices, in the belief that this was the best prospects for an equitable and expanding world economy.

In global negotiation involving trade, developing nations are on a razor's edge. The attitude of the countries of the North is: "Give us access to your natural resources and we will also open our doors more widely to your products". Furthermore, regional trade preferences, such as the Lome scheme, often run counter to GATT's ideology, and could be seen as undermining the multilateral system. EU's partners (US and Japan) have often criticized EU's preferential arrangements. The US has opposed discriminatory trade arrangements, such as the Lome regime. Ironically, beyond the US' version of the GSP (granted to all developing nations as a whole), Washington also granted selective preferences under the Caribbean Basin Initiative (CBI), and the free trade agreement with Israel-preferences that were not granted to Europe's ex-colonies in Africa.

The opposition to Africa's preferences come from several sources. The first group of critics involve nations outside of Europe and her peripheries in the ACP world, principally the US and her satellite nations in Latin America. The second group involves European critics - nations and firms that are affected by competition from the ACP camp. EU preferences granted to African countries could be diminished if the EU retains non-tariff barriers (NTBs) in the so-called sensitive sectors. The deployment of NTBs against imports from outside of the EU could be political-to pacify EU member countries that might face adjustment difficulties, especially in agriculture, clothing and steel. As for the ACP nations, they are worried about EU's enlargement of the arena of preferences to include non-Lome countries.

The enlargement of the ACP to include the Dominican Republic and Haiti in 1989 is crucial for competition in the rum market in the EU. Some Caribbean and Central American states have expressed the desire to join the ACP, so as to gain access to the preferential treatment and financing agreement available under the Lome Convention. In applying to join the Lome Convention, the Dominican Republic's main concern was membership in the Sugar Protocol which allows some ACP states and India as a non-member, to export a set sugar quota into the EU at a preferential price.

The problem with the allocation of the sugar quota is that more prosperous developing nations like Barbados, Fiji, Guyana, Jamaica, Mauritius, and Trinidad and Tobago, receive a higher percentage of the transfer due to their high quotas. Haiti and Dominican Republic's accession could pave the way for other South American and Central American states. African countries are concerned that an enlargement of the Lome Convention could mean an adulation of the Lome preferences. In the EU, some developing countries with preferential access have been placed at a disadvantaged position, partly as a result of the new uniform treatment of trade originating from outside the EU. This has implications for the exports of Ghana's cocoa, and bananas from Cote d'Ivoire, to mention but a few.

Boom or doom?

The "1992" unification process could be described both as an opportunity and as a challenge. For Africa, and third parties in general, "1992" is going to have some trade-creating effects. Speaking on the theme, "The Impact of Europe in 1992 on West Africa", during an African Leadership Forum in Brussels, a former President of Nigeria, Olesegun Obasanjo, conceded that at the level of generalities, no one can doubt that the completion of the Single Market in Europe will offer considerable opportunities, in addition to strengthening the international trading system.[6] Even though the "1992" process could be largely seen as an "internal" deregulation offensive, it will have a major impact on the Community's partners-the major ones being the stimulation of world trade and competition, and the growth of the world economy.[7]

In the first place, an increase in the EU's GNP, relative to what it would otherwise be, could raise the demand for primary product imports. If this happens to be the case, then African exporters of primary products are likely to gain. However, the extent of EU import demand for African commodities would also depend on import elasticities of the commodities concerned. A major stimulus to the growth of the EU economy could come from trade diversion, and that the stimulus to EU imports from Africa may be limited, relative to the increase in the EU's GDP.

To the extent that there is more trade diversion, it is likely to be higher with regard to manufactured goods than primary products-where the degree of market segmentation and the scope from import substitution by EU producers is limited.[8] Furthermore, the removal of technical barriers and national quantitative restrictions to intra-EU trade could have trade-inducing effects. Through the principle of mutual recognition, a product which has legally been imported from Africa into one member country in the EU, and meets its requirements, can freely circulate throughout the Community. Third, the removal of excise taxes on some primary commodities (eg. coffee in Germany and in Denmark) may increase demand for these products.

The harmonization or mutual recognition of legislation, and the principle of free movement of goods within the EU, would make it possible for African nations to benefit from the Single Market, with all the known advantages of economies of scale. Harmonization of regulations would facilitate increased transparency, production of greater quantities at lower unit costs, etc. The European Market would be more uniform as a result of harmonization and mutual recognition of standards.

The impact of fiscal harmonization on the export of African countries could be positive or negative, however, depending on whether such a policy leads to an increase or decrease in the price paid by the consumer. While technical harmonization offers some "windows of opportunity" in access, there is the issue of "upward harmonization". The Single European Act requires harmonization at the highest level in the areas of health, security, environmental, and consumer protection.

Mutual recognition has now become the norm. This principle enables products which are legally manufactured and sold in any EU member country to circulate freely throughout the Community. This principle applies to not only goods that originate in a member country, but also those which have been legally imported into a member state and entered for free circulation.

Furthermore, the tests to which products will be subjected in the country of first importation, and the certificates issued there, are valid throughout the Community, and no further analyses, tests, or certification can be required. In theory, this practice would help the exports of African countries, since they benefit from opportunities which hitherto had been restricted to the markets of individual member states.

The harmonization of tax rates within the Community is a purely internal matter, though it is not without effects on third countries. The harmonization of taxes within the Community leads to greater mobility of goods, including imported goods.

For African countries, EU's harmonization of standards has a price tag. The inability to meet deadlines regarding technical standards will mean a loss of the EU's economic pie. The faster the clock of European unity tickles forward, the more worried African policy makers become about potential loss of market shares in the EU Single Market, where raw material supplies are being diversified, with cocoa, for example, coming from Malaysia. The elimination of frontier controls in intra-community trade would lead to a reduction in costs. There could be some "pull-in" effects. New markets that were previously small, or inaccessible, may be developed, as a result of internal liberalization. This may come as an added opportunity for Africa, especially if those markets happen to be those where African exporters have comparative advantages.

Trade diversion effects

On the other hand, the "1992" program could also have some trade-diversion effects. As the removal of internal non-tariff barriers is implemented, the cost of importing from the Community countries would fall. All other things being equal, this could encourage trade diversion from third country suppliers. Another possibility for trade diversion would come, if the removal of national barriers are accompanied by a strengthening of common external barriers.

Even though EU's exports constitute a high proportion of its GDP (equivalent to 9 percent of GDP, compared with 6.7 percent for the U.S.

and 9.3 percent for Japan),[9] it is reasonable to assume that at lower than estimated growth rate, trade expansion (with LDCs) will also be slower. The US imports two-thirds of manufactured exports of developing countries, compared to less than 25 percent by the EU, and less than 9 percent by Japan.[10] Furthermore, before the Community puts its own internal market in order, it is not likely to embark upon full-scale liberalization. Aware that market unification involves severe competition from third countries, interest groups, particularly European industrial lobbyists, have fought against unrestrained liberalization.

The abolition of National Quantitative Restrictions and the special restraints imposed by member states, in addition to the simplification of customs procedures, will facilitate developing countries' exports to the EU. However, the outlook for a number of sensitive items which are of special importance to developing countries-textiles, footwear, television, etc. remain uncertain.

While market access for the sensitive sectors (sectors where protectionist tendencies may be higher in the EU) may not be of immediate concern for the largely primary commodity-exporting countries of Africa, there are other factors worth taking into account. Even though African countries may not be in direct competition with EU producers, they are competing with non-EU producers. Only 51 percent of the Community's primary products originate from developing countries; the remaining portion comes for North America, EFTA and Eastern Europe. Developing countries lost their share in total EU imports from 43 percent in 1965 to 37 percent in 1986.[11]

On the demand side, a number of factors have caused a steady decline in raw material imports from Africa, despite continued, although weaker, growth in the economies of industrialized countries. For example, over the past decade and half, the annual average growth rate of world trade has been particularly slow, or even negative for major commodities of interests to Africa. What is worse, Africa's share in the supply of these commodities has fallen.[12] This phenomenon could be viewed from different angles. First, there are new products requiring small quantities of raw materials. Natural products have been partly replaced by synthetic materials. Second, the consumption of many food products from Africa, e.g. coffee, has reached a saturation point in Europe and in North America.

Third, the income and price elasticities of world demand for most commodities traditionally exported by African countries are not only low, but even appear to be declining in some cases.

The removal of borders in Europe would mean the dismantling of the national quantitative quotas. The external implications of this policy would depend on what the current national quotas are replaced with. If high external tariffs are imposed on a Community-wide basis, then it is reasonable to assume that imports will be replaced by domestic goods, where possible.

National Quantitative Restrictions appear to have little effect on African nations. The EU Commission compiled an inventory on NQRs, the majority of which concerned state-trading countries and Japan. In the case of the ACP countries in general, NQRs remained for only nine agricultural products. The inventory further showed that a significant number of these restrictions remained on paper, and were either not applied by EU member states, or are no longer supported by the protective measures under Article 115 of the Treaty of Rome.[13]

The sectors that are involved in the NQRs constitute the hard core of the problem for the Community. However, they concern products which are generally of little interest to Africa countries: few of the developing nations produce and export them. They include motor vehicles, electronic goods, footwear, tableware, and toys.

Carrying coal to Newcastle

It appears that in some cases, Africa may just be "carrying coal to Newcastle". African nations see that raw material supplies are being diversified, with coffee coming from Malaysia (this has implications for Ghana, Nigeria, and the Cote d'Ivoire,), coffee from Latin America (implications for Kenya), and bananas from Central and Latin America. African exporters will have to compare their competitiveness with European and third-country suppliers. For many African countries, the major risks associated with dependency are already evident. There is the fear that the EU will become increasingly self-sufficient in tropical commodities. In that event, the share of the EU in the supply of these commodities might increase in the future. This, however, is a trend that is not necessarily related to the "1992" process.[14]

Added to the rapid growth of non-EU markets, particularly in the Pacific Rim, there is also increasing self-sufficiency in the Community in energy supplies. It is largely as a result of the combination of these developments that African countries have insisted on a firm guarantee that EU's Plan to remove national frontiers would not endanger the special treatment accorded to the products which are of particular importance to their economies.

Ability to compete

Competition within and outside the EU pose challenges or African suppliers. The formation of EU-wide research programs was out of the concern that Europe's technological performance had been impeded by lack of cooperation, and duplication of research effort.

European firms have the advantage of marketing and advertisement via direct satellite broadcasting. Lack of access to superior marketing technology puts Africa at a competitive disadvantage. There is unfair competition, as the financial services of the LDCs enter the world financial market as unequal partners, and end up with unequal results.

Adebayo Adedeji, former Executive Secretary of the UN Economic Commission for Africa, noted that Africa, a major exporter of lint cotton, has no processing industry capable of meeting even its own textile and clothing demands, let alone Europe's. Adedeji also lamented that most ACP countries run a deficit in the services trade.[15] This is a strategic loss to Africa, since service liberalization is a key aspect of the "1992" program. In order to be competitive in the tourism industry, there is the need for changes in Africa's policies toward investment, and preservation of the environment.

The German Institute of Development Policy pointed out that exports of finished products from Sub-Saharan Africa is less competitive, as compared with South-East Asia because of high labor cost, lower product quality, and rudimentary innovative capacity at both government and company level.[16] Furthermore, even where African countries have comparative advantage, there are protectionist barriers in importing developed countries.

Gloomy scenario

According to the UN, exports of LDCs represent 0.3 percent of total world exports. This contrasts with the figure of 1.4 percent in 1960, 0. 8 percent in 1970, and 0.8 percent in 1980 respectively.[17] Given the small share of LDCs in global trade, there is scope for an increase in the exports of LDCs to the markets of Industrialized nations, without seriously threatening those industrial markets. The UN concluded that "privileged access to the market of industrialized countries should be part of the international policy on LDCs".[18]

Unfortunately, the UN's expectations have not been realized. Experience shows that the preferences accorded to the LDCs have not played a significant role in helping the diversification of the products and exports of Third World nations. For example, despite the Lome preferences, there is a mediocre African export performance in manufactured goods, due to shortfalls, in some cases, as a result of internal policies. Of total world export, only US $ 100 million (i.e. 4 percent) originate from Latin America. Even though this figure is two-thirds that of South-East Asia's, it is twice the figure for Africa.

At the ACP level, the situation is not different. Despite the increase in the membership of the ACP since 1975, the group's share in the EU market in the 1990s has drastically dropped from 8 percent to only 3 percent.

Africa's share of developing countries agriculture exports fell from 17 percent to 8 percent between 1970 and 1990. In 1990, Sub-Saharan Africa's share of world manufacturing value-added declined, and remained at less than half of 1 percent. Also, Africa's share of global foreign investments declined from 4.5 percent in 1980 to 0.7 percent in 1990. As one observer noted, "Africa plays hardly any part in world trade any more...If Africa disappeared off the map tomorrow, the world economy would hardly miss it".[19]

As Table 6.1 indicates, intra-EU trade has expanded since 1958, at the expense of EU's trade with the rest of the world.

Table 6.1
The regional structure of EU 12 trade, 1958-1990

	Partners										
		Western Europe			*Eastern & Southern Neighbours*				*Rest of the Word*		
	Year	*EC-12*	*EFTA*	*Total*	*Eastern Europe*	*Mediterranean Countries*	*ACP*	*Total*	*Developing Countries*	*Industrial Countries*	*Total*
E	1958	37.2	12.2	49.4	2.7	7.8	6.6	17.1	15.3	18.2	33.5
x	1965	49.6	13.0	52.6	2.9	4.8	4.4	12.1	9.4	15.9	25.3
p	1970	53.4	11.7	65.1	3.4	4.8	3.6	11.8	7.1	16.0	23.1
o	1975	52.4	10.6	63.0	4.9	6.7	3.6	15.2	9.6	12.2	21.8
r	1980	56.1	11.2	67.3	3.5	5.9	3.5	12.9	9.2	10.6	19.8
t	1985	55.2	10.0	65.2	2.8	5.2	2.3	10.3	8.7	15.8	24.5
s	1990	61.2	10.4	71.6	2.3	4.2	1.6	8.1	7.3	13.0	20.3
I	1958	35.2	9.3	44.5	2.9	4.5	6.8	14.2	19.2	22.1	41.3
m	1965	44.9	9.0	53.9	3.4	4.7	5.2	13.3	12.7	20.1	32.8
p	1970	50.3	8.7	59.0	3.2	4.7	4.4	12.3	10.3	18.4	28.7
o	1975	49.5	7.9	57.4	3.5	3.8	3.8	11.1	16.3	15.2	31.5
r	1980	49.3	8.6	57.9	3.7	4.2	3.8	11.7	15.6	14.8	30.4
t	1985	53.4	9.4	62.8	3.9	5.1	3.5	12.5	9.8	14.9	24.7
s	1990	59.0	9.6	68.6	2.7	3.8	1.8	8.3	8.2	14.9	23.1

Source: Andre Sapir, "Regionalism and the New Theory of International Trade: Does the Bells Toll for GATT?: An European View, *The World Economy*, Vol. 16, No. 4, July 1993, p. 428.

African countries' concerns about the future trend of their commercial relations with the EU is partly related to some aspects of EU's past protectionist policies and non-tariff barriers towards the Third World. They include EU's domestic price policies, government subsidies, EU's preventive surveillance agreements, Voluntary Export Restraints Agreements (VERs), technical regulations, certification difficulties, and quantitative restrictions. Some of these protective instruments are particularly more severe on low-skilled labor intensive products that are of significance to developing countries. It is largely due to the implications of "the shape of the things to come"[20] (because of "1992"), that a Nigerian Paper, *The African Concord*, concluded that Africa's future is "gloomy" with "1992".

EU's protectionism is severest in the sensitive sectors, particularly in textiles. Before the Single European Act (1987) was promulgated, individual member states could protect their national markets, thanks to Article 115 of the Treaty of Rome. However, to achieve the same level of protection post-1992, an EU-wide border measure would be necessary, and some European interest groups even call for state subsidy for ailing European industries. Given the current emphasis on competition, there is a risk that a EU-wide protection could be the preferred avenue. The accession of three Southern European countries (Greece, Spain, and Portugal) to the EU, increased the protectionist interests and pressures within the EU, especially in sectors of interest to developing countries.

There is the concern that Africa may be "pushed-out" of the EU market for some of these reasons, which are not necessarily related to Africa's lack of competitivity. Siegfried Schultz, an official at the World Bank has noted that "the export prospects of developing countries have worsened considerably ... due to the marked leveling-off of US economic growth and the moderated development in other OECD countries".[21]

While African nations face the basic challenge of coping with the intensification of competition in their traditional markets, they also need to seize new opportunities offered by a dynamic world economy.[22]

Redistributive effects

In addition to trade creation and trade diversion, some redistributive effects of "1992" are possible, in the sense of substitution of one developing-country supplier for another country supplier. Redistribution is likely to result from the removal of national restrictions involving preferences for certain groups of developing countries. At present, implicit restrictions exist tending to favor colonial suppliers. To an extent, the "1992" process will tend to bring about more homogeneity in geographical import patterns with potential redistributive effects. Supply capabilities among developing countries (Africa vs. Asia, for example) would mean that some group of countries may be able to respond to the new opportunities and challenges in Europe more quickly than others.

The change in the purchasing power among the member states of the EU could have important effects on different regions of the Third World. On the impact of "1992" on LDC primary exports to the EU, Alan Matthews and Dermot McAleese, for example, made a comparison of EU member countries' import patterns.[23] Their analyses showed a more diverse picture at the EU national level. In the U.K. market, Africa holds a stronger position compared to Latin America, Middle East and Southern Europe. There is an opposite scenario in the case of Spain, with its market more oriented towards Latin America. Africa has a stronger position in France compared to Latin America, the Far East, and Southern Europe. In Italy, the bias in favor of Africa and Southern Europe is less marked than in other EU member countries. The sharp difference in the import pattern existing among the members of the EU must be taken into account when assessing the impact of "1992" on Africa. Member countries' trade patterns seem to be influenced by geography, history, language, and national preferences. Such factors, which could determine whether Africa may be "pulled-in" or "pushed-out" of the EU economy, are less likely to dramatically change in post-1992.

Africa's challenge as a result of "1992" is the challenge of being able to overcome three interrelated problems: intra-European politics of deregulation, country - and commodity-specific factors, and external factors regarding loss of African market share through loss of competitivity, or dilution of preferences. The erosion of preferences could be triggered by, among other things, the extension of Lome benefits, or the General System of Preferences (GSP) to other developing countries.

Sugar is an example of the commodity that helps to shed some light on the interaction of the above problems.

The case of sugar

When the UK entered the EU, the British government negotiated special conditions of access for cane sugar for certain countries in the ACP that belonged to the British Commonwealth. In 1973, the sugar protocol was negotiated and attached to the Lome I Convention. There is a paradox here. While the EU produces surplus beet sugar, it has committed herself to import ACP sugar.

As Carol Cosgrove has observed, sugar can be regarded as "a highly political product in the context of EC-ACP co-operation".[24] The casualty list in the sugar battle includes nations of the West Indies which, incidentally, also have limited alternative crops, given the hurricane, cyclone, soil conditions in the region. Hence their fate depends on the political goodwill of the EU, and particularly the UK, to perpetuate the Sugar Protocol.

Since 1975, the EU has accumulated surplus sugar production. The EU agreed under the Lome Convention to pay a fair guaranteed price for a limited amount of imported cane sugar (the main beneficiaries being Mauritius, Fiji, Jamaica, and Swaziland). A major issue raised by "1992" is that there will be increased competition between EU beet sugar and cane sugar imported from developing countries. Despite the existence of the Sugar Protocol, the future access of beet sugar from developing countries onto the EU market depends on the continued existence of a viable EU cane sugar refining industry. As checks on cross-border trade in the EU are removed, it will be easier to transfer refined sugar across the Community.

France is a low-cost producer of beet sugar, and produces more sugar surplus than any other EU member state.[25] This surplus will be boosted by the proposed legislation in the Single Market removing the restrictions insisting on the use of sugar in French soft drinks. As this surplus is concentrated in Northern France, France is well poised to invade the UK market - the traditional market for former colonies of the UK.

In addition to trade implications, the social dimensions of European unity poses a major challenge for African nations. At a time the Africa needs its talents most, there is an exodus of Africa's brains to Europe and other parts of the world. By 1987, Africa had lost about one-third of her skilled labor force to Europe. At the same time, the continent lost remittances from its migrant workers in Europe, especially those who had been kept out of higher paying jobs.

For a large undocumented Africans, the welfare gains of the Single Market, if any, will come through the unofficial process by which illegal migrants are able to send money to their relatives back in their native countries in Africa. Africa's welfare gains from the EU would decrease, as a result of a decrease in migrant income that would follow stringent controls on illegal immigration and discrimination against legal and qualified African residents in Europe.

African residents in Europe are not immune from the crisis of unemployment. According to Jean-Pierre Garson, three factors influence the unemployment of foreigners in European OECD countries (see Table 6.2): the extent of their skills, their ability to speak the language of the host country, and their age.

Table 6.2
Change in unemployment of foreigners and total unemployed in Belgium and Germany, 1986-1990 %

	1986	1987	1988	1989	1990
Belgium					
foreigners	-4.0	-1.5	-3.5	-7.4	-1.8
total	-5.5	-2.5	-9.0	-10.0	-4.8
Germany					
foreigners	-2.1	-5.7	-2.8	-13.7	-12.8
total	-3.3	-0.0	-0.6	-9.1	-7.6

Source: Jean-Pierre Garson, "International Migration: Facts, Figures, Policies", *OECD Observer*, Vol. 176, June/July 1992, p. 24.

Elements of disparity

Market integration has in-built inequalities. A major disturbing aspect of EU integration is the varying capacity of EU's partners to take advantage of the opportunities offered by the Single Market. Global trade liberalization (and the inevitable erosion of the preferential margin enjoyed by developing countries) would lead to greater competition for access on EU's market. It implies that the weakest nations of the world, be they in Africa, the Caribbean, or Asia, would find the going to be tougher.

As a continent, Africa would count on EU's distributive justice, in ensuring that there is equity in dispensing EU's preferences. African nations are justified in their fear that foreign investors might find the Single Market so attractive, and so important, that investments in less developed countries could suffer as a result. For African countries, the stakes for foreign investments and market access in Industrial nations are high.

The case of the Southern African nations illustrates this point. The countries belonging to the Southern African Development Community (SADC) have realized that their previous policy that emphasized infrastructural development would be meaningless, if there are no goods to be carried on the roads and the railways. This brings into focus the urgent need for increased production. When we talk of increased production and diversified exports (to include more manufactured goods), then the issue of market access (to industrialized nations) becomes a crucial matter. For example, newly independent Namibia will be blessed with a more favorable access to the EU for its beef exports.[26]

To an extent, Eastern Europe provides a second chance for third country firms to enter the EU market. In this regard, though, African countries are disadvantaged, as compared with other developing regions such as Asia. Countries like Poland and Hungary have been granted GSP preferences by the US. Many of the Asian nations have begun to capitalize on the preferences enjoyed by countries in Eastern Europe, in order to side-step trade quotas placed by the US on similar products manufactured in the ASEAN home markets.

Eastern Europe represents an area where the ASEAN nations can maximize their economic potential through opening new market for manufacturing industries, and initiating joint ventures. By this way, ASEAN can gain a footing in prospective EU-member countries, and consequently into the larger and more powerful EU market.[27] Late-comers from Africa and other developing nations, who were not in a position to capitalise on the advantages of early entry into the EU, would also be lucky to have a second shot at the EU market via Eastern Europe.

Fading colonial ties

In chapter one, the author introduced the concept of *proximity factors* (factors that increase the closeness of non-union members to an economic bloc). In the case of Africa and the European economic bloc, colonial ties have contributed to Africa's privileged status in Europe. An examination of the policies of major European powers and their relationship with Africa would be illustrative here.

(A) Francophone Africa

France's links with Francophone Africa are the most extensive of all the Euro-African links. The existence of about 71 million French speakers in Africa allowed France to claim linguistic parity in a world dominated by English speakers.

France's attempt to maintain links with her former colonies in Africa dates back to the negotiation of the Treaty of Rome (1957) that established the EEC. Despite Germany's objections, France insisted on including in the Community accord, agreements that Paris had maintained with her former colonies. For Africa, such colonial deals had both pull-in effect (for Francophone Africa) and push-out effect (the case of Anglophone Africa). The agreements would guarantee Francophone Africa (unlike Anglophone Africa) preferential access to the EEC market. The entry of UK into the EEC in 1973, and the signing of the Lome Convention in 1975, ended the disparate treatment that was accorded former British colonies in Africa.

For its former possessions in North Africa, which are outside the ambit of the Lome Convention, Paris cut a separate deal with her European partners that permitted Algeria, Morocco, and Tunisia to export large amounts of agricultural products into France on preferential terms.

Even after independence, French companies - including the *Compagnie Francaise de l'Afrique Occidentale* (CFAO) and *Societe Francaise de l'Afrique Occidentale* (SCOA) - controlled large commerce in Africa.

At the dawn of European unity, colonial ties between Africa and France are receding. The emergence of democratization movements, and revolutions against African dictators supported by Paris, has fuelled Africa's condemnation of French *neo-colonialism* in Africa.

In the 1990s, France's relationship with Africa has been affected by several factors that include Paris' increasing ties with Europe, Africa's economic recession, and rising oil prices. There is the fear that further integration of the EU would loosen Paris' economic ties with Africa (a push-out scenario).

Thirty years ago, about one-third of French exports went to Africa. By 1990, exports to Africa accounted for 7.4 percent of France's global shipments of $17.4 billion: in the same year, shipments from Africa accounted for a mere 5.2 percent of France's $19.3 billion import bill.[28] Despite the "ziggings and zaggings" in Franco-African relations, Paris has put more effort in retaining its relation with Africa than any of the European powers.

Nevertheless, France's special relations with the continent are undergoing extensive changes that may alter the power balance on the African continent. The demise of African autocrats controlled and propped by France, has robbed Paris of the magic of influence in Africa. In place of the "Old Guards", there is the emergence of new African elites who are looking elsewhere, particularly to the Untied States.

Behind France's wooings and moorings in Africa is the desire to exploit Africa and its resources. This is how William Drozdiak, writing in the *Washington Post*, put it:

> Behind the guise of paternalistic care lies an ugly image that France has treated black Africa like a cash cow, exploiting its resources and markets, protecting dictators that do Paris' bidding and even using those countries as conduits to channel funds to French political parities.[29]

(B) **Britain and Africa**

Colonial attachment has, to some extent, served as a gravitational pull-in force that has brought Anglophone Africa closer to the British Commonwealth and to the EU. The imperial system of trade preferences, that London bestowed on its colonies in Africa, survived Britain's "retreat from empire" that occurred in the 1950s and 1960s. However, such preferences were affected by Gaullist politics that pushed the UK out of the EEC until 1973. As part of her membership deal in the EEC, some of Britain's trade deals with former colonies were scrapped. There was an exception: almost all sugar consumption in the UK come from Mauritius and Jamaica. This is a living symbol of the Commonwealth Imperial Preferences scheme that was initiated by Britain

Commonwealth Africa is worried about the future of British preferential treatment. Even before the "1992" process gained momentum, UK's trade with the Commonwealth countries had declined. Britain bought more from France in 1990 than it did from the former colonies. What is worse, Britain now trades more with Australia and Canada than it does with Africa. Australian companies invested in the EU in the 1980s, using UK as a launching pad. The challenge for Anglophone Africa is to use the Metropolitan link to pull themselves into the EU Market as Australia is doing.

To a large extent, Africa's relationship with Europe could be affected by a shift in intra-European politics and preference towards competing developing country regions. Former colonial powers are interested in preserving some advantages for their former colonies. Spain, for example, advocated the enlargement of the Lome Convention to include those countries within its former sphere of influence in Latin and Central America. At the same time, Spain would like to protect its own banana production on the Canary Island.

Globalization or monopolization?

The proliferation of trading blocs darkens Africa's prospects for economic survival. The emerging trading blocs, alongside the EU, have resulted in the shrinking of global horizons to hemispheric (Enterprises for the Americas), continental (European Community), or even regional (eg. East-Asian) dimensions.[30]

These blocs could accelerate the push-out effects (on Africa) of the

Single Market. According to Jack Scarborough, "the stronger international competition the Europeans are trying to create by unifying their market will intensify competition elsewhere, generating more pressure on firms to carve out defendable niches".[31]

In February 1993, the first meeting of the Foreign Ministers of the 10-member Economic Cooperation Organization (ECO) was held in Quetta, Pakistan. This bloc brings together Iran, Turkey, Pakistan, Afghanistan and six Muslim countries from the former Soviet Union.[32] Iran, one of the strongest members of the group, has advocated an Islamic orientation of the bloc. Contrary to Tehran's ambition to turn this into an "Islamic Common Market", countries like Turkey have tried to downplay the group's religious undertones. The potential global implications of this bloc cannot be hidden, though: ECO members envisage forming the world's second biggest trading bloc, with a population of about 300 million.[33]

The challenge of access

Compared to other regions, Africa has some comparative advantages, one of them being geographical proximity. In addition to that, there are preferential trading arrangements between the EU and the continent. All things being equal, there should be no reason why Europe should buy tropical products from distant non-ACP countries. Comparative advantage factors are necessary pull-in factors. It is up to African nations to exploit all their proximity factors.

(A) **Misunderstanding "1992"**

Africa must understand EU protectionism and learn how to fight it. Understanding the sensitive sectors is also important. It is in these sectors that EU protectionism is severest. For example, Eurofer, the EU steel producers's organization which lobbied against improved market access to Eastern European countries, also launched an anti-dumping complaint against Polish steel beams.[34]

European petrochemical companies claimed that a free trade pact between the EU and the Persian Gulf States would place them (EU companies) at a disadvantage against their US and Far Eastern competitors.

The Persian Gulf countries are among the world's most prolific oil producers, and their costs of production are low. The Gulf states have tried, since 1981, to get the EU to eliminate duties on their petrochemical. According to European lobbyists, then, a free trade with the EU would be tantamount to bringing a Trojan Horse into the EC.[35]

The sheer volume of information and the technical complexity of EU regulations and procedures present a particular problem for resource-poor nations that intend to follow developments in Brussels. For example, Robert E. Cawthorn, the Chairman and CEO of Rover Group Inc (USA) noted:

> To put the 300 provisions of this Act [the Single European Act] into perspective — the Lords Prayer has 56 words. The Ten Commandments combined have 296 words. But just one of the 300 EC directives has 26,911 words.[36]

African suppliers must understand that many changes will occur in marketing, production, and infrastructure:

(B) **New changes**

(i) **Marketing**

In marketing, African firms must be aware of these possible changes:

(1) Customs and buying power will change, as a result of "1992."

(2) There will be increasing pressure to reduce the cost of distribution.

(3) Downward pressure on prices will occur.

(ii) **Production**

(1) Costs will be affected by the removal of barriers to trade.

(iii) **Infrastructure**

(1) African companies will need people who can operate in the international context.

(2) Top management will need increased access to information, in order to plan about the European market.

The most salient factors that African exporters should take into consideration are supply, quality and price. The supermarket customer in Europe is a discerning purchaser, so there is the need for critical quality control.

(iv) **Consumer awareness**

(1) European consumers are increasingly becoming concerned about the level of pesticide residues in fruits and foodstuffs. Codes of practice involving the level of pesticides residues are already in effect in the EU.

(2) Packaging of goods is becoming more important. Any unfamiliar foreign insect, even a dead one, could be a turn-off for the European consumer, and a blow to the reputation of the country of origin. African exporters must be aware of such things. Food packaging must meet the toughest standards in use in the EU. The size of packaging must comply with commercial and marketing demands, as well as European waste management and recycling codes.

(v) **Linkages**

(1)African nations must forge linkages between producers and exporters in order to share information about the EU market.

(vi) **Research**

(1) There should be research in high-yielding, pest-resistant crops adapted to different agro-economic zones, in order to sustain supply to Europe.

(C) **Market risks**

Africa faces uncertainties about possible changes in the European market, and their effect on Africa. It is possible that demand may shift from a higher-cost, less competitive, national producers in other European Union countries to lower-cost producers inside the Union. If the higher-cost producers are unable to compete, they may collapse. The result will be a depressing effect on these regions where the high-cost (and hence less efficient) firms are located. If these countries, or regions happen to be Africa's partners in Europe, then Africa could be affected too.

The other source of uncertainty remains the future demand for Africa's products, and the future of EU's external policy. For example, synthetic substitutes in the form of raw material and semi-finished goods have been given a boost in European manufacturing industries.

A major hope for Africa's chances of market access, in the short-term, would be the retention of the traditional preferences. While these preferences are likely to remain for a while, they are likely to be important for their political symbolism than their economic significance to Africa.

EU's political commitment to liberalization is not total absolute. For example, the Cecchini Report noted that "the expectation may be that a dynamic European market, trading with the world on a footing of revamped competitivity, will provide a much needed short in the arm for other markets and economies in less buoyant shape".[37] At the same time, Paolo Cecchini also noted that "there must be a fair share out of the burdens of global economic responsibility, with market opening measures extended internationally on a firm basis of clear reciprocity".[38]

Overcoming the problem of access

African nations must use international negotiations in order to "push" their interests onto EU decision making agenda. The Uruguay Round of GATT negotiations may not be totally dysfunctional in this matter. As Ad Koekkoek has suggested, the Uruguay Round "offers a chance to let internal liberalization [in the EU] be accompanied by external liberalization".[39]

The EU has granted preferences to products exported from Eastern Europe, without looking at the implication of any preferences accomplished in the context of the Lome Agreement between the EU and ACP states. It is partly as a result of this unpalatable omen that Olesegun Obasanjo, has noted that African nations are "pushed more and more by evolving world events to the periphery".[40] This predicament could be seen in the areas of development aid, investment and monetary relations.

Notes

1 Joseph Rocher, "GATT—The Non-Agricultural Round: The South on a Razor-Edge", *The ACP-EEC Courier*, No. 139, May-June 1993, p. 87.
2 On some of the problems of access related to GATT negotiations, see *Ibid*.
3 Michael Davenport, "Africa and the Unimportance of Being Preferred", *Journal of Common Market Studies*, June 1992, p. 233.
4 Mary Alexander, quoted in *West Africa*, June 29, 1992, p. 1092.
5 *EEC-ACP Courier*, July-August 1992, p. 97.

6 Olesegun Obasanjo, "Leverage Against 1992", Excepts of his Speech in *West Africa*, 8-14 May 1989, p. 716.

7 Paolo Cecchini, *The European Challenge 1992: The Benefits of the Single Market*, Brussels, The Commission of the European Communities, 1988.

8 On this issue, see for example, Michael Davenport, "The External Policy of the Community and its Effects Upon the Manufactured Goods of the Developing Countries", Paper prepared for meeting convened by the Netherlands Economic Institute and the Ministry of Foreign Affairs on 'Europe 1992 and Developing Countries', The Hague, 6-7 October 1989.

9 See Bimah Ghosh, "1992: Third World in the Margin", *European Affairs*, Fall 1989 p. 118.

10 Michael A. Samuels, "The Decline of Multilateralism— Can We Prevent It?", *The World Today*, January 1990, p. 7.

11 Alan Matthews, Dermont McAleese, "LDC Primary Export to The EC: Prospects Post 1992", Paper prepared for Expert Meeting Convened by the Netherlands Economic Institute and organized by the Dutch Ministry of Foreign Affairs on Europe and Developing Countries, The Hague, 6-7 October 1989, p. 2.

12 OAU, "Addis Ababa Declaration of African Ministers Responsible for Trade and Development Preparatory to UNCTAD", E/ECA/ Trade/70, 18 March 1987, p. 14.

13 See Dieter Frisch (Director-General for Development, EC Commission), "1992 and the Developing Countries", Address Given in Boon, 25 October 1988.

14 Based on an interview with an EC official in Brussels.

15 Quoted in *African Business*, November 1992, p. 9.

16 Jurgen Zattler, "The Effects of Structural Adjustment Programmes", *Intereconomics*, November-December, 1989, p. 284.

17 *Africa Recovery*, No. 2, 1990, p. 10.

18 *Ibid.*

19 Cited in *"Development and Cooperation"*, #1 1993, p. 12.

20 Europe in 1992: The Shape of the Things to Come", *Africa Concord*, (Nigeria), 24 April, 1989, p. 24.

21 Siegfried Schultz, "Third World Foreign Debt Crisis: Which Way

Out?", *Development and Cooperation*, No. 2, 1985, p. 4.

22 "Trade Issues in the Context of Lome IV and 1992", *ACP-EEC Courier*, No. 123 Sept-Oct. 1990.

23 Alan Matthews, Dermont McAleese, "LDC Primary Exports to the EC: Prospects Post 1992".

24 Carol Cosgrove, "The Impact of 1992 on EC-ACP Trade", in I William Zartman, Europe and Africa: The New Phase, Boulder, Lynne Rienner, 1993, p. 66

25 Edward Mayo, *Beyond 1992: The Effects of the Single Market on the World's Poor*, The World Development Movement, London June 1989, p. 14.

26 Based on presentation in European Parliament in Brussels by a SWAPO representative.

27 Howard Richards, "Developing Relations Between the EC an the Association of Southeast Asian Nations", *European Research*, January 1991, p.25.

28 Jane Sasseen, "Out of Africa", *International Management*, May 1992, p. 70.

29 William Drozdiak, "French Ties to Africa Undergo Key Change", *Washington Post*, January 22, 1993, p. A. 10.

30 Jack Scarborough, "Global Vulnerabilities: Opportunities in International Niche Markets in An Environment of Economic Growth in Developing Countries", Paper presented at Academic of International Business Annual Conference, Baltimore, June i-2, 1992, p. 9.

31 *Ibid.*

32 These Muslim countries are Azerbaijan, Turkmenistan, Tajikistan, Uzberkistan, Kazhakstan and Kirghizia.

33 "New Islamic Economic Bloc", *Development and Cooperation*, No. 3, 1993, p. 6.

34 Robert D. Haslach, "The Bright Lights of Eastern Europe", *Europe*, March 1992, p. 7.

35 "European Petrochemical Firms Hit EC-Arab Free Trade Plan", *Journal of Commerce*, March 23, 1988.

36 Robert E. Cawthorn, Chairman and CEO of Rover, Inc. "Are US Multinationals Ready for the US of Europe?", *Vital Speeches*, Vol

XL No. 2, 15 August, 1989, p. 654.

37 Cecchini, *op cit*, p. xix, reference 7.

38 *Ibid*, p. xx.

39 Ad Koekkoek, "1992 and the Developing Countries: Fortress Europe or Outward Orientation", Ministry of Foreign Affairs, Directorate General for Information and Cooperation, the Netherlands, December 1989.

40 Olesegun Obasanjo, Hans d'Orville (ed.) *The Impact of Europe in 1992 on West Africa*, New York, Crane Russak, 1990, p. 201.

7 Development, investment and monetary relations

The European Single Market initiative has tremendous implications for Africa's survival in the world economy. Changes in regimes that the EU integration would generate, could affect Africa's trade balance, hence its development.

Due to internal opposition and external pressure, many African nations are embarking upon a new process of democratic transition.[1] But stable democracies are not born out of hunger. The EU's development assistance for democratization will help create stable political conditions for Africa's development.

Ironically, at a time that Africa needs external help most, there is "aid fatigue" in the Northern countries. In the US, there is a right-wing backlash against US foreign aid - a policy platform that is noticeable in Patrick Buchanin's Presidential campaigns (1992 and 1996). The Republican Presidential campaigns in the US were fought with conservative and neo-isolationist ideological rhetoric. Because of President Clinton's emphasis on domestic agenda, many US foreign aid programs have been phased out, to the detriment of African nations that are highly aid-dependent.

The EU concedes that it cannot totally abandon Africa. It tried to demonstrate its commitment to helping Africa, when it signed a five-year financial protocol with North Africa that is geared towards countering perceived threat of instability, Islamic fundamentalism, and rapid immigration (to Europe) because of poverty in North Africa. EU aid will be essential to bolster the political standing of secular regimes in Islamic North Africa that are trying to win political legitimacy at home.

Development aid implications

Africa's vulnerability must be seen primarily from its overly dependence on the EU's market. A key to Africa's economic recovery will include EU's external aid, improved market access, and investments in Africa. Private foreign investment, a major booster for sustained development in Sub-Saharan Africa, are primarily directed towards export industries, where the EU's market remains the most crucial for Africa at the moment. As Michael Davenport has argued:

> If access to foreign markets is impaired by changes in trade regimes, foreign direct investment (FDI) flows may be reduced with long-term implications for the balance of payments constraints and thus development.[2]

One of the major implications for Africa, as a result of EU integration, concerns foreign aid. The gap between the developed and developing nations is increasing at a frightening pace. The European Parliament's suggestion that industrial nations ought to give one percent of their GNP as foreign aid will do little to arrest such gross imbalances in wealth, unless Africa's foreign debts are also canceled.

Africa's survival in the world system has been affected by developments now occurring in Europe. In the first place, the "upward harmonization" of European-wide technical standards EU could potentially exclude Africa's exports. Already, EU's CAP policies are affecting world prices of commodities. Furthermore, the EU integration process might have served as a catalyst for the decline in foreign direct investments in Africa (the *push-out* scenario).

As their continent is highly dependent on external aid, particularly from Europe, African policy makers harbor uncertainties regarding a potential shift in EU's aid policy that may accompany European unification. The tying of aid - both project and adjustment supply-to supplies from donor countries tend to reduce the possibility of intra-African trade.

The aid provided by the EU and its Member States accounts for a large share of total world ODA (some 40 percent in 1988-89). EU's aid remains largely focussed on the ACP states, and in particular, sub-Saharan

Africa. Including the member states, the EU contributes 56 percent of total aid to Sub-Saharan Africa. EU's role in this domain must be assessed on the recognition that aid accounted for more than 10 percent of Africa's GNP during the period 1988-89, and financed over half its investments.

Because of the collapse of the Eastern bloc and the end of the cold war, Africa has already lost its geo-strategic position in the West's global political calculations. Aid contribution of EU donors has become increasingly subjected to "efficiency" and other political standards, that African nations may find hard to meet.

There exist divergent viewpoints about the primacy of foreign aid in Africa's development. While some scholars have hailed foreign aid as indispensable, others have questioned its utility. Teresa Hayter, for example, described foreign aid as "imperialism".[3] Despite these divergent opinions, the importance of external aid to Africa cannot be overemphasized. Foreign aid becomes crucial, particularly for those African nations with limited development potential. The development plans of most African countries are based virtually on the supply of commodities whose prices are unstable, because of the vagaries of the environment, or because of the oligopolistic structures of the world market.

One of the dimensions of the aid problem relates to the amount of aid. Unlike trade and agriculture, EU's aid is partly "Communitised". A major concern for African leaders and policy makers is whether "1992" is going to mean a reduction, or an increase, of EU economic aid to its traditional partners.

The Counselor for Development Affairs of the EU Delegation to Washington suggested that the creation of the Single Market will increase EU's "capacity to dispense aid"[4] to its traditional recipients. Despite official assurances from the EU, African countries and leaders are watching anxiously at any EU aid orientation. This watch is largely focussed on EU's relations with other countries, particularly Eastern Europe.

Future increases in the economic growth of the EU, as a result of the deregulation of "1992", implies that even if the EU's contribution to African development aid as a percentage of GDP remains the same, there will be a larger volume of EU aid to Africa. However, it may be unrealistic to expect that EU's growth will increase by the margin that had been earlier projected by the Cecchini Report.[5] The implicit assumption underlying the Cecchini Report is that most of the barriers enumerated by the 1985 EU White Paper will be removed. In a less optimistic mood, the IMF, for example, lowered the growth estimates of industrial countries in 1992 and 1993, from 1.8 and 3.3 percent to 1.7 percent and 2.9 percent respectively.

The concerns expressed by African countries about the Single Market need to be understood in the contexts of the changing North-South and East-West relations. Industrial nations have become increasingly preoccupied with their own domestic problems. Also, the mood at the September 1992 annual meeting of the IMF and the World Bank reflected the industrial world's preoccupation with changes that are occurring in Europe. As Bimah Ghosh has noted, particularly in relation to the "1992" process, the Third World is "in the margin" [6] of post-Cold War global concerns.

There is a new convergence of interests among the East and the West, particularly the Group of 7 (G7) Nations-U.S., Germany, Canada, Great Britain, France, Japan, and Italy. Initially held in the early 1970s to develop united response to OPEC's success in quadrupling oil prices, annual summits of the G-7 have since continued as a vehicle for leaders of the Industrialized North to jointly coordinate their economic polices.

Since the Paris Conference of the G-7 in 1989, the Industrial Nations have been preoccupied with the political and economic transformation of the former Eastern Bloc. Thus, former Soviet leader, Mikhai Gorbachev's public appeal for Moscow's membership in the G-7 got immediate and dramatic response. Ironically, the G-7 then designated the EU to coordinate Western efforts to integrate the Eastern European economies into the Western economies. Six months later, in January 1990, 17 foreign ministers of the EU, meeting in Dublin, called for a 35-nation summit to explore, among other things, the possibility for long-term free trade agreement with the Eastern bloc nations.

The EU and the United States have teamed up in the assistance towards the former Eastern bloc (see Table 7.1).

Table 7.1
Assistance to Eastern and Central Europe

(Jan. 1990 through June 1991)	EU	US
G-24 Assistance committed to Eastern and Central Europe, excluding former USSR (billions)	$22,588	$2,373
As a % of total G-24 assistance	73.1%	7.1%

Source: "G-24 Assistance to Eastern and Central Europe", Commission of the European Communities, DG1, Brussels, 11 November 1991.

EU-US cooperation in assisting Eastern Europe have included the following programs:
(1) PHARE (Poland and Hungary Assistance for Restructuring of the Economy). Coordinated by the EC Commission, PHARE is a multilateral aid program that was established in 1989 to assist Poland and Hungary. In 1990, the program was expanded to include other Central and Eastern European countries committed to "democratic principles" and market economies.
(2) EBRD (European Bank for Reconstruction and Development): Beginning operations in June 1991, the EBRD fosters the transition toward open market economies and promotes private and entrepreneurial initiative in Eastern Europe. The EU, including its member states, is the majority shareholder (51 percent) of this Bank. The US holds 10 percent of the shares.[7]

In addition to multilateral initiatives, bilateral aid has been generously extended to Eastern Europe. Germany set aside a fund of 115 billion deutschmarks as start-up capital for reunification assistance. When the former President of the World Bank, Barber Conable, visited Bonn in June 1990, one of his main preoccupations was to find out what the process of German re-unification means for future German aid policies.[8] Further assistance in the future, in addition to Germany's role in the East, particularly the former Soviet Union, has created uncertainties in the minds of the aid community as to Germany's future role in the developing World.[9] Germany's aid policies are very crucial for developing nations, because Bonn is the economic heart of the EU.

One important thing about the relationship between European integration and Africa's development must be recognized here. Most dependency theorists argue that development in the core nations does not, and would not, benefit the peripheral nations. Consequently, they are skeptical about any positive development scenario for Africa via incorporation into the EU's Single Market. The current EU's tightened immigration policy would seem to support this pessimistic assessment. The 1992 *Human Development Report* published by the UNDP has calculated that LDCs lose about $250 billion annually in potential income transfers, because of restricted migration to the developed world . This is about five times the amount of development aid given to those countries-provided that migrants are gainfully employed in targeted countries.

In Chapter 5, this author examined the current trend of EU's immigration policies that seem to justify such pessimism. As a result of interviews conducted with African migrants in Brussels in 1989-90, this author found out that many African nations depend on their nationals resident abroad for a large amount of development projects. These include private transportation, the provision of housing and educating relatives.

Africa and the aid fatigue

Even European nations that have traditionally been more sympathetic with aid, such as Sweden (see Table 7.2), are now critical of development aid. Sweden considered a 10 percent cut in foreign aid in September 1992.

Table 7.2
Net overseas development assistance from OECD Countries in 1989

	As % of GNP	$ Billion	
Norway	1.04	Japan	8.95
Sweden	0.97	US	7.66
Netherlands	0.94	France	7.45
Denmark	0.94	Germany	4.95
France (a)	0.78	Italy	3.61
Finland	0.63	UK	2.59
Belgium	0.46	Canada	2.32
Canada	0.44	Netherlands	2.09
Italy	0.42	Sweden	1.80
Germany	0.41	Australia	1.02
Australia	0.38	Denmark	0.94
Japan	0.32	Norway	0.92
UK	0.31	Finland	0.71
Switzerland	0.30	Belgium	0.70
Austria	0.23	Switzerland	0.56
New Zealand	0.22	Austria	0.28
Ireland	0.17	New Zealand	0.09
US	0.15	Ireland	0.05
Total DAC	0.33	Total DAC	46.68

(a) Including DOM-TOM

Source: OECD-"Development Cooperation, 1990 Report Highlights" (Paris: 1990), reprinted in James Gustave Speth, "A New US Program for International Development and the Global Environment", *Issues and Ideas*, (World Resources Institute), Washington, DC., March 1992, p. 6.

Table 7.3
The geographic concentration of developed nations' aid

Africa	France	Germany	Italy	UK	US	Japan
Sub-Saharan	54%	36%	56%	50%	14%	13%
North Africa	10%	26%	14%	5%	48%	9%
and Middle East	10%	26%	14%	5%	48%	9%
South Asia	3%	12%	4%	27%	10%	17%
Other countries in Asia and Oceana	14%	14%	6%	10%	7%	52%
Latin America and Caribbean	19%	11%	20%	8%	20%	8%
Milliards de Dollars	5.1	4.9	3.6	2.6	7.6	8.9

APD% - Base moyenne des annees 1989-90
Source: CAD-OCDE 1991

It is evident from Table 7.3 that France, UK, and Italy give more than half of their aid to Sub-Saharan Africa countries. There are historical reasons for this pattern of aid giving-their past colonial ties with Africa, and sympathy towards the plight of the continent. The question is: How long will this trend in foreign aid persist? Since apartheid is officially dismantled in South Africa, Southern African nations are gradually losing the West's sympathy. The Japanese government, which committed $50 billion in foreign aid to the Third World for the period, 1982-92, concentrated a large portion of that aid on South-East Asia.

Following the historic PLO peace accord with Israel in September 1993, the West has been interested in rewarding the Middle East actors with economic assistance and political support. The EU promised to pour more than one billion dollars in West Bank and the Gaza Strip. According to a Report carried by the *Washington Post*,[10] the World Bank promised a $3 billion development plan for the West Bank and Gaza. Israel and the PLO are seeking assistance from the US, Japan, and the Gulf States.

After being overshadowed and sidelined in the recent Israeli-PLO peace negotiations, the EU did not hesitate to bask in the shadows of peace. William Drozdiak, who captured EU's motivation behind her aid pledges to the PLO, noted that the EU was eager:

> To jump on the peace bandwagon and to capitalize on their experience in establishing economic integration among former enemies, such as that between Germany and France after World War II.[11]

The EU also promised 200-bed hospital and 50,000 housing units for the Gaza Strip-one of the world's most crowded enclaves. EU Commissioner for Development, Manuel Marin, held talks in Brussels with Nabil Shaath, a senior advisor to Yasser Arafat.

Africa used to be accorded global sympathy because of the continent's plight. Vladimir Vigand has concluded that the Lome Accord, that grants privileges to African nations, "signified acknowledgement by the EC [EU] of colonialism's responsibility for the backwardness of these [African] states".[12] This sympathy is shifting, in the financial heart and eyes of Japan. For example, Tokyo has argued that Asia contains the largest number of the world's poor, and disagrees that Africa should be the major focus of foreign aid.

Japan contributed $150 million to Poland and Hungary. It is the "Eastern factor" in recent aid policies of the Industrialized North that worries EU's traditional aid beneficiaries, such as those in Africa. As the Acting Administrator of the US Agency for International Development (USAID) put it: In a zero-sum game of foreign aid, "no one gets more unless someone else gets less".[13] There is no question that Africa is going to get less, while Eastern Europe gets more.

A change of EU's ideology regarding aid offers will also impact on EU's aid assistance programs in Africa. While officials in Brussels often point to the "non-political" character of the Lome Convention, the political and ideological undertones of EU's aid policy are discernible. There are indications that structural adjustment ideology will continue to shape EU's development agenda in Africa. The Lome IV Convention signalled a change in EU cooperation policy in the sense that there are new changes introduced, that were absent in the previous Conventions, such as the support for structural adjustment in the ACP countries, and the introduction of conditionality clauses.

EU nations have begun to use the degree of pluralism, respect for human rights, and in some cases levels of defense spending, as criteria for allocating assistance. These conditionalities constitute a threat to the sovereignty of the African state.

African critics are disdained by the West's selective application of the political conditionality doctrine. For example, the principle of "democracy" was enforced in Nicaragua because the US wanted to topple the "Marxist" Sandinista regime; in Angola (because the US supported Jonas Savimbi) and Haiti (because the US resented the radical politics of ousted Haitian leader, Aristide), but not in Algeria (because of US aversion to Islamic fundamentalism).

Africa has lost control over her economic policies, as a result of Structural Adjustment conditionalities that have resulted in the increase in the influence of external actors in the economic decision-making in Africa. If the World Bank and the IMF have their way, the roads, airports, power installations, railways and harbors built with public money would be handed over to private companies.[14] The EU has been co-opted by the Breton Wood development establishment in pursuance of the policy of Structural adjustment.

The social ailments that accompany structural adjustment (eg. the present drastic cuts in Africa's health and education budgets) appear to run counter to Africa's long-term development aspirations. Consequently, policy re-evaluation by the EU in the domain of SAPs would be in the right direction. A closer and more meaningful coordination between the EU and other donor agencies would be needed, in order to integrate measures that would support the promotion of Africa's development.

Alongside the erosion of Africa's trade preferences, we can also notice that there is an erosion of the colonial paternalism that, for example, undergird Gaullist African policies in France. In Africa, too, there is the demise of the "Old Guards" [African politicians] who fought the Cold war on the side of the West, and who were politically attached to, and well accepted in, European capitals. The death of Houphouet Biogny of Cote d'Ivoire, the electoral defeat of Kerekou of Benin, the "dumping" of Mobutu in Belgium are just but a few of the recent political changes in African politics. With the death of the legendary President Houphouet Boigny of the Cote d'Ivoire in 1993, perhaps, a new epoch in Euro-African relations will be born.

In European capitals, too, the emergence of young bureaucrats or politicians in policy circles, who have little attachment to, or sympathy for, Europe's colonial ties with Africa, has diluted Africa's leverage in European politics. In the EU itself, internal politics [particularly among ex-colonial powers] has also tilted the balance. Some African observers, for example, lamented that the retirement of the pro-African Dieter Frisch as the EU's Director-General of Development might have negatively affected the future of the Lome Convention.

Africa would have to watch the overall colonial links, and the possible shifts in alignments. Spain and Portugal, since joining the EU in 1986, have mounted an intensive diplomacy to include Latin America in aid programs. The "Latinization" of EU policy may shift the balance of privilege that Africa enjoys in Europe.Given the state of the American economy, this is not the best time for African nations to line up in the American foreign aid queue. Three popular countries - Israel, Egypt, and now Russia - received the lion's share of the $13 billion US foreign aid bill for year 1993. Meanwhile, the $800 million Development Fund for Africa - the primary direct funding source for more than 30 countries in Sub-Saharan Africa - was cut by $16 million.[15] As the *Washington Post* emphatically put it, "the timing is especially bad for the countries of sub-Saharan Africa".[16]

Development specialists are still worried that Africa's gloomy days still lie ahead. The US Administration is planning to replace its 32-year old Foreign Assistance Act. This new Act removes the concentration of funds designated specifically for Africa's economic development. Second, the legislation may result in a situation whereby poorer African nations would have their limited funds being siphoned by those with more political clout in Washington.

There is a call for a transfer of capital to developing nations, now that the Communist threat has been neutralized. Some observers have even called for a Marshall Plan (which provided $13 billion annually to Europe) for Africa. However, there is no agreement about the relevance of the Marshall Plan in rebuilding Europe. Second, the Marshall Plan was an effort to restore already developed, not underdeveloped, Europe. There is limitation on the capacity of aid as a catalyst for development. Critics cite corruption, debt burden, and neocolonialism. As a result of these internal and external factors, there has been a general failure of development aid as an instrument of positive change in underdeveloped regions of the world.

Regardless of divergent ideological positions on foreign aid, there is a "moral deficit" in recent donor attitude towards Africa. For example, there are more people per capita starving in Africa than in Eastern Europe, but largely for geo-political considerations, the World's attention is being shifted toward the East.

Africa and the future of EU's aid

On the positive side, perhaps, is the fact that the liberalization of public procurement in the EU could widen the recipient countries' choice of suppliers, and also enhance the cost effectiveness of aid-giving. As at 1990, government procurement accounted for 15 percent of EU member's GDP, but only 2 percent of government contracts went to non-national firms. In post-1992, the possibility for Community-wide choice and competitive bidding would limit the tendency of aid tying often associated with EU member countries' bilateral aid policies.

Nonetheless, national sentiments and parochial interests, which have often characterized European public procurement, would not just vanish after 1993. For example, it has been difficult for EU member countries to surrender power to the Community to suspend the award of unfair contracts.[17] Edward Mayo concluded that to the extent that EU member countries have been using aid tying as a means to preserve public support for development cooperation, pan-European liberalization of procurement may result in a diminution of this support, and could adversely impact on the future flow of EU aid, since the direct domestic benefit of aid to the donor country could not be effectively demonstrated.

According to Bimah Ghosh, coordinator of the Swiss-based Committee on North-South Issues, pan-European liberalization of public procurement will not only widen recipient countries' sources of supply, but will also improve the cost-effectiveness of aid. Ghosh, however, ended on a pessimistic note in regard to future aid disbursement to developing nations following public procurement liberalization. EU-wide procurement, Ghosh noted, may reduce the propensity of individual EU member country to dispense aid, "since they will no longer be sure of an automatic reverse flow of aid money to boost exports and employment at home".[18]

As European integration gathers momentum, increasing pressure has mounted that could result in the diversion of additional funds to less advantaged regions in the EU, as part of solidarity assistance, and as a "compensation" for adjusting to the vagaries of internal liberalization. As Table 7.4 indicates, EU's aid to less developed regions in the Community increased from 7.2 percent in 1987 to 14.5 percent in 1993.

Table 7.4
EU aid to less developed regions in the EU and industrial spending by structural funds (1988 prices, billion ECUs)

Year	Percentage
1987	7.2
1988	7.7
1989	9.0
1990	10.3
1991	11.6
1992	12.9
1993	14.5

Source: Bimal Ghosh, "1992: The Third World in the Margin", *European Affairs*, No. 4, 1987.

There is a "cohesion fund" for the EU's poorest nations-Spain, Portugal, Greece and Ireland. In order to strengthen the social and economic cohesion in the EU, the later has made an effort to reduce the gap between the rich and poor regions in the EU. The European Investment Bank gives loans and guarantees for financing projects in less developed regions in the EU. The Integrated Mediterranean Program (IMP) was set up by the Council Resolution in 1985, for a seven year period, to improve the socio-economic situations of Southern regions as they deal with problems associated with the enlargement of the EU.

A pessimist observer, who has been skeptical about the prospects of increased EU's aid towards Africa (as a result of expected increased income in Europe), has noted that the EU spends about $32 billion a year in income redistribution from relatively wealthy EU member countries-such as Germany and Britain - to less wealthy countries such as Greece, Ireland, and Portugal. By 1997, this amount is expected to increase by 25 percent[19]. If this trend persists, then, Africa cannot put its hopes on Europe.

The financial pillar of the EU-ACP Accord is shaky. For example, STABEX, a system designed to stabilize the export earnings of the ACP countries, is not stable itself. In the wake of falling commodity prices, STABEX funding has been a source of controversy in EU-ACP relations. According to the Rapporteur for the ACP-EEC Joint Assembly, Francis Wurtz, while structural aid to the less favored regions within the EU is trebled, development aid's share of the EU's budget "is marking time".[20] At the EU-ACP negotiating session in Luxembourg in November 1989, several ACP delegates stressed that the Community, distracted by the "1992" deadline for the creation of the Single Market, and by its new involvement in the political and economic reform process in Eastern Europe, was paying less attention to its ACP partners. The EU's failure to come up with a convincing offer on the key trade and aid chapter of Lome IV Convention heightened the criticism.[21]

A shortfall in EU development aid to Africa has affected, particularly, the politically vulnerable countries which, not only are debt-ridden, but are also largely dependent on EU aid for revamping their economies, while carrying on the herculean task of structural adjustment. Africa's external debt increased from U.S. $ 128 billion at the end of 1982, to U.S.$ 169 billion at the end of 1985. The OAU noted that by the end of 1995, the average annual debt service payments are expected to reach about $31 billion, or 48 percent of Africa's export earnings.[22]

There are some scholars who have taken a different view about the whole idea of foreign aid to African countries. According to them, inadequate (or lack of) assistance to Africa is not the issue. The major obstacle to Africa's development is the corruption of a political class-the African elite. This viewpoint is not only supported by EU officials and other external donors, but also some African scholars. For example, George Ayittey, a Ghanaian professor of Economics at the American University in Washington, DC, has described Western aid to Africa as tantamount to "the looting of Africa"[23] . According to Ayittey, every franc that is given to Africa by France comes back to France, or is smuggled to Switzerland. An estimated $15 billion - more than what Africa receives in foreign aid - flees Africa every year.[24] Partly as a result of corruption, Egypt has foreign debt nearly equal to its GDP. According to a social critic from Cote d'Ivoire, this wealthy West African country is the nation with the most millionaires in the world, and also has the dubious distinction of having the most thieves in the world.[25] It is estimated that about $130 billion francs ($450 million) is taken out of Cote d'Ivoire every year.[26]

Environmental threats

The EU Commission has the responsibility to see to it that EU member states do not impose trade barriers under the guise of environmental protection. At the same time, too, the European Commission must address the concerns of environmental activists that ecological protection be stepped up, if the negative impact of the Single Market are to be negated.

In Germany, the country where the Green Movement started, the government has imposed the strictest laws and standards on industry. The implication for Africa is obvious. Germany's initiatives are sometimes harbingers of EU-wide policies, and Bonn supports the adoption of the strictest environmental standards (its own) at the EU level.

There is a linkage between EU's technical standards and environmental protectionism. Newly legislated technical standards have affected a variety of products and industrial performance: labeling of hazardous materials, protection of engendered species, recycling, etc.

Already, EU environmental policies have had a toll on Africa. For example, African birds - captured, caged, and transported overseas are prohibited for sale in the lucrative European market. The EU is the world's largest market for wild birds. A campaign against the sale of birds was launched in Britain by three major organizations: the Royal Society for the Protection of Birds (RSPB), the Royal Society for the Prevention of Cruelty to Animals (RSPCA), and the Environmental Investigation Agency (EIA). The ban on the import of wild birds into the EU is being orchestrated by a partnership of animal welfarists and conservationists.[27]

In order to assess how the new European standards could affect Africa's interest in the EU, we need to consider the loss of export revenue, and the financial cost of adopting to new environmental standards. Consumer and environmental protection in the EU could place undue burden on African exporters, who are expected to meet high quality packaging and sealing requirements.

The negative consequences of EU's industrialization has already spilled over to Africa. There have been complaints about the dumping of toxic waste in Africa that is made possible thanks to the collusion between some African officials and foreign multinational companies. For Africa, the industrialization and growth that the "1992" process is supposed to generate in Europe may be achieved at a high cost to Africa, in terms of technological costs involved in cleaning up the wastes that European firms dump in Africa.

According to TransAfrica, as Washington-based African-American lobbying group, the countries in which toxic wastes have been dumped include Benin, Equitoria Guinea, Gabon, Guinea Bissau, Guinea, Nigeria, Sierra Leone, South Africa and Zambia.

At the May 1988 OAU Summit in Addis Ababa, "toxic terrorism" became a major issue on the agenda. Reacting to reports that some Italian firms had dumped toxic waste in Nigeria, the Government of Nigeria recalled her ambassador in Rome, demanded that Italy recall its ambassador in Lagos, seized an Italian ship, and arrested 54 people, and in addition mandated the death penalty for subsequent toxic dumping.[28] Table 7.5 provides a sample of the dumped wastes and their effects.

Table 7.5
Substances dumped in Africa and their effects: A sample

ASBESTOS: Causes mesothelioma (a virtually incurable cancer that occurs in the chest and abdomen).

CYANIDES: Induces confusion, nausea, and slow gasping respiration. They also attack the liver, kidneys, and the central nervous system.

DIOXINS: Its effects include spontaneous abortion, cancer and chromosomal aberrations. One such aberration is suspected in epilepsy.

MERCURY: Causes tremor, insomnia, irritability, indecision, fatigue, irritation of eyes, and skin and affects the lungs.

PAINTS (Lead): Paints containing lead can cause lead poisoning which (1) lowers IQ in children, (2) causes miscarriage among pregnant women and (3) hypertension in middle-aged men.

PCPs: Carcinogenic, they are known to cause cancers, jaundice, vomiting, anorexia, and nausea.

PESTICIDES: External contact causes skin disease while internal injuries affect most frequently the lungs, the gastrointestinal tract, and the central nervous system.

SOLVENTS: Short term exposure causes light headedness, nausea, and mental confusion; contributes to heart attack; and is a potent carcinogen.

Source: "Toxic Dumping Alarms Africa", *TransAfrica Forum*, Vol. 7, No. 3, Winter 1988/1989, p. 3.

Monetary implications of '1992'

The European Monetary System (EMS) was created with the objective of linking a number of European currencies which could only be allowed to fluctuate with each other, within a defined floor and ceiling. The purpose of this monetary system was to stabilize exchange rates between major European trading partners in the interest of trade. Such a system was needed after the US, then as the world's hegemon, abandoned the gold standard of fixed exchange rates in 1973, which had been put in place in Breton Wood in 1944, in order to restore order in the world's economy, and stimulate global trade after World War II.

The Delors Committee Report on Economic and Monetary Union (EMU) declared itself in favor of a movement towards monetary union.[29] The EU Council of Ministers Summit, which was held in Madrid in June 1989, agreed to initiate the first phase of this plan in July 1990. This phase has involved cooperation and coordination between member states in the EU in the monetary field.

The second and third phases of the plan will require changes in the EU Treaty and the establishment of European Monetary institutions. Speaking to the European Parliament after the signing of the Maastricht Treaty, the then EU President, Jacques Delors, stressed that between January 1, 1997 and January 1, 1999, the EU countries would embark on the third phase that would facilitate the establishment of a single currency, and a fully independent Central Bank. However, differences among the EU member states have led to uncertainties, so it is difficult to guess the pace of developments in the monetary field. The European Currency Unit (ECU), the unit of account used for the European Monetary System (EMS), is mushrooming into a true EU currency which, some EU leaders predict, could be in place by the end of the 1990s.

As an indication of the stability of the EMS was the decision of the Swiss central bank, earlier in 1989, decided to hold some of its reserves in ECUs.[30] It could be possible that an European Monetary System could be an ideal opportunity for Europe to define an international role for European currency that could assist African countries facing exchange rate instability. [31]

The European Exchange Rate Mechanism (ERM) was built around the

German mark because of the strength of the mark. After Germany's reunification in 1990, the Bonn Government decided to exchange the East German mark with that of West Germany on a one-to-one basis. As a result of this transaction that involved the printing and injection of billions of deutchemarks to the East German economy, money supply in reunified Germany rose to inflationary levels. European monetary integration has financial implications for African countries, particularly the Franc zone countries and those bordering them.

The CFA currency arrangement

The Francophone African nations fear greater loss of control over their exchange rate determinations as a result of European monetary integration. The lack of competitiveness of the Francophone nations was attributed to the fact that the CFA currency was overvalued. With an integrated monetary policy in Europe, Francophone Africa would be unable to influence collective EU action, especially when France's attention is distracted by EU policy imperatives.

The monetary arrangement between France and Africa can be best analyzed within the theoretical prism of dependency and neo-colonialism. France's objective in the currency arrangement was to facilitate the external (French) control and orientation of the Francophone economies. The CFA monetary arrangement has enhanced France's objective of using the wealth of the colonies to improve the economy of the "Mother country" that had been ravaged by war.

One of the hitherto advantages of the CFA currency had been its parity with the French franc, which gave the CFA franc a relative stability compared to most of the African currencies. This monetary parity reassured investors that capital invested in the franc zone will retain its value. Economic decline in Francophone Africa in recent times, has repudiated the myth of the franc zone's payment reliability. Investors are worried about the possible disintegration of this zone, as a single European currency is in the offing.

European and African officials differ in assigning blame for the causes of financial crises and divestment in Africa, and what part the Single

Market might have played in accentuating this phenomenon. For example, during the Franco-Africa Summit in Morocco in 1988, the French Cooperation Minister, Jacques Pelleter, called for an urgent restructuring of what he termed, the deteriorating banking sector of the West and Central African countries involved in the Franc zone.

There is a dilemma for both French and Francophone African officials. France would be hesitant to repudiate its support for the franc zone, for this would mean a diminution of Paris' political and economic leverage over its former colonies. Keeping the French franc as a peg will be difficult, as Europe moves towards a monetary union that would largely reflect the low level of inflation in Germany, more than the higher rates that had been in France until recently. This could place further stress on the franc zone.[32]

On August 1, 1993, Finance Ministers and Central Bank Governors of the EU met in Brussels, in an intense acrimonious discussion which lasted till two o'clock in the morning of August 2, to decide the fate of the Exchange Rate Mechanism (ERM). A week of interest speculation on the European exchanges saw the French franc drop below its flow in the ERM. This had a direct impact on the CFA zone.

On August 1, 1993, the West African Monetary Union (UMOA) announced that it had suspended the repurchase of CFA notes exported outside of African member countries of the CFA. This hasty decision, and its bad timing for Africa, led N. Susungi to ask a question about the future of the Franc Zone.[33]

When the CFA currency was devalued by 50 percent in the early part of 1994, it sent a political shock wave throughout the African continent and beyond. Parents in Cameroon who have their children studying in neighboring Nigeria found it more difficult to use CFA notes to finance their education in Nigeria as before.

The first casualty of any currency crisis in Francophone Africa is intra-African cooperation. This is because, traders outside the Franc zone will not accept CFA notes, once it is no longer freely convertible in French franc for importing goods from abroad.

European officials may not have any major objection to the idea that France maintains the link between the CFA franc and the French franc. However, EU's official might not be prepared to contribute towards maintaining a fixed exchange rate between the CFA and the European

Currency Unit (ECU). In deed, some EU experts acknowledged that since the total circulation of the CFA franc represented less than 2 percent of the value of the total circulation of the French franc, the problem was within France's capability to manage.[34]

Several policy options are open to the Francophone countries to solve the CFA dilemma. However, given the dependency structure inherent in Franco-African relations, there is a greater possibility for realignments of some sort, rather than total abolition of the CFA zone. Perhaps, a more conservative policy would be to maintain the status quo (i.e. to leave the arrangement intact), because of the popularity of the French franc in Africa.

Table 7.6
African nations linked to the Franc zone

Country	Population	GNP Per Capita (US$)
Gabon	1,168,000	$3,780
Congo	2,350,000	1,120
Cameroon	11,881,000	850
Senegal	7,625,000	720
Ivory Coast	12,360,000	690
Togo	3,773,000	410
Central African Republic	3,086,000	390
Benin	4,886,000	380
Equitoria Guinea	427,000	330
Niger	7,911,000	300
Burkina Faso	9,272,000	290
Mali	8,707,000	280
Chad	5,826,000	210
Comoros	586,000	540

Source: World Bank, 1993 Statistics.

The Franc zone consists of countries with different economic experiences and relations with France (see Table 7.6). In the first 30 years of the establishment of the Franc zone, several African countries left the zone to establish independent currencies. In 1984, Mali rejoined the zone after 22 years of absence. In 1985, Equatorial Guinea became the first country, to join the Franc zone, which had no colonial or close economic links with France,

In recent years, critics of North-South monetary arrangements, as exemplified in the case of France and the Franc zone, have come out of both sides of the Atlantic. European critics of the CFA zone allege that this imperial monetary arrangement-between Metropolitan France and its African satellite nations-facilitates Francophone African elites' access to hard currency that is used to import luxury goods, at the expense of national development.

These critics often regard as irrelevant the argument that the CFA zone has "stabilized" the economies of the African countries, since to them only few African elites benefit from it. Also, because of the widening gap between the value of the CFA and other currencies such as the Ghanaian Cedi and the Nigerian Naira (see Table 7. 7), products from CFA countries are harder to sell in neighboring countries.

Table 7. 7
Exchange rates of selected African currencies
Value Equivalent to One (1) US dollar

Country	Currency	Value
Algeria	Dina	21.47
Benin	CFA Franc	254.475
Cape Verde	Escudo	62.63
Ghana	Cedi	486.00
Madagascar	Franc	1872.37
Mauritania	Ouguiya	106.00
Mauritius	Rupee	15.49
Nigeria	Naira	19.45
Sierra Leone	Leone	500.00
Tunisia	Dina	0.847
Zimbabwe	Dollar	5.1785
Zaire	Zaire	115.0017

Source: Bank of America, 28 October, 1992, quoted in *The African Mirror*, November 1992, p. 35.

Devaluation of the CFA franc is often suggested in many financial quarters - both within and outside the Franc zone. However, devaluation is politically suicidal because, it could lead to mass protests and political unrest.

Another option available to the Franc zone countries will be to seek a new parity between the CFA and the French franc, or the European currency, the ECU. According to William Zartman:

> The historic response [to European monetary system] would be an African franc (or all-currency) zone attached to the emerging European currency in some fashion, just as a French African colonial zone had its aid and preferential trade relations multilateralised thirty-five years earlier in the Treaty of Rome.[35]

A more drastic alternative for African countries is total delinkage from imperial currency arrangements. It is possible that European monetary integration could serve as a catalyst for Africa's monetary integration. Here, then, lies one of the positive catalytic impacts of European monetary integration on Africa.

EU-related investments: Potential and scenarios

One of the major theoretical discussions on the effects of customs unions has focussed on the stimulation of direct foreign investments. Foreign direct investment in the EEC was a major booster for the European economies. During the 1970s and early 1980s, the managerial and technology gap between Western European and US transnational corporations was reduced, except in the more technology-intensive industries. In the period 1981-1987, almost 28 percent of global flows of FDI went to the member countries of the EU.

As a result of European integration, non-EU firms that face Quantitative Restrictions (QRs) on their exports turned to increased investment in production facilities within the EU. The integration process has already had a significant effect on existing investment patterns. The upsurge in US investment in the EU reflects the profitability of past investments. The growth of Japanese investments in the EU reflects the limits placed on the imports of many Japanese goods. It also reflects the medium to long-term prospects for growth in the European Community.

The major concern for Africa is: How would EU integration impact on Africa's investment opportunities both in Europe and in Africa? Major restructuring in the services sector in the EU will definitely create new opportunities for investment in the Community. However, major investment opportunities in the service sector are largely applicable to firms in the EU, than those located in Africa. In the first place, the service industry in African nations is in its embryonic stage and thus, these countries may not be able to offer any major competition vis-à-vis European firms. It is possible, however, that service liberalization will strengthen European firms, and could consequently increase their presence in Africa. This will happen at a time that some African countries are embarking upon structural adjustment programs. For example, in Ghana and in Nigeria, large public enterprises have been privatized. In Southern Africa, too, new promising political developments, such as independence of Namibia, peace prospects in Angola, and the emergence of a multi-racial regime in South Africa, could usher in political stability conducive to foreign investments.

Since the 1970s, when the expropriation of TNCs reached its peak, there have been significant changes in Africa's attitude toward foreign direct investment. In some African countries, economic expansion plans have been linked to an increased flow of foreign investments.

There might be a ray of hope for African suppliers. Even if EU's new standards and certification procedures impede their exports to the EU, direct investment in the EU will ensure that African firms could still benefit from increased intra-EU trade. However, this prospects will depend on the ability of African firms to overcome, or circumvent, the various barriers to entry, such as strict local content requirements.

For some more aggressive non-EU member countries, one strategy of circumventing Voluntary Export Restraints (VERs) restrictions in (host) EU member countries has been the resort to direct investment in the EU. Of course, that strategy is not wholly faultless. The resultant conflict is vividly illustrated by France's opposition to, and attempt to block, imports of UK-based Nissan cars.[36]

In addition to direct investment potential in the EU itself, European integration has major consequences for investments flows to other regions, including Africa. At this stage, it is difficult to have a full picture of the effects of the single market on the flow of foreign investments to, or divestment from, Africa. Already, African leaders have seen investment withdrawal from their countries.

At the dawn of EU integration, EU investors are targeting Europe-both the East and the West. The number of mergers and acquisitions involving, at least, one of the top 1,000 EU firms steadily increased from 155 in 1984 to 227 in 1986, and 303 in 1987.[37] This was in response to the EU White Paper published in 1985, and the Single European Act that followed in 1987. According to the EU, the sharp increase in mergers and acquisition that took place in 1987 was to accelerate in the run-up to the Single Market in 1993.

For African and developing nations, "1992"-related investments in Europe itself raise a concern about diversion of investment funds from other (less competitive) regions. Industrializing developing countries are themselves investing in Europe, in order to safeguard future access (eg. South Korea in Northern Ireland, and Brazil in Portugal).

Comparative assessment

A comparative assessment of possible investment flows, attractiveness of regions, and capabilities of firms and countries provide important insights into Africa's competitive position or lack there of, in the investment equation.

(A) **Western Europe**

Largely as a result of the single market, Western Europe has already proved to be a magnet to foreign and European investment. The EU would continue to be a preferred location for US and Japanese MNC activity in the 1990s. The EU has several location advantages: the reduction of intra-EU barriers and the perceived need of non-EU firms to be "insiders" in the Single Market would result in increased intra-EU investments, as well as investment by other non-EU investors.[38] European firms could count on home political support to shield them from outside competition. Free trade could be suspended for internal political reasons.

(B) **Central and Eastern Europe**

Southern and Eastern European nations increasingly compete for the FDI which might otherwise have gone to developing nations. The Eastern Bloc presents a large, highly skilled labor force which, for the time being, will work almost as cheaply as workers in the poorest developing nations, including Africa. There is the East's logistical advantage over Africa. For example, products manufactured in Eastern Europe can just be put on trucks, and delivered to Eastern Europe, rather than shipped or flown as is the case in Africa.

The East will also be able to compete with African countries in the later's own market. This author agrees with John Guess' assessment that the relaxation in East-West tensions and the euphoria about security and disarmament means a loss of employment, income, international market competition, and even a weakness of developing nations in their own markets.[39]

Eastern Europe offers competition with traditional EC partners for investment due to several reasons: (1) geographical proximity to the EU; (2) higher development levels; and (3) suitability of products. Poland, for example, has a per capita income of $2,000 a year; the world's 42 poorest countries have an average of less than $300 a year.[40] If the economic and political crisis in the Cote d'Ivoire, once regarded as a capitalist haven for investment in Africa is anything to consider, then, Africa's chances for EU-related investment look more gloomier. In Eastern and Central Europe, the strategy of creating the ideal environment for private investment from the West and other countries has involved, among other things, (1) price reforms, (2) privatization of state enterprises, and (3) improving internal trade and debt rescheduling. Other incentives include the provision of tax benefits and the permission to repatriate profits. Many of the CEE countries, particularly Czechoslovakia, Poland, and Hungary, have extended the scope of investment possibilities open to Western investors. [41]

Eastern Europe's aggressiveness in attracting EU-related investment is exemplified by the efforts being made by Hungary, the country which is, perhaps, best positioned for gains because of her comparatively greater endowments. Not only have Hungary's economic reforms policies been, perhaps, the most advanced so far, but also the country has the greatest experience with Western investments. Hungary's legislative reforms resulted in the tripling of the number of joint ventures in Hungary during 1990 (see Table 7. 8). By late 1991, there were over 9,700 joint ventures in the country, the vast majority of them in the services and trade sectors.[42]

Table 7. 8
Western joint ventures in Hungary (August 1990)

Country	Number of Joint Ventures
West Germany	1,117
Austria	960
USA	264
Switzerland	230
Italy	176
Great Britain	149
Sweden	147
Other	1,386
Total	4,469

Source: Ruth Downes, John Bachtler, "Foreign Investment in Central and Eastern Europe", *European Business and Economic Development*, July 1992, p. 24.

As regards investment partners in Hungary and Czechoslovakia, there is an even split between the EU and EFTA countries which account for 40 percent each of the total number of joint ventures. In Poland, EU countries account for nearly two-thirds of joint ventures and invested capital, with EFTA countries contributing about a quarter of the total.[43]

In terms of sectors, the auto industry has benefitted from a high degree of foreign investment. This is partly due to the large consumer market for cars in the CEE region, and partly as a result of the presence of a large market base for re-export and supplies to Western Europe. Major world automobile producers, such as GM, Mercedez-Benz, Susuki, Daihatsu Fiat, and Volkswagen have all invested in the region - primarily in Hungary, Czechoslovakia, and Poland. Some of the major deals include Volkswagen's 3.4 billion deal in Skoda in Czechoslovakia, and Fiat's 473 million deal with FSM in Poland.

Located between the EU and former Soviet Union, Eastern Europe has traditionally been a buffer zone between the two regions. As a result of the fall of the Soviet empire, the "Eastern Corridor" become a link between the two regions. Eastern Europe has about 113 million hungry consumers who are eager to obtain Western goods, services, and technology.

Compared to Africa, Eastern Europe has several advantages as location for foreign (EU related) investments. Politically, Eastern Europe is more stable than Africa. There is also a cultural advantage. Because of its location, Eastern Europe has been exposed to Western political and economic lifestyles for decades. There is also an "*external push*" factor. The economic and political reforms that are taking place in the East are being fully supported by Western nations, under the assumption that a successful transition to democracy in the East will serve Western ideological and economic interests.

Economic recession in Industrialized nations, the after effects of the Gulf War, the gloomy economic performance of the former Eastern bloc, and the disintegration of the former Soviet Union (FSU) have cast doubts about the prospects of massive foreign investments that were expected in that region. Investment in the Commonwealth of Independent States (CIS) would depend, to a greater degree, on the preparedness of the Eastern European nations to support market opening and industrial restructuring programs.[44]

(C) **The NICs of Asia**

The most rapid progress in attracting direct foreign investment would seem to have been made by the Asian tigers (Hong Kong, Singapore, South Korea and Taiwan), though other developing countries from Asia seem to follow. Since the first half of the 1990s, Thailand has followed on the footsteps of Taiwan and South Korea. However, on account of its larger population, industrial base, and its oil revenue, Indonesia, perhaps, enjoys one of the more promising long-term prospects for foreign investors. Business persons are been lured by the booming economies of South-East Asia and the potentials of the emerging Chinese market. To be able to compete in the "Pacific Century", foreign firms would want to have a strategic presence in South-East Asia.

(D) North America and Nafta

In addition to the EU, a major challenge for Africa has been unleashed by the North American Free Trade Agreement between the US, Canada and Mexico. In addition to encouraging greater trade competition internationally, NAFTA has encouraged greater European and Asian investment in the North American region. For European firms to gain preferential treatment in NAFTA, they will have to satisfy Mexican and US "residency" tests, and be established in either of the two countries as "subsidiaries", not as branches. Can ada, in keeping with its international policy, will grant companies national treatment, only if they are controlled by a NAFTA partner.[45] This exclusionary policy could compel foreign, including European firms, to locate in NAFTA countries.

European companies have not lost sight of Mexico's advantages, as compared to other developing nations such as Africa. Using Mexico as base, European firms can not only capitalize on the country's cheap labor, but could also have an open access to the huge American market. As at 1994, the UK was on top of the list of European nations in Mexico, with an estimated direct investment of $2.3 billion, followed by Germany, Switzerland, France, and Spain.

Europe is Mexico's second largest trading partner, accounting for 13 percent of exports and 18 percent of imports.[46] For the European firm, NAFTA opens Mexico's closed financial market with a $146 billion potential market, and improved access to Canada's worth $285 billion.

E) Africa in the competition

Africa differs from other developing nations for two reasons: (1) it is at an earlier stage of development, and (2) has followed a different type of development path. It differs from the NICs, because most FDI that has moved into manufacturing activities has been import-substituting, rather than export-oriented, and differs from Latin America in as much as foreign led import-substituting industrialization has been far more related to the previous structure of the existing FDI in extractive sectors.[47]

There is a possibility that increased growth in the economies of the EU countries would propel an increase in the demand for raw materials which could generate more investment in developing countries in general. Here, African countries are concerned that investments could be located anywhere, not just in Africa.[48]

As Table 7. 9 indicates, European nations have increased their investments in Southern Europe. They also have reduced their investments in Sub-Saharan Africa, while their activities in North Africa and the Middle East remain weak. On the contrary, the Europeans are strengthening their presence in Asia and in Central America.

Table 7.9
Europe and the North-South investment pattern
(in billion dollars)

	1982	1988
Southern Europe	8	15
Sub-Saharan Africa	19	3
North Africa and Middle East	5	4
Asia	5	21
Central America	13	21
South America	19	16

Source: *Jeune Afrique*, No. 1659, 28 October 1992, p. 21.

Foreign direct investment tends to concentrate on relatively few developing countries. On average, over the period, 1981-86, Brazil and Argentina accounted for 11 percent of investment flows to developing countries, and three Asian countries — Hong Kong, Indonesia, and Singapore, accounted for 15 percent (EU, 1988). By its nature, such investments are not attracted to poor countries with few natural resources and unskilled labor.

According to the *World Investment Report* (1992) compiled by the UN, Africa's small share of global direct investment fell to $2.2 billion in 1990.[49] What is worse, it is concentrated on few African countries. For example, the Report noted that in 1989, oil exporting countries received over 80 percent of Africa's $4.3 billion in FDI.

The *Financial Times* [50] has noted that at current growth rates (5 percent for GDP, 3 percent for population), it would take Ghana twenty years to join the lower middle income countries. Private investment in Ghana in 1990 amounted to 8 percent of GDP, compared to 18 percent in all developing countries, and 32 percent in Thailand.

Amid the gloomy prospects for investments, there are exceptions, however. Based on a research that was published in the *North Carolina Journal of Investment Law and Commercial Regulations* (1992), four of the major African countries that may be attractive for investment include: Zaire, Cameroon, Cote d'Ivoire, and Kenya.[51] According to the authors, the relative attractiveness of these four nations as location for FDI is based on several factors. The above countries:

(1) Profess market-oriented economic philosophy, and have courted foreign companies;

(2) Enjoy political leadership willing to denationalize formerly state-owned enterprises;

(3) Have favorable conditions for take-off of export manufacturing and import-substitution industries; and

(4) Have a record of relative 'political stability ' over the last quarter of the century.

However, while some commentators would refer to Zaire, the Cote d'Ivoire and Kenya as "economic models", others refer to them as enclaves of neocolonialism, because of the nations' subservient policies towards the West.

In the past, Africa, like so many developing nations, placed prohibitive restrictions on FDI. Given the experience with colonialism, foreign presence was received with a great degree of suspicion. Among the prohibitive policies that African states imposed on foreign investors included ceilings on foreign equity ownership and employment of expatriates, unfavorable tax laws, and restrictions on repatriation of capital and profits. As other developing nations are jockeying for positions as hosts of FDI, policy changes regarding foreign investment will be needed, if Africa is not to be left behind in the realm of competition.

Two major problems that cloud Africa's future as a location for foreign investment relate to (1) the concentration on few countries and (2) the falling rate of investments. According to the *Financial Times* (September 1, 1993), several developments are occuring in the global economy with implications for Africa.

In the first place, investment flows to Africa relative to GDP are half the levels of those that exist in other regions. After averaging at $1 billion annually in the first half of the 1980s (of which three-fourths went to oil exporting countries), FDI accelerated during the 1987-91 period, averaging $1.7 billion.

Almost half of FDI in Africa went to Nigeria, and another $190 million to other oil exporters.

Second, while FDI flow to other continents have diversified into manufacturing and services-away from resource-intensive activities, Africa's chief attraction remains in energy and mining sectors.

Investment relocation scenarios

Two major scenarios are possible in so far as Africa's stake in EU-related investments. Under the pessimist scenario, Africa would be a net loser in the investment equation, as the continent is unable to take advantage of investment boom in Europe, and as investments are also diverted to other regions outside of Africa. Under the optimist scenario, Africa may gain from EU-related investment, counting on some proximity factors such as geographic location close to Europe, historical ties, and other country-specific factors such as cheap labor (see Chapter 1 for an analysis of the effects of economic blocs).

(A) **Pessimists' scenario**

Since the 1980s, as a result of Structural adjustment policies, some African countries have tended to link their economic expansion to increased FDI. However, moves towards the Single Market could jeopardize such plans. Globalization of markets, financial deregulation, and increased cost of research have resulted in cross-border mergers and acquisitions in the EU. Japan's strategy to be an "insider" in Europe was partly based on some political considerations. The European attraction would consequently exacerbate the problem of investment diversion away from developing nations.

Unfortunately, structural adjustment policies have not created ideal conditions for FDI in most of African countries. Critics even argue that Ghana could not be the so-called "model" for the World Bank-IMF sponsored structural adjustment in Africa. According to Julius Ihonvbere and Terisa Turner:

> Africa's sacrifice through forced implementation of structural adjustment program does not alter the fact that European investors, with the exception of certain mineral extractors, have lost interest in African economies and are now looking elsewhere.[52]

To support their argument, the authors cited specific cases about Nigeria. The authors further assert that the Conference on Investment Promotion in Nigeria that was sponsored by the Confederation of British Industries in 1990 was embraced with a lukewarm attitude by the British industrial establishment. The British Minister of Trade argued that Nigeria had not "liberalized enough". Ihonvbere and Turner noted that, this lukewarm attitude towards investment in Nigeria has nothing to do with the fact that Nigeria has not "liberalized" enough. The authors cited Nigeria's bold liberalization program to include:[53]

(1) A 100 percent five-year tax-free holiday to pioneer industries; 30 percent five-year tax concession for export-oriented industries that exports not less than 60 percent of their products; 100 percent tax holiday for companies investing in deprived areas.

(2) British Oil giant, BP, was invited back in Nigeria, after being expelled in the late 1970s for supporting apartheid in South Africa.

(3) Abrogation of the "indigenization" decree of the 1970s;

(4) Devaluation of the Nigerian currency, the naira.

(5) Privatization of public enterprises.

Even before they gave Africa any second look, pessimists had already ruled out any brighter prospects for Africa. According to Joseph Cantwell:

> It is fairly clear that in terms of the changing international division of labor, and of regional shifts in the location of productive activity, that Africa will not attract the level of FDI flows that are directed to Asia and Latin America, at least not in the foreseeable future.[54]

Of the total stock of foreign direct investment (FDI) of firms based in eight major industrialized countries in 1981, just over a quarter was located in developing countries. Of this stock of FDI in developing countries, 12.7 percent was directed to Africa.[55]

Africa has already seen the gloomy side of the Single Market. Take, for example, the liquidation between mid-1990s and early 1991 of the *Banque Internationale Pour l'Afrique Occidentale*, a 138 year old establishment that once financed trade throughout the French empire in Africa. The company reportedly incurred losses estimated at more than 6 billion French francs (ECU 867.9 million).[56]

Some European firms have left Africa. Most European companies that have not completely left Africa want to retain a minimal presence, in order to safeguard a reputation built over the years, and have shut down most of their unprofitable operations. Table 7.10 indicates that some European companies, such as the Societe Generale (from Belgium) invested in Africa since the pre-1914 period.

Table 7.10
A list of some of the most historically significant investors in Africa

Company	Home Country	Host Country	Date of Entry	Sector
Anglo-French Sisal Co.	UK/France	Kenya	1931	Sisal Growing
Associated Portland Cement	UK	Kenya	1933	Building Mat.
BAT (Imperial Tobacco)	UK	Kenya	1907	Tobacco
BAT (Imperial Tobacco)	UK	Zimbabwe	1917	Tobacco
BOC	UK	Zimbabwe	1930s	Industrial gases
BP (APOC)	UK	Kenya	Inter-war	Oil distribution
BSA (British South African Co	UK	Zimbabwe	Pre-1914	Railways,plantations
Balfour Beatty	UK	Kenya	1922	Power generation
Bird and Co.	UK	Kenya	1920	Merchant trade
Brooke Bond	UK	Kenya	1924	Tea & coffee process.
Brooke Bond	UK	Tanzania	Inter-war	Tea & coffe plantation
Brooke-Bond-Liebig (Liebigs)	UK	Zimbabwe	Pre-1914	Cattle ranching
Brooke-Bond-Liebig (Liebigs)	UK	Kenya	1935	Metal processing

Source: John Cantwell, "Foreign Multinationals and Industrial Development in Africa", in Peter J. Buckley, Jeremy Clegg (eds.) *Multinational Enterprises in Less Developed Countries*, London: Macmillan, 1991, p. 207.

The fortunes of French companies, Renault and Peugeot, have been damaged in Africa. Renault closed the last of its commercial subsidiaries in sub-Saharan Africa in 1991, selling only 15,000 cars that year.[57] Peugeot also has faced the same problem. Peougeot's African sales dropped from 90,000 vehicles in 1982 to 41,000 in 1991.

In Cameroon, French companies owed about 1.6 billion French Francs. While many giants like Bouygues have cut local production to a minimum, others have abandoned the market altogether. Mounting political turmoil in Algeria, Cote d'Ivoire, and Zaire have exacerbated the problem of foreign investment. Car manufacturers such as Volkswagen, Fiat, and Opel, as well as the furniture manufacturer, IKEA, are investing in Eastern Europe. Australia also invested about $300 million in Hungary alone.[58]

Some analysts conclude that when talking about the implications of European unification, and the possibilities of investment diversion, it is unfair to lay the blame solely on Europe. According to them, investments in Africa had declined, anyway, since the mid-1980s. Apart from oil exploration by Elf Aquitaine, the only investments made by French companies in recent years have been those geared towards the maintenance and consolidation of existing operations.[59]

The problem of attracting investment in Africa are partly rooted in Africa's physical and ecological environment. The decline in health standards, particularly as a result of the AIDS epidemic, has affected Africa's attractiveness as a location of FDI. Some pessimists conclude that foreign investments in Africa (which accounts for only a fraction of world investments) may dry out, if the health condition deteriorates.

Africa's vulnerability in the global system can be partly explained by the political psychology of the international media that stereotypically portrays Africa as "a continent of AIDS and diseases". According to forecasts, if the AIDS crisis continues at an alarming rate, there could be a decline in regional trade in Africa, as governments restrict the free flow of labor and foreign investors see AIDS as a reason to put their money elsewhere.

(B) **Optimists' scenario**

A number of analysts, including some EU officials, have emphasized that EU integration will mean greater opportunities that will be available to all countries, and that the prospects for third-country investments in the EU is good. Again, EU officials note that investments will flow to Africa, provided there are adequate incentives for prospective business partners, and structural adjustment policies are working. Ironically, the case of Ghana, perhaps, lends some credence to this argument.

German companies, particularly, have made inroads into the beer industry in Ghana, as a result of the divestiture program which was implemented in the wake of the Economic Recovery Program that was launched by the Government of Ghana.

Africa's attractiveness in the investment equation is enhanced by several country-related factors, including the continent's large reservoir of cheap labor. The increase in wages, that has accompanied the industrialization drive of the NICs, has improved the attractiveness of an African location. The value of Indian investments in Nigeria, for example, is perhaps the greatest in any individual country outside of Asia.

We must think of a possible "spill-over" effect of EU integration in Africa. Western European multinational companies could, in fact, increase competition between these firms and those from the US and Japan for markets in developing nations. MNCs from the US and Japan might find it advantageous to invest in developing countries associated with the EU in the framework of the Lome Convention, in order to gain access to the EU market. This could be an opportunity for African countries to gain some benefits from association with the EU.

Industrialized countries, particularly the US, have imposed trade quota arrangements on South-East Asian textile exports. The trading policies of industrial nations have compelled firms based in the NICs to diversify home production, moving in the direction of more sophisticated products. The manufacture of more basic lines can be relocated to countries with more favorable conditions of access to industrialized country markets.

In the case of Sub-Saharan Africa, the Lome Convention provides an opportunity for a third-country firm that is eager to enter Europe through the "backdoor". According to John Cantwell, this is what has already begun to happen in the case of Hong Kong's investment in Africa in general, and Mauritius in particular.[60]

Some African countries have the capacity to become involved in the new international division of labor in the textile sector, in which they have already been host to German and Italian investments. Even though these investment have focussed on North Africa, it has extended to Sub-Saharan Africa, and according to Cantwell, "there appears to be an emerging opportunity that has not yet been fully exploited".[61]

According to the African Development Bank, most of the countries in Africa experienced economic growth in 1991, following seven years of contraction. Studies conducted by the World Bank also suggest that as a result of Structural Adjustment Policies, African nations have improved on fiscal discipline, have eliminated production subsidies, divested state-owned enterprises, and liberated trade and investment regulations.

African attractiveness may be given an extra boost by the perception that post-apartheid South Africa will become the engine that would drive the continent. The positive assessment of Africa is based some observations. For example, Nigeria supplied more than twice as much crude oil to the US as did Kuwait and Iraq combined, prior to the "Operation Desert Storm" in 1990.[62] According to statistics compiled by the US Department of Commerce, US trade with Africa is more than three times as large as US's trade with all Eastern Europe and the former Soviet Union. US's exports to Sub-Saharan Africa grew by 12 percent in 1992.

Andre Azaulay, chief economic advisor to King Hassan of Morocco, predicts that a decisive stimulant of the Moroccan economy would be [Arab] diplomatic recognition of Israel. There are more than 500,000 Jews of Moroccan descent in Israel and many more in the US and Canada.[63] They are ready to invest in Morocco, if Rabat recognized Israel.

Perhaps, of more significance than quantitative measurements of growth is the changing attitudes regarding foreign investments in Africa. There is a change in the once-prevalent view in Africa that foreign companies are undesirable exploiters. President Rawlings of Ghana, once a demonologist of "capitalist exploitation" -who, in 1979, even threatened to bomb alien-controlled industrial enclaves in Ghana—has transfigured himself into an apostle of capitalism. Ghana, under his rule, has become the World-IMF's "model" in Africa.

Some *proximity* factors work to the Africa's advantage. The colonial relationship between Europe and Africa that has existed for over five centuries, place Africa in an advantageous position vis-á-vis other developing countries. Historically, the bulk of FDI was located in LDCs, and was often associated with colonial ties, and for this reason Africa was prominent, especially for French, British, and other European investments. British, French, German, and Italian companies had above average shares of their investment in less developed countries (LDCs) in Africa. Of the total stock of FDI in the LDCs, Africa accounts for 58.7 percent in the case of France, 30.7 percent for UK, 28.4 percent for Italy, and 19 percent for Germany.

There are some European companies that are well known in Africa, due to their historic presence and role on the continent. This is particularly true of some British companies in extractive and trading activities, as well as in the construction of railway systems. UK firms with investments in Africa before 1914 included Imperial Tobacco (now BAT), the British South African Company in Rhodesia (now Zimbabwe), Liebigs (which became part of the Brooke Bond group), Mitchell Cotts, and Lever Brothers (now Unilever).[64]

American and Japanese investment in Africa also need to be taken into account here. While their activities in Africa do not hold the same relative weight in their global productive activity, MNCs from the US and Japan are important to many African countries. Although the US corporate outlook is becoming more global, as it must compete with Japan, the EU, and Asian nations, it has given little attention to investment opportunities in Africa.[65]

As discussed earlier, the comparative attractiveness of other Third World regions for EU-related investments is a factor that would determine the margin of overall gains or losses that African nations would sustain from EU market unification. In the 1980s, a slip back of FDI in Latin America occurred, owing to the region's debt crisis. The prolongation of such crisis in Latin America could benefit other regions like Africa that are competing for FDI.

There are differential capabilities and disparities in terms of African economies. Such disparities will partly determine which African nations would gain the most from potential investment flows. For example, FDI flows to Nigeria have traditionally been higher, as compared to Mali or Ghana, partly due to the investments in oil-related sectors in Nigeria . Nigeria's favorable position, however, has been affected by recent economic recession and the depreciation of the naira.

The extent to which firms from Africa can increase their trade and FDI activities in the EU will depend on their supply capabilities vis-à-vis both EU and non-EU firms. Africa's relative competitiveness will also depend, in part, on the policies pursued by the EU towards trade and foreign direct investment between EU and non-EU countries. EU's protectionist policies could also potentially dampen Africa 's ability to penetrate the manufacturing sectors in Europe, as African firms progress on the ladder of international competitiveness.

There is also a technological dimension of the challenge. Lack of technological sophistication have limited the success of African nations diversifying from raw material production to the production of manufactured goods.

African nations have the initial difficulty of securing funds in order to bring production and quality up to European levels. There is also the management deficit. African firms must improve on their management development. African countries must also improve their marketing skills and technological sophistication, so they can compete on the same level with Western European counterparts.

The other issue of concern is political stability. For example, while the dismantling of apartheid offers a glimmer of hope for new investments in South Africa, predictable or brighter future for the continent depend, of course, on continued political stability. If EU investments in Africa looks gloomy, the possibility that African companies could invest in Europe and benefit from "1992" looks more gloomier. The establishment of plants in Europe is ruled out for most African countries on account of the sheer financial costs involved. For these countries, therefore, marketing assumes critical importance, and that the concern for them is the extent to which new barriers to entry are created, as a consequence of European unification.

African countries could use their preferential status (thanks to the Lome Convention) as a "Trojan Horse" to penetrate the EU market. It is possible that countries such as Japan or the "Asian Tigers" could invest in Africa, in order to take advantage of the Lome benefits that are enjoyed by the host African nations.

The EU has remained alert about the "Trojan Horse" strategy, though. For example, following its anti-dumping actions in 1986, the EU tightened up its rules of origin and local content requirements. Now, EU's anti-dumping duties can be applied to products made in the so-called "screwdriver" assembly plants (including those located within the EU)- that use components imported from outside the EU. This was particularly the case of the Japanese affiliated Ricoh Company (a photocopier manufacturer in California) that suffered from the EU's anti-dumping rules because of its Japanese parentage. More stringent criteria have been established in rules of origin for radios, television, ball bearings and integrated circuits. These stringent trade policies have compelled Japan, the US and some NICs - Brazil, South Korea and Hong Kong - to increase their investments or production facilities in Europe.

Negotiating with EU firms

Africa's capability to negotiate with European firms in terms of investment will be essential. The Lome Convention, which some of its adherents hail as a "model", has forged some sort of partnership, albeit, asymmetrical, between Africa and Europe. As a developing country, Africa lacks enough bargaining power to deal with the EU. The World Bank Report on Africa (1989)-*Sub-Saharan Africa: From Crisis to Sustainable Growth*-is a synthesis of the problems affecting the continent. According to that report, overall economic growth in sub-Saharan Africa has averaged 3.4 percent a year since 1961, only a fraction above the continent's population growth. While growth took place in 1972, it stagnated until 1980, and declined since then.

Edward Mayo observed that the influence of developing countries in negotiating with the EU is likely to decline further, as the EU "holds the cards of a rich integrated market".[66] The Secretary of State for Belgium, Anne-Marie Lizin, captured the asymmetry of power between Europe and Africa when she noted that once European firms strengthen their muscles - through increased mergers-African countries would come to find European firms more powerful to negotiate with.[67]

For the sake of fairness and uniformity, if ACP nations grant automatic extension of concessions equally to all EU firms, it could undermine the bargaining position of African states in negotiating with the EU. There is a paradoxical situation where Africa's potential has been wasted by war and mismanagement. No country in Africa has been blessed with greater resources than Angola which possesses oil and diamonds, fertile agricultural land with rivers that flow all the year, natural harbor, and an area five times the size of Britain, but only 10 million people. Would-be investors in Africa will be riddled by formidable obstacles, ranging from complex legislation to corruption, slow-moving bureaucracy, short of skilled personnel, and an infrastructure ruined by war.

That European unity has implications for Africa cannot be over emphasized. European investments in Africa could create employment in Africa, and could stem the tide of outward emigration of African talents to Europe. For example, French investments in Africa translate into 600,000 jobs in Africa.

One important point needs to be stressed here: that is, European unification would have differential effect on Africa, depending on both country and sectors-specific characteristics. Chapter 8 discusses some of these factors.

Notes

1 *New African*, June 1992, p. 25.

2 Michael Davenport, "Africa and the Unimportance of Being Preferred", *Journal of Common Market Studies*, No. 2, June 1992, p. 234.

3 Teresa Hayter, *Aid as Imperialism*, Harmondsworth, England: Penguin, 1971.

4 "Third World Watches Anxiously as Aid Flows to Eastern Europe", *Financial Times*, 12 Dec., 1989.

5 Paolo Cecchini, *The European Challenge: The Benefits of a Single Market*. Brussels, EU Commission, 1988.

6 Bimah Ghosh, "1992: The Third World In the Margin", *European Affairs*, Fall 1989, .

7 The EU, *Facts and Figures on the European Community and the United States*, Brussels, March 1992.

8 "Conable in Boon", *Development and Cooperation*, No.4, 1990, p. 32.

9 See "German Unity and Global Survival", *Ibid*, p. 2.

10 *Washington Post*, Sept. 17, 1993.

11 William Drozdiak, "EC Pledges $1 billion In West Bank, Gaza Strip", *Washington Post*, 17 September, 17, 1993.

12 Vladimir Vigand, "Africa, the EEC and the CMEA", *Development Policy Review*, Vol. 6, 1988, pp. 362-3.

13 Quoted in *Ibid.*

14 *West Africa* 26 October-1 November 1992, p. 1818.

15 *Washington Post*, 29 October, 1993.

16 "Saving Aid for Africa", editorial comment, *Washington Post*, October 29, 1993.

17 Ghosh, *op cit*, reference 6.

18 Bimah Ghosh, "The Single Market Means New Tests for Third World", *Wall Street Journal*, 9 May, 1989.

19 Mark D. Isaacs, "Forcing a United Europe", *New American*, 16 November, 1992, p. 7.

20 Frances Wurzt, Joint ACP-EEC Rapporteur on the Effects of the Singe Market, Interview in *ACP-EEC Courier*, No. 118, p. 3.

21 Shada Islam, "EC-ACP Confusion", *West Africa*, 6-12 November 1989, p. 1840.

22 Organization of African Unity, "African Common Position on Africa's External Debt Conditions", EAHG/2 (III), Addis Ababa, p. 5.

23 George Ayittey, "Looting of Africa", Excerpts of his book cited in *The African Mirror*, November 1992, p. 31.

24 *Ibid.*

25 This is attributed to Professor Laurent Gbagbo, and cited in *Ibid.*, p. 32.

26 *Ibid.*

27 "European Conservationists Seek Ban on African Birds", *African Business*, July 1991, p. 46.

28 "Toxic Dumping Alarms Africa", *TransAfrica Forum: Issue Brief*, Vol. 7, No. 3, Winter 1988/1989, p. 1.

29 European Commission, Comite pour l'etude de l'union economique et monetaire, *Rapport Sur l'Union Economique et Monetaire dans la Communaute Europeene*, (Delors Committee), Brussels, April 1989.

30 "Europe 1992 Countdown", *Belgian American Trade Review*, Fall 1989, p. 27.

31 Patrick Guillaumont, Sylviane Guillaumont, "The Implications of European Monetary Union for African Countries", *Journal of Common Market Studies*, Vol. 28, No. 2, December 1989.

32 *Financial Times*, 17 July 1990.

33 N.N. Susungi, "What Future the France Zone", *West Africa*, 4-10 October 1993, p. 1756.

34 Francois Misser, "European Single Currency Won't Kill CFA Zone", *African Business*, June 1992, p. 29.

35 William I. Zartman (ed.), *Europe and Africa: The New Phase*, Boulder, Lynne Rienner, 1993, p. 4.

36 On this issue, see V.N. Balasubramanyam, David Greenaway, "Economic Integration and Foreign Direct Investment: Japanese Investment in the EC". *Journal of Common Market Studies*, June 1992, p. 189.

37 European Community, "Horizontal Mergers and Competition Policy in the European Community", *European Economy*, No. 40, May 1989, p. 33.

38 John Dunning, "International Direct Investment Patterns in the 1990s", Key Note Address Delivered at the 1992 Annual Meeting of the Academy of International Business, Northeast USA, Baltimore, June 1-3, 1992, p. 23

39 John Guess, "The Effects of Relaxed East-West Tension on the Third World", *Urban Profile* (US), Spring 1990, pp. 14-15.

40 "World 's Poor Cry Betrayal as EC Cuts Export Funds", *The Times*, 13 Oct., 1989.

41 Ruth Downes, John Bachtler, "Foreign Investment in Central and Eastern Europe", *European Business and Economic Development*, Vol.1, Part 1, July 1992, p. 23.

42 *Ibid.*, p. 24.

43 *Ibid.*, p. 26.

44 Dunning, p. 22, *op cit*, reference 38.

45 Renne Riley-Adams, "America Builds its Single Market", *International Management*, November 1992.

46 *Ibid*., p. 45.

47 John Cantwell, "Foreign Multinationals and Industrial Development in Africa", Dept of Economics, University of Reading, 1989, p. 357.

48 "Worries For the Future", Interview by Kaye Whiteman With Edwin Carrington, former Secretary-General of the African, Caribbean and the Pacific (ACP), *West Africa*, October 24, 1988.

49 Cited in *Africa Recovery* (UN), August 1992, p. 30.

50 *Ibid.*

51 Terrence P. Steward, Margaret E.O. Edozien, "Toward a Truly Global Marketing Strategy: A Need to Consider Trade and Investment Opportunities in West Africa", *North Carolina Journal of Investment Law and Commercial Regulations*, Vol. 17, No. 1, Winter 1992.

52 Julius Ihonvbere, Terisa Turner, "Africa in the Post-Containment Era: Constraints, Pressures, and Prospects for the 21st Century", *Round Table*, No. 328, 1993, p. 452.

53 *Ibid*., p. 452.

54 Cantwell, p. 16, *op cit*, reference 47.

55 *Ibid*., p. 2.

56 *International Management*, May 1992, p. 70.

57 *Ibid.*

58 *Europe*, March 1992, p. 7.

59 *International Management*, May 1992, P.70.

60 John Cantwell, "Foreign Multinationals and Industrial Development in Africa", p. 363.

61 *Ibid.*

62 *Washington Post*, 25 November 1993.

63 *New York Times*, November 11, 1993.

64 Cantwell, *op cit*, reference 47.

65 Terrence P. Stewart, Margaret E. O. Edozien, *op cit*, reference 51.

66 Edward Mayo, "Beyond 1992: The Effects of the Single European Market on the World's Poor", World Population Movement, London, June 1989, p. 7.

67 Interview with Anne-Marie Lizin, Secretary of State for Belgium, by Francis Kpatinde, in *Jeune Afrique*, No. 1504, 30 Oct., 1989, p. 48.

8 Analyses of Africa's vulnerability: Country and sector - specific issues

The analogy of an African boxer

Perhaps, the best analogy that could be used to compare Africa's vulnerability in the EU market, is that of an African boxer who faces a challenge: to fight an European champion in the latter's own turf. The African boxer would be more vulnerable to injury, if not defeat, if he were not well-trained. His chances of winning would be slim, if his boxing gloves did not fit him well, or if he was unfamiliar with their use. The European weather will be against him, because he is not accustomed to a cold climate. The African should not be surprised, if he were told that he would have to abide by European boxing rules, not international ones. The African boxer will also have to understand the psychology of European spectators, and how they react when their idols lose. Few of them [European spectators] would cheer a winning African boxer on European soil, but most would probably boo at him. Few boxing fans would expect that the African boxer would even survive the first round. Before the fight begins, European commentators and the media might even rule the African out! At the end of the day, if the African is not able to persevere, he is likely to lose the fight.

The analogy of the African boxer can be applied to Africa's ability to survive the vicissitudes surrounding the European Single Market. Years of psychological conditioning has created the myth that Africa is doomed to failure, and is uncompetitive. Consequently, there is a need for a psychological reconditioning in order to boost up Africa's confidence to compete globally.

As the African boxer must understand the psychology of European spectators, so must the African supplier understand the political, social and cultural contexts of the Single Market. European unity will not mean complete homogenization. Tastes will still be different in the EU, despite market integration. For example, Nestle coffee sold in different countries may taste differently. European integration seems to be encouraging the concentration of business sectors in different European capitals. The "1992" process may lead to some regional specializations.

- London's stock exchange could make London the principal financial market in Europe.
- Frankfurt may be Europe's high-tech center and silicon valley.
- Milan is capitalizing on her competitiveness in fashion.
- Paris may be a major advertising center.
- Brussels is Europe's political capital.

Furthermore, experience that would be a determining factor in the boxing arena will also be a major factor in the marketing field. EU unification has enhanced the globalization of international markets in the twenty-first century. This means that African exporters will have to be familiar with the EU market very well.

An important prerequisite would be endurance. There will be heavy punches from the European side. Some of them could be avoided, others cannot. In the EU market place, African countries must be able to withstand intense competition, and circumvent cumbersome restrictions, if need be.

As in the boxer's analogy, African suppliers or competitors will have to overcome the disadvantages of their "outsider" status. This requires that African firms and nations must maintain a physical and political presence in Brussels. It must be recognized that the EU market is European, and Africa will have to play by "European rules". It is against this background that a better assessment of Africa's vulnerability and capability in confronting the European Single Market can be made.

At the present time, many Afro-pessimists see Africa as a lost continent of conflicts, AIDS, and unwanted immigrants.[1] When Africa is in the Western media these days, it is more and more portrayed as a disaster area. No matter how anyone looks at the EU unification, Africa nations remain vulnerable in confronting it.

In order to examine how Africa is prepared to face the "European Challenge", we have to look at Africa's past, its present structures, and its "no-choice" option in dealing with an unequal international system. At the time of independence, the role of Africa in the international political economy had been predetermined. African nations remained under either the Western capitalist orbit or under Soviet tutelage. There was no credible third option, the rhetorical espousal of "non-alignment" notwithstanding.

Political vulnerability

The general failure of economic integration and development in Africa is partly attributed to the fragility of the European-imposed multi-ethnic state system. Basil Davidson wrote about this problem when he discussed what he refers to as the "curse of the nation state" that has remained the "Black man's burden".[2]

The Cold War created political contradictions in African development. African institutions were fragile when autocrats were bolstered by external support. Today, the fragility of African institutions may be further undermined, as the support system linking African despots to the major powers are cut.

Political stability and good leadership are very important in Africa's search for nationhood. Africa needs a new breed of leaders to a provide a vision at the national and continental levels. Decades after political independence, many African nations have failed to create political and economic systems in which development can flourish. There is lack of accountability to the governed, as well as the encouragement of innovation that can help liberate the continent from anarchic structures and lethargy.

While many an analyst has focussed on sub-Saharan Africa when commenting on the bleak prospects of Africa's development and survival in the international system, North Africa, too, deserves attention. In the 1990s, the Mediterranean, so close to Europe, is going to offer, perhaps, the greatest "African challenge" to a unified Europe.

In Algeria, for example, virtually all secular opposition to the government has disappeared, leaving the Algerian regime in precarious struggle against an Islamic movement that is gaining a symbolic value that the FLN regime has lost.[3] Attempts by Islamic fanatics to create an Islamic State in Algeria constitute a "Southern threat" to the Northern shores. Islam represents an ending opposition to the form and content of the type of nationalism earlier used by the Algerian state to bolster its legitimacy.

In addition to internal problems in North Africa, there are external ones-those embedded in the region's relationship with the EU. Of all political challenges facing North Africa, Islamic fundamentalism is seen in Europe as the most disruptive to dialogue and cooperation between the EU and her partners to the South. The EU has been alarmed by lack of economic and political liberation in North Africa, particularly for the *mustadhafen* (the "disinherited"). As a result of problems in Euro-Maghreb relations, bilateral agreements with the EU have been revised, trade fairs canceled, and immigration policies tightened. Remember the riots in Brussels and in Paris that were initiated by second generation Maghrebi immigrants. At a time when Western European nations would want to bury their political hatchet, civil unrest is spreading through a host of African countries, amid deepening economic recession. In the Cote d'Ivoire, the government had to propose a 40 percent cut of the salaries of public workers, and a 10 percent "solidarity tax" on private sector workers, because of falling revenue caused by the collapse of coffee and cocoa prices.

Participants at the International Conference in 1990 [on the Popular Participation in the Recovery and Development of Africa] concluded that they were united:

> In our conviction that the crisis currently engulfing Africa...is a crisis of unprecedented and unacceptable proportions manifested not only in abysmal declines in economic indicators and trends, but more tragically and glaringly in the suffering, hardship and improvishment of the vast majority of African people.[4]

While African nations gained political independence more than three decades ago, economic independence is yet to be won. The economic infrastructure of African nations - transportation, communication and industries - were, and are still mainly, designed to support industries in Europe. For example, Zaire's economy is largely dominated by Belgian, and French MNCs. This situation falls short of the expectations of African nationalists. Remember the advice that Kwame Nkrumah gave to his fellow statesmen in Africa: "Seek ye first, the Political Kingdom, and all else will be added unto thee". Yet, after political independence, African nations have lost their sovereign power to determine their own economic future. Their economic plans are being controlled by donor agencies and nations, and are often sadly mismanaged by external interests, who are not held accountable for mismanaging Africa's development.

Europe's economic growth, post-1992, will not substantially alter the structures of dependency that exist in Euro-Africa relations, in a way that would benefit Africa's development. Charities are ringing the alarm bells in Somalia today. Perhaps, the bells will ring for drought in the Sahel region tomorrow. Europe's attention span for Africa is becoming shorter and shorter, as it gets preoccupied with her own internal problems, while Africa's problems multiply.

In Sub-Saharan Africa, the transition to democracy offers some glimmer of hope for political stability in the region. But democracy is not the end, though. After elections, what next? Ghana faces a "ballot box test", as Jerry Rawlings finds it tough to pursue hard IMF-World Bank imposed structural adjustment policies (SAPs).

The scope of Africa's political crises encompass coup detats, debt, class conflicts, and political decay. Also, there is bank corruption, declining competition, de-industrialization, and nine-fold increase in foreign debt.[5] Western-sponsored structural adjustment policies have tended to increase African political crises, and the delegitimization of the African state.

In a chronicle of the African crises, Gavin Williams noted that:

> By 1990, African states were bankrupt. Their economic policies were in the hands of the International Monetary Fund (IMF) and the World Bank. African leaders whether drawn from civilian politicians or military officers, had

> lost moral credibility as a result of arbitrary and corrupt government and increasing economic, and personal, insecurity.[6]

The collapse of Eastern Europe delegitimized Marxist regimes in Africa. Africa's "margin of maneuver" in the game of international politics has eroded since the demise of the Cold War. There is a closure of the strategic space within which Africa could bargain with the West by playing "the Soviet card". The emergence of the Eastern Bloc as a counter-hegemonic bloc is entering a decisive phase. In the 1960s and 1970s, socialism provided alternative paradigm of development for Africa, but no longer. Soviet scientific achievements in the era of the Cold War served as an attraction to Africa. Following the Soviet model, African leaders often supported doctrinaire experiments in agriculture and industry that achieved little benefits for the continent. Autocrats who were nurtured by the East-West confrontation were basically anti-development, whose power base was linked to external, rather than internal, support.[7]

According to David Aaronson:

> Mobutu pillaged his country with scarcely a murmur of dissent from his Western sponsors...There were two reasons for this: first, Zaire is an important supplier of minerals, including industrial diamonds, copper, and cobalt (needed for the alloys used in military aircraft); and second, Mobutu allowed his country to be used as a base for covert American military and diplomatic expeditions into Angola and Chad. His stature as one of America's most important assets in the region was underlined in 1988 when Mobutu became Africa's first head of state to meet with President George Bush. [8]

The Lome regime was Europe's strategic response to the Socialist onslaught in the West's capitalist backyard in Africa. In a world without a Cold War, Africa will have to adjust to the changing global arena, in order to survive therein.

Socio-economic vulnerability

As Fantu Cheru has noted in *The Silent Revolution* in Africa, even those African countries that once were recognized as Africa's models (Cote d'Ivoire and Kenya) have tarnished image.[9] Since 1985, the combination of declining commodity prices, lax domestic and fiscal policies, and the appreciation of the French franc has meant that the CFA zone in Africa has suffered a huge real exchange rate appreciation of more than 30 percent.[10] The effect of this fiscal crisis was a loss of competitiveness of exports from the Franc zone in Africa. By 1991, for example, average wages in Senegal (as a proportion of average income) had risen to three times the level in Ghana, and six times that of Indonesia.

While some analysts have mentioned Africa's lack of competitiveness as the main source of concern, this author looks beyond Africa's [un]competitiveness. Like Africa, most competitive developing nations (including South Korea, Taiwan, Hong Kong and Brazil) are concerned about the EU Single market, because of a) the introduction of reciprocity clauses in some of the EU's proposals; b) the tightening of anti-dumping rules; and c) the uncertainties regarding import quotas. As the competition between communism and capitalism recedes, industrial nations are likely to resort to protectionism against the more competitive developing nations.[11] This is the cradle of Africa's vulnerability.

Population explosion now threatens Africa's survival. First of all, massive population growth has a bearing on Africa's economic development. Second, it makes Africa a target of EU's stringent immigration policies in the context of "1992".

According to a World Bank Report, Sub-Saharan Africa had a population of 450 million in 1987 - more than double the figure that existed at the time of independence. In that year, too, Africa had a total Gross Domestic Product (GDP) of around $135 billion-about the same as that of the EU member country of Belgium that has only 10 million people.[12]

The subject of population explosion particularly strikes a sensitive chord in North Africa - a region that sits on a 'human volcano'. A ballooning population in North Africa, so close to Europe, is causing anxiety on both sides of the Mediterranean. Islamic theologians see increased population as a source of (Islamic) strength. *Sharia* law says that Muslim countries need a growing number of people. [13] Consequently, contraceptive use by married people is not permitted in Muslim societies. It is estimated that the population in Morocco, Tunisia and Algeria will double by the year 2025. The Maghreb population is growing at the rate of 1.5 million per year.[14] At least, 1.5 million of this population would more likely escape to Europe.

At a Population Conference in Rabat in the Spring of 1993, Princess Lall Menem, daughter of King Hassan of Morocco, conceded that Morocco must choose between birth control and the threat of famine. The EU sent a delegation to the Population Conference, in order to urge population control.

According to the Moroccan Minister for Health, Abderrahim Harouchi, if the current trend in population growth continues, then Morocco will have to:[15]

- Invest 6 percent of its GDP to absorb population growth.
- Build 9 new hospitals every year.
- Supply 85,000 classrooms.
- Build 15,000 new homes.
- Provide an annual employment of 280,000, until the year 2007.

With its share of 12 percent of world population in 1992, Africa will account for 34 percent of projected population growth in the world in the 1990-2050 period, according to the State of the World Population Report (1992), published by the UN Population Fund.

In a Statement delivered before the European Parliamentary Committee on Development and Co-operation, the former Executive Secretary of the UN Economic Commission for Africa, Adebayo Adedeji, noted that:

> Almost three out of four Africans are afflicted by poverty. The illiterate population has increased to 162 million in 1985 up from a level of 124 million in 1960. The average share of health and education in public expenditure dropped from over 26 percent at the beginning of the 1980s to only 19 percent in 1988. Over a quarter of the African population is now undernourished or malnourished, while endemic diseases-which had actually been brought under control by the 1970s-have re-emerged on the continent.[16]

Some African countries are also affected by warfare and severe social conflicts, with subsequent disruption of productive activity, and the creation of large mass of refugees. Unless they receive external aid, these countries are less likely to maintain a national existence, let alone be able to compete with Europe. Like the African boxer, Africa is already too weak to compete with, or in, Europe.

The AIDS epidemic has taken a toll on Africa, either in terms of the loss in productivity, or international discrimination. Figures from the World Health Organization (WHO) show that more than half of the world's 15 million sufferers of AIDS are in Africa. It is estimated that the AIDS virus has already killed 1.2 million Africans and that 14 million people will be affected by the year 2000.[17] Tougher restrictions on African immigrants in European capitals will be AIDS-related.

Is Africa in a "transition" or in decay? This seemingly sarcastic question may be relevant in the present debate about Africa's New World Order. To Afro-optimists, Africa is currently engaged in a great surge that will sweep overboard tyranny, and bring about political pluralism, trade liberalization, and growth.

The pessimist, however, may discern some signs of decay, or sliding back into barbarism, even where there appears to be a new dawn. Consider the massacres in Liberia and the civil strife in Somalia and Rwanda. Africa accounts for only 2 percent of the world's economic product, 2 percent of its trade, and less than 3 percent of global investments. The ironies are best captured by Desmond Colborne who noted:

> What a change from the sixties when a country like Ghana produced as much as South Korea and when decolonization catapulted leaders like Nkrumah, Sekou Toure and Senghor at the world scene.[18]

Farm output in Africa has dwindled, and food imports have increased to five times what they were in the 1970s. Traditional services - those connected with the development of banking, health services, education, and so on - have declined. The emerging insurance and banking services have also slipped behind, and their budgets are being cut, thanks to the structural adjustment policies recommended by Western donor agencies.

The need to borrow for investments, the terms on which such loans are secured, and the dynamics of the world trading system, have all contributed to generate heavy indebtedness. Africa's external debt, as at 1993, stood at $282 billion.

Structural imbalances

African nations must overcome their structural vulnerability vis-à-vis the EU. The term "structural vulnerability" has been defined by the UN as follows: "a country is structurally vulnerable when its development risks being retarded by factors which in the short or medium-term are independent of its economic policy".[19]

Africa lacks control over its economic destiny, and cannot determine the prices of her exports. Arrghiri Emmanuel's concept of unequal exchange[20] was explained in simple practical terms by one African observer who noted that, "anytime I go to the supermarket in Holland, the price of coffee is dropping. At the same time, the price of Western products are pushing upwards".

Africa, the poorest of the World's continents, accounts for two-thirds of the UN-designated least developed countries. By mid-1990, 28 of the 41 of such countries were African. One of the major limitations of African nations is (small) size. Africa has more than its fair share of the countries in the world that are classified as "least developed" (see Table 8.1).

Table 8.1
The least developed countries of the world

Africa	Others
Benin	Afghanistan
Botswana	Bangladesh
Burkina Faso	Bhutan
Cape Verde	Haiti
Central African Republic	Kiribati
Comoros Islands	Laos
Djibouti	Maldives
Equitoria Guinea	Myanmar
Ethiopia	Nepal
Guinea	Thvalu
Guinea-Bissau	Vanuata
Lesotho	Yemen
Malawi	
Mali	
Mauritania	
Mozambique	
Niger	
Rwanda	
Samoa	
Sao Tome & Principe	
Sierra Leone	
Somalia	
Sudan	
Tanzania	
Togo	
Uganda.	

Source: *Africa Recovery* (UN) No. 2 August 1990. p. 3.

Another source of vulnerability is the continent's dependence on a handful of commodity exports. For 23 of African countries, the top three export commodities accounted for an average of 76.9 percent of total foreign exchange earning in 1980. By 1989, this figure had worsened to 79 percent.[21]

Africa has been sustained by handouts from the EU. This external dependency has created some contradictions. Handouts from external agencies have allowed Africa to enjoy a level consumption that is not compatible with the continent's level of production, productivity, and global competitiveness. Change in the trade relations between Africa and the EU would only realize positive results for African partners, if there are substantial changes in Africa's production system, so as to render the continent externally competitive, and internally resilient.

Furthermore, African nations which might have gained the most from EU's preferential treatment stand to lose the most in an era of world trade liberalization, where new nomenclatures, such as the "level playing field", have become vocabularies of economic relations.

Africa's adjustment fatigue

Despite the pains of adjustment, EU member nations have pushed their way towards political and economic unification. On the contrary, as drought and economic crises intensified in the 1980s, African nations abandoned the Lagos Plan of Action (1980) that was to be the blue print for sustainable development in Africa. Instead of collective self-reliance, national survival became the main concern of individual African nations. This "adjustment fatigue" will constrain Africa's ability to forge a "united front" strategy against the EU bloc. This is because, the pains of adjustment may preclude the necessary collective self-reliance strategies that could put African economies on a sound competitive footing. Consequently, there is a limited possibility for Africa, as a collectivity, to act as a counter-weight to a united Europe.

The state in Africa is wrecked with bureaucratic corruption.[22] Public bureaucracies are overstuffed, poorly managed, and their productivity has declined. The deterioration of universities, the degeneration of paved highways, and the collapse of judicial and banking systems are just some of the evidence of Africa's institutional decay.

The EU is attempting to position European firms more favorably in relation to world giants in US and in Japan. In pursuant of this strategic initiative, Europe is building pan-European institutions. Noteworthy of such collaboration include the ESPRIT Program (European Strategic Program for Research and Development in Information Technology) and RACE (Research and Development in Advanced Communication Technology).

Africa is comparatively vulnerable when we consider the continent's preparation for the twenty-first century. By comparative vulnerability, this author refers to Africa's relative disadvantaged position as compared to other regions. It has been concluded elsewhere that" A f r i c a plays hardly any part in world trade any more...If Africa disappeared off the map tomorrow, the world economy would hardly miss it".[23]

As Table 8. 2 shows, Africa's share of global exports in 1991 was 1.1 percent as compared to East Asia's 7.5 percent.

Table 8.2
Africa: Facing the competition

	Sub - Sahrara Africa	East Africa
Population Growth rate 1980-91	3.1	1.6
GDP Growth rate % p.a. 1980-91	2.1	7.7
GNP per capita 1991 (US$)	350.0	650.0
Inflation 1980-91 (% p.a)	18.4	8.3
Investment (% of GDP 1991)	16	35
Savings (% of GDP 1991)	14	36
Exports of goods and Services		
(% of GDP 1991)	28	-
Government consumption (% GDP 1991)	30	
Share of global exports 1991	1.1	7.5
Global imports	1.0	7.6
Annual Growth		
Rate of exports		
1980-91	2.7	10.2
Imports	-4.0	8.4
Terms of Trade: Change 1985-91		
External Debt % if GNP 1991		
Debt-service ratio 1980	10.9	13.5
1990	20.8	13.3
% Enrolment primary eduction		
Primary		
1970	46	88
1990	68	127
Secondary		
1970	6	24
1990	17	49

Source: World Bank

If all regions were in the same boat as Africa, then Africa would not be vulnerable. In confronting the EU Single Market, Africa must redress its disadvantaged position vis-à-vis other competing developing regions.

In order to position themselves as "local" companies, ensure their access to the EU market, or comply with local content requirements, the NICs are establishing manufacturing plants in Europe. South Korea's auto manufacturers are there, so too are Hong Kong's textile manufacturers.

Among the strategies that other nations are adopting in the context of European economic unification include increasing direct investment in the EU. Japan and other Asian developing nations are establishing their presence in the EU, in order to get market share. Africa is conspicuously absent in these aggressive activities.

Unlike African nations, South Korea, for example, has developed a niche strategy in the aerospace market. Lack of technological innovation has put Africa at a disadvantaged position. The Taiwan-based Evergreen company is the world's largest shipping line. Taiwan planned to purchase Airbus jets from Europe. This policy makes a good political sense in that, this business deal would tie Taiwan with the EU.

Another troubling situation is the income disparities among regions. In the last few decades, the distribution of global income has become more unequal. A group of countries in Asia have achieved rapid economic growth: in contrast, there has been a continuous marked decline in growth in Africa. According to the World Bank, the GDP of sub-Saharan Africa grew at an average of 2 percent during the 1980s. On a per capita basis, though, this is a mere 0.3 percent due to population explosion. This figure compares unfavorably with 1.8 percent in South Asia, 1.9 percent in Latin America, and 5.2 percent in East Asia.[24] The rapid growth in population is exerting pressure on resources in Africa. Most of the Asian countries have overcome this structural impediment, by successfully redirecting their exports towards manufactures.

According to the *Financial Times* (1 September, 1993), Sub-Saharan Africa will enjoy 3.7 percent annual growth rate over the coming decade (or 0.6 percent growth in per capita GDP). At such rates of growth, Africa will wait 40 years to enjoy the per-capital income that it had in the mid-1970s.

Why have African economies not responded to structural reforms? African nations have taken reforms as in Latin America and China, but there are problems: there is little reform program coordination among different African countries. For example, when Nigeria devalued its currency over a period of five years, there were no devaluation of the CFA that is pegged to the French franc. Reforms in the banking system in Africa eliminated ailing banks, but failed to provide local alternatives. Consequently, they starved the local markets of the much needed medium and long-term financing. In the end, Structural adjustment policies failed to generate investments that could boost economic growth.

Structural adjustment policies, that supposedly seek to alter the international non-competitiveness of African nations, have so far fallen short of expectation. Some critics of SAPs have asked the question: Are they necessary for Africa? For several reasons, SAPs may be a wrong tonic for Africa's woes. African nations are small and are highly dependent on external trade. They have a narrower range of non-trade goods, and a particularly weak service sector. It is doubtful that SAPs could significantly alter these structural problems. As compared with other regions, Africa's chances of industrialization are limited.

Boasting about EU emerging industrial prowess, a senior official of the EU told this author a story. According to the official, industrialization shifted from Europe to America: It then moved to Japan. It will come back to Europe, thanks to the "1992" program. The official did not mention Africa, and this author was not surprised. The pendulum of industrialization is shifting away, leaving Africa behind. The center for manufacturing has shifted from Britain to the US, to Japan and Germany and has moved to places like South Korea and Malaysia. Few countries in African countries, like Mauritius and Nigeria, could follow closely, if they pursue the right policies.

Structural changes in the global economy, rapidly growing North-North axis (consider the West's improved relations with the East), and the steady decline in Africa's trade, work to Africa's disadvantage. The collapse of Communism in Eastern Europe, and the attendant civil war there, have meant that Eastern Europe and the Middle East would be able to compete for a geo-political spot in EU's global agenda. While South-East Asia exploits its economic magnet in the Pacific Century, Africa's hitherto geo-political and economic attraction to Europe are slowly evaporating, leaving Africa, perhaps, with a "humanitarian" magnet that is losing its force of political sympathy.

Boris Yeltsin, the Russian President, has used the threat of a fascist or a hard-line Communist take-over as a diplomatic card to pressure Western donors to expedite Western transfer of development aid to the Commonwealth of Independent States (CIS). Even though pro-democracy movements occurred in some African countries (Ghana, Togo, Ethiopia) before *perestroika* and *glasnot* in Eastern Europe, a major difference remains that pro-democracy movements in the East, not Africa, have received full and unalloyed Western support.

Weakened bargaining power

Lack of independence and autonomy in the international political economy translate into Africa's lack of bargaining power in the international system. Africa's heavy debt repayment obligations, coupled with decline in commodity prices, have meant that Africa would have to dance to the tune of donor nations.

In bargaining with European partners, the continent of Africa has the cards stacked against her. Africa - the largest regional grouping of countries in terms of size and numbers - contains the most land-locked and least developed states in the world. It is the continent most affected by the crisis in energy, drought, refugee explosion, and political instability.

According to the UN, the standard of living of Africans, in particular, has declined substantially. About 85 percent of the African population are below the 'bread line'. At the time of the Paris Conference on the 'Least Developed Countries' in 1981, there were 21 African nations in the "least developed" category, but in 1989, there were 28 - a third more.[25] Given the above structural problems, it is not difficult to see how vulnerable African is in bargaining with a unified Europe. World trade is basically world politics, where power is the underlying determinant of gains and losses. One of the nagging questions remains: Can Africa retaliate against the EU if the later becomes protectionist?

One of the major achievements of the Treaty of Rome has been the consolidation of an European trading bloc with substantial power to persuade US officials and other economic powers such as Japan, that protectionist measures will be met by Europe's retaliation.

Unlike major economic powers such as Japan and the US, Africa and the developing nations do not possess enough power to retaliate against protectionist policies of the EU. Once an international actor knows that the international power of a competitor is real and substantial, it is likely to treat the competitor with respect and caution, if not as a co-equal. For example, since the rise of Japan as an economic superpower, Tokyo has been accorded a lot of respect in the comity of nations - respect that was denied Japan when it was producing 'low-class' products for the global market.

The developing world's lack of power to retaliate against discriminatory protectionism of the EU are due to several factors:

(1) Despite lower wages, most African nations are not capable of meeting the competition from light manufactured goods exporters. A surprising number of African nations did not reach the low textile and clothing quotas allocated to them by the EU. African textile exporters are weak, for example, against China's competitive potential.

(2) Even the more industrially advanced developing nations in South-East Asia are vulnerable, thanks to European unity. This is so because a very large fraction of EU's imports comes from few countries which have little bargaining power in dealing with the EU.

(3) Diplomatic or political factors may constrain even the more competitive developing nations in retaliating against the EU. For example, since Hong Kong is a colony of an EU member nation, a trade war between Hong Kong and the EU would be disastrous both to Hong Kong's and Singapore's trade. Taiwan's international situation also calls for caution, as does South Korea's need for US military support and Western investments.

(4) The strongly protectionist policies pursued by some developing countries have excluded most consumer goods from their imports. They, therefore, cannot afford the import cuts from advanced nations - a policy that may be necessary to implement an effective retaliatory policy.

(5) African countries have been unable to constitute effective bargaining units in international politics. The Group of 77, of which most are from Africa, has been described by one observer as "an instrument for the dramatized expression of dreams".[26] Ironically, the size of the number

of countries in Africa has been of little significance in terms of bargaining power. Political cleavages that exist on the continent cut across linguistic lines: Francophone vs Anglophone: geographic, or even racial lines, such as White North (Arab) Africa vs. Sub-Saharan (Black) Africa.

At a workshop on the proposed African Economic Community, in Abidjan, Cote d'Ivoire, in June 1992, there were cleavages that were based on linguistic lines. Participants from Anglophone Africa maintained that the CFA franc should be devalued, in order to bring it in tune with the real economic conditions in the countries of the CFA zone. Delegates from Francophone Africa, however, opposed this suggestion, arguing that Africa's economic problems did not lie with a particular currency, but with finding a workable monetary system.[27]

The divisive tendencies in inter-African relations are paradoxical, especially considering the fact that Africa needs unity to be able to bargain with united Europe.

Since the decline in influence of the OPEC countries, no organized bloc in the developing world has been in a position to influence the contours of international trade negotiations from a position of strength. If past EEC-ACP negotiations over the Lome Conventions are any thing to consider, then it can be concluded that Africa's leverage against the EU is quite limited.

The limits of interdependence

North-South schemes such as the Lome Convention and the Caribbean Basin Initiative dramatize the limits of interdependence. The "privileges" that the US offered the Caribbean nations proved to be less beneficial, because the US canceled out Caribbean products which competed with US products, particularly textiles and sugar - off the list of preferences. This problem is also applicable to the Lome Convention. There are important tropical products on which the EU still maintains tariff barriers: these include bananas, coffee, cocoa, spices, and tobacco. Others are cut flowers and fish.

This author identifies three types of preferential erosion in North-South schemes. In the first place, protectionist policies of the preference grantors may erode preferences. This, the author refers to as *vertical erosion*. In the second category, involving *lateral erosion*, preferences may be diluted because of competition from new grantees. A third predicament exists that involves *preference extinction*. Here, preferences may exist, but because grantees are unable to use them or take advantage of them, they may become extinct or useless. All these possible scenarios pose challenges to the preferential regime that is supported by the Lome Convention to which Sub-Saharan Africa nations are party.

An enlargement of the EU could trigger vertical erosion of preferences. In order to examine the challenges posed by the enlargement of the EU, we have to examine the characteristics of the new entrants (into the EU), and the structure of their economies, particularly to the extent that they compete with, or complement, the exports of African countries. Before Spain and Portugal entered the EU in 1986, North African countries, such as Morocco, lost part of their market share in Europe, as a result of Spain's and Portugal's competitiveness (lateral erosion). Furthermore, when Spain and Portugal gained entry into the EU, they contributed to vertical erosion of preferences accorded to North Africa.

The "devil's relationship" between EU's (or ACP's) enlargement and preferential erosion is due to the fact that new entrants often compete with existing beneficiaries of EU preferences. For example, the enlargement of the ACP to include the Dominican Republic and Haiti reinforces the competition in the rum market in the EU. Some Caribbean and Central American countries have expressed the desire to join the ACP group, so as to gain access to the preferential treatment and financing agreement available to the ACP. Spain has advocated for the enlargement of the ACP bloc to include those countries within Madrid's (former) sphere of influence. At the same time, Spanish authorities would like to protect banana production on the Canary Island. Politics among European powers regarding their colonial attachments are important in such redistributive issues.

Sector-specific issues

Any impact assessment of the "1992" process on African nations must examine EU's legislative measures that: (1) have general impact on the EU (or global) economy; (2) are specifically related to the sectors in which African nations operate, and (3) are related to other sectors that may have indirect effect on Africa.

A combination of factors would determine which sectors and parties stand to benefit the most, or otherwise, as a result of EU's Single Market initiative. Some of these factors that have already been discussed in the previous chapters, include technical standards (whether they are high or low) that will determine the ease of access; the competitivity of different countries, enlargement of the EU, or the ACP, and preferential erosion or extinction.

According to a study conducted by the Directorate General for Economic and Financial Affairs at the European Commission in Brussels (1988), the Single Market will have some impact on different sectors due to a combination of factors, such as:

- Reduction in costs due to economies of scale.
- Improved efficiency in enterprises, rationalization of industrial enterprises, and setting of prices closer to cost of production.
- Adjustment between industries on the basis of comparative advantages in an integrated market, and
- Flow of information, introduction of new products, and new processes.

For the purpose of analysis, the following sectors are selected:

(A) **Agriculture**

As a sector, agriculture is a critical issue for Africa, largely because Africa is an agricultural country, and that EU's CAP policy is protectionist. The effect of EU's integration on world agriculture is partly based on product categories. Several analytical perspectives could be used to examine the possible impact of the EU Single market on Africa's agricultural exports to the EU. The effect would vary according to whether or not an African product falls within the following categories:

(1) Products which are not produced in the EU (coffee, cocoa, spices, coconut)

(2) Products not produced in sufficient quantities in the EU (banana, cotton, tobacco)
(3) Products whose prices are too expensive in the EU, and hence, are purchased cheaper from developing nations (soya beans, manicot).

Developing nations face a pyramid of risks when dealing with the EU, as new agricultural products are subject to CAP (*protection* effect); productivity in a particular product increases in the EC (*productivity* effect); a particular product can be replaced by another produced in the EU (*substitution* effect).

The EU made sure that protectionist clauses were inserted in the Lome IV Convention that was negotiated in 1989, according to which EU's trade concessions to African nations could be suspended anytime they resulted in "disruptions" of the EU economy.

Both the Uruguay Round negotiation and the "1992" process will combine to impact on Africa's agricultural trade with the EU. Fair agricultural practices mean that the EU and the U.S. could find a truce in their "grain war" in Africa. Ironically, agriculture is the area in which African nations, largely developing, could potentially reap their so-called Richardian comparative advantage. Unfortunately, the EU's policy in this sector has been protective.

EU's CAP system was established in the 1960s to address the economic problems of European agriculture. At the present time, the CAP's *raison d'etre* is mainly political. The EU has offered food aid - taken from agricultural surpluses - to Africa and other developing regions. However, this type of aid could hardly make African nations agriculturally self-sufficient, and second, globally competitive. African peasant farmers are likely to be driven off the land, as they are unable to match the prices of highly subsidized exports from the EU and other industrialized nations, such as the US and Japan.

The US Food Security Act (1985) is of particular importance to African nations. Under the Bonus Incentive Commodity Program, US exporters of major products received bonuses, which enabled them to lower their prices in international markets. Between 1980-1985, the US and the EU spent $61 billion on agricultural support programs; Japan also spent $51 billion for the period 1980-83.[28]

(B) **Food Industry**

The European Food industry purchases agricultural products from Africa and other developing nations. The industry is one of the most barrier-ridden, with a wide range of different national standards and restrictions. However, two factors could work to Africa's advantage. The possibility that the Euro-consumer will become more global in the choice of food, and also the growing concerns about health foods may benefit African producers using less intensive farming methods, or natural tropical products.[29]

(C) **Beef**

The EU imports limited quantities of boneless beef from specific countries, most particularly from Botswana. The upward harmonization of pysto sanitary conditions remains as the main concern for African beef exporters to Europe. The battle on the beef market is fought on two fronts. The first theater is Europe, and the weapon is the deployment of psyto-sanitary regulations that would restrict Africa's beef exports to Europe. The second theater is Africa, where the EU dumps cheap beef. The EU has sold thousands of tons of heavily subsidized frozen beef in West Africa at half local prices. As a result of EU's subsidy, locally-produced beef costs CFA 300 per kilo more in Abidjan than beef imported from Europe.[30] Since the mid-1980s, the beef-importing coastal states of Ghana, Togo, Nigeria and Benin have turned to the cheaper EU meat rather than buy from their traditional suppliers in West Africa, such as Burkina Faso.

Africa is continuously worried by EU's dumping of meat on the African market. Farmers in Burkina Faso and Mali have asked development organizations in Europe to campaign against the dumping of subsidized European beef in West Africa. According to the Brussels-based Eurostep lobby, EU's beef exports to West Africa increased from seven to 54,000 tons in 1991. France, the Netherlands, Germany, Denmark,, and Ireland are the main suppliers.[31]

According to *African Business*, the Sahel region of Africa has lost its share of the local beef market, as a result of the EU "beef invasion" of Africa. For example, the Sahelian share in the Ivorien market has fallen from two-thirds in the early 1980s to less than one-third in 1993. The Sahelian countries mostly affected by the European competition are

Burkina Faso, Mali and Niger. Translated into economic terms, this market loss is a big blow to those Africa countries because, live stock accounts for 9 percent of GNP in Burkina Faso, 16 percent in Mali, and 14 percent in Niger.[32]

(D) **Mineral Products**

Environmental and technical harmonization have affected a number of mineral products exported by African nations. One of the major issues raised by the "1992" program is the restrictions on the cadmium content of phosphates exported by African nations. The nations that are affected include Senegal, Togo and Mauritania. This issue raises a financial burden for the affected countries who have to invest in more expensive equipment to be able to meet the new Europe-wide standards.

(E) **Crude Oil**

Oil is an important strategic material, and that the impact of European unity on crude oil supply needs to be examined. African exporters of crude oil to Europe include Algeria and Nigeria. One of the challenges that these African oil suppliers face is the possibility that the EU may diversify their sources of crude oil imports. Nigeria and Algeria face possible supply diversion to the North Sea. Diversification of sources of supply is a strategy of dependency reduction. Europe is striving towards energy self-sufficiency. The fall of the Soviet Union could enhance opportunities for Western Europe in tapping Soviet oil, as the former Soviet Union develops closer economic relations with the West.

(F) **Coffee and Tea**

One of the major structural constraints of Africa's economies is the cash-crop export dependency. EU's internal liberalization would affect Africa's coffee and tea exporters. As regards fiscal harmonization, standard VAT rates may be good news for exporters, especially where high rates have been set on certain products. Similarly, the abolition of domestic taxes should boost the demand for some commodities. In Germany and in Denmark, for example, removal of national excise taxes on coffee should benefit major producers such as Nigeria and Cote d'Ivoire.

Most of the economies of sub-Saharan Africa have slowed down, because of the significant decline in the prices of coffee and cocoa, which account for about 40 percent of agricultural exports in sub-Saharan Africa.[33]

The coffee trade (and that is also true of tea), as one observer noted, "is dominated by Western dealers. It has been calculated that for every pound of coffee the peasant receives only 8 percent of the money, the government gets 17 percent while the rest, 75 percent gets to the Western dealers".[34]

According to estimates calculated by Michael Davenport, the elimination of EU tariff on coffee could lead to reduction in Africa's export values of US $66 million (or 3 percent of export values).[35] According to Davenport, the biggest losers under such a scenario would be Cote d'Ivoire and Kenya. Similarly the major losers in respect to export revenues in the case of cocoa are Nigeria and Ghana.[36]

(G) **The Cocoa Episode: Effects of 'upward harmonization'**

Cocoa demonstrates a dangerous precedent about the impact of technical harmonization on Africa's access to the EU market. The African exporters of cocoa are concerned about the "upward-harmonization" of standards because of the fear that they may not be able to compete. They are particularly worried about the principle of mutual recognition of standards because of the very precedent—that of cocoa.

The cocoa episode occurred when the EC Commission decided to get the standard in use in the UK and Denmark applied at the Community level. If that had been the case, there would have been the likelihood that cocoa could be partly replaced by vegetable fat. This could have resulted in the drop in the imports of cocoa, especially when a competing product came to the market. The UK uses a lot less Vanilla in their ice cream; they also use vegetable oil, rather than cocoa butter to make their chocolate, or "vegetate", as the French mockingly call it. In the future, a directive such as that on cocoa could have a detrimental impact on cocoa exporters in Africa.

Another major EU policy that could affect African cocoa exporters is the possible elimination of EU tariffs on cocoa products. Davenport has estimated that the major beneficiaries of major EU's tariff reduction would be Latin American and Asian competitors (in particular Indonesia and Malaysia). These nations would gain because of trade diversion, and also due to a rise in world prices that would occur as a result of increased world demand.[37] Malaysia and Indonesia have strong competitive advantage in the palm oil and cocoa market. Technically speaking, these countries are lowest cost producers.

(H) **Sugar**

The EU Sugar Protocol protects African exports of sugar cane to the EU, despite the fact that the EU has a large surplus of sugar beet. The completion of the Single Market and the arrival of cheaper transportation (thanks to the Channel Tunnel link) - could give EU sugar beet producers a competitive advantage. Also, the position of sugar cane exporters would be further weakened by the abolition of special EU green currency rates, which in 1987, gave them one eighth more income than beet producers.[38]

Carol Cosgrove refers to sugar as "a highly political product in the context of EU-ACP cooperation". [39] The countries that are affected by the sugar problem include Mali, Togo, and the Caribbean states. The EU guarantees prices (in practices close to those received by EU producers) for specific quantities of sugar from ACP countries - in Africa, notably Mauritius. These special arrangements depend on the existence of EU's Common Agricultural Policy.

One of the major problems regarding sugar preferences is a redistributive one - the disparities in the share of sugar quotas. More prosperous countries like Barbados, Fiji, Guyana, Jamaica, Mauritius , and Trinidad and Tobago, receive a higher percentage of transfers due to their higher quotas. The ascension of Haiti and Dominican Republic to the Sugar protocol could pave the way for other South and Central American nations. This would be detrimental to some African countries since it could mean a dilution of Lome preferences.

ACP exporters of sugar are concerned that the guarantees supported by the EU-ACP Sugar Protocol may be compromised by GATT negotiations or CAP reforms. In August 1993, it was reported that ACP supplies of sugar were denied access to the Portuguese market.[40]

(I) **Manufactured Goods**

While manufactured products constitute one of the more promising exports in the European market, competition with European industry make access to this sector slippery. The US imports two-thirds of manufactured exports of developing countries, compared to less than 25 percent by the EU, and less than 9 percent by Japan. Thus, the EU is not a major importer of manufactured goods from the Third World.

The small percentage of manufactured items in Africa's exports to the EU largely originates from European firms which have cooperation projects or local branches in African countries. Some European firms in Africa have already withdrawn, or are on the verge of withdrawing from Africa. A withdrawal of such firms from African nations is likely to worsen the situation of manufactured exports by African countries.

Many African countries lack the technical power to sustain large scale manufacturing. They are also likely to face barriers related to rules of origin requirement, and local content restrictions. In the first place, there is little prospects for trade-creation in the manufacturing sector that may favor Africa. Africa lacks the Ricardian comparative advantage in manufacturing, despite low wage structures. The percentage of government expenditure devoted to R&D in Africa is minuscule. It is least likely that most low-cost producers in manufactures will be located in Africa.

(J) **Services Liberalization**

One of the greatest challenges that the market integration of Europe poses for Africa is rooted in Africa's lack of competitiveness in the services sector. The services sector has become one of the major focus in the Uruguay Round of GATT negotiations. This reflects the rapid internationalization of the service sector. For Africa, negotiating in new service fields is difficult, because the continent is in less of a position than say the US or Japan, to identify its interests. At the same time, too, African nations will also find it harder to defend their interests, because of their weak negotiating position.

As Table 8.3 indicates, the share of services in the foreign exchange receipt of Cote d'Ivoire is negligible (0.0 percent). On the other hand, as table 8.4 suggests, Cote d'Ivoire is included in the countries where services share is more than 50 percent of imports.

Table 8.3
Selected ACP states earning less than one-sixth of their foreign exchange receipts through services sectors

Country	% Share in Foreign Exchange Receipt	
	Services	Raw Materials
Nigeria	3.5	95
Ghana	7.5	82
Zaire	7.7	82
Liberia	0.9	88
Congo	0.0	89
Zambia	0.5	90
Gabon	0.8	84
Niger	0.5	83
P.New Guinea	0.1	81
Cote D'Ivoire	0.0	52
Mauritania	0.2	75
Madagascar	0.5	71
Uganda	0.2	73
Zimbabwe	0.6	60

Source: *EEC-ACP Courier*, No. 118, November-December 1989, p. 9.

Table 8.4
Share of services in total imports of ACP states

Service share/country		
Less Than 20%	25%-50%	50 % and More
Lesotho	Gambia	Cote d'Ivoire
	Ethiopia	Congo
	Niger	Gabon
	Uganda	

Source: *EEC-ACP Courier*, 3, No. 118, November-December 1989. p. 12.

About 19 ACP states earn more than one third of their foreign exchange receipts through the service exports,[41] while most of the ACP states like Cote d' Ivoire, Congo, and Gabon buy services, using 20 to 50 percent of their foreign exchange receipts (see Table 8.3). Also, for more than half of the ACP states, the service sector is the most importance economic sector, in terms of its share of the GDP.[42]

The inclusion of services in the Lome IV Convention raises questions about:

(1) Africa's access to the services sectors in the EU. African firms are already positioned in certain service activities in Europe: shipping, air transport, travel agencies and information technology. Africa will have to monitor EU regulations involving the right of establishment and the treatment of foreign firms in the EU.

(2) The nature and the extent of reciprocity that African countries could grant EU services firms.

(3) Non-discrimination between African countries and EU Member States.

The EU, as an economic bloc, has taken a serious look at the services industry where it derives greater competitive advantage. Here, the EU could use its newly-found trade card: the demand for reciprocity. African nations could be asked to treat EU insurance companies, banks, and law firms, for example, the same way they treat domestic (African) firms. Can African nations claim infant-industry status for their service industries?

In addition to the "1992" program, international rules may seal Africa's doom. The services agreement of the GATT would open up the services sectors of Third World nations to foreign banks, financial, business and professional companies. In Africa, some smaller local enterprises would be outcompeted, and the development of a indigenous industry nibbled in the bud.

Francis Wurtz, the EEC-ACP Rapporteur on the effects of the Single Market on the ACP States:

> Saying that they [African] nations only fear Fortress Europe is giving a limiting view of the reality...They fear protectionism and their fear excessive liberalism, both of

> them, and the risk is that these countries will get caught between the devil of protectionism and the deep blue sea of ultra-liberalism.[43]

(K) **Air Transport**

Africa's participation in the service industry in general, but air transportation in particular, demonstrates the sad paradox of a "David-and-Goliath" affair. European nations have supported the Airbus project. On the other hand, many national airlines in Africa have sunk into decay. In 1991, the Gambia experienced a 12 percent fall in arrivals, because of the withdrawal of British Airways' flights to the Gambia and Sierra Leone. Many things have gone wrong with African airlines, which have reduced their competitiveness vis-à-vis European airlines. Air fares are too high. Routes between Africa and Europe are not very profitable.

The problem of technical harmonization has taken a toll on the African air transportation industry. The EU would regulate the maximum decibel level of noise that may be permitted in aircraft engines. This constitutes a loss to the aging African aircraft industry.

Immigration control policies have also affected the African air transportation industry. According to the *West Africa* magazine, the Ghanaian Airways owed the British Government 400,000 pounds sterling by 1993, being fees accumulated from fines imposed on the airline for carrying passengers possessing invalid travelling documents to Britain.

From the African side, the problem of procrastination has resulted in a big loss. Even though the International Civil Aviation Organization (ICAO) warned about the technical regulation concerning aircraft about 10 years, African nations came too late - 18 more months later - with excuses that they bought the old planes from the same industrial national that made those rules.[44]

(L) **Tourism**

The challenge for Africa in the tourist industry is to be able to compete with other regions, including Europe and the Caribbean islands. To increase her attractiveness, Kenya is seeking to diversify tourism from traditional beach and safari packages into more up-market field of water sports, golf, incentive travel and cruiseship with safari. Africa would need improvements in infrastructures, services rehabilitation and improvement of the environment, if the continent is to register gains in the tourist industry.

Country-specific factors

Despite differences in opinion, both African and European officials concede that Africa faces a crucial challenge in competing in the EU Single Market. African countries differ in the degree of attractiveness to EU-related investments. There are countries that, due to their structural vulnerabilities, have little potential of attracting any significant industrial investments (for example, Chad). Some countries are rich in mineral resources in which resource-based MNCs have already invested heavily in extractive activity. There are also countries that are exporters of oil (Nigeria, Gabon, Libya) and strategic materials such as copper (Zambia, Zaire), uranium (Niger, South Africa), and phosphates (Morocco, Tunisia).

Some larger countries with bigger markets, such as Nigeria, already have substantial foreign investments. In the more fortunate countries, expatriate firms to links with local elites and trading companies have established local, market-oriented, and trade-related investments in the past. Other African countries have other potentials based on some legal incentives such as liberal taxation (Kenya, for example). In these countries, foreign MNCs have invested in export-oriented and trade related activities. There are countries that possess little attraction for investment, either because of political instability, or economic decay or both (eg Angola and Somalia). The implication is that the potential for gain arising from EU-related investments might trickle down to few "semi-peripheral" African states. These relatively well-off states could advance selfish, even non-African, interests at negotiating with Europe.

The Asian miracle: Can Africa replicate it?

In order to understand the enormity of the challenge that African nations face in dealing with the Single Market, one must compare Africa with other developing regions of the world. David Vick contrasts Africa's economic policy and strategy with Asia's and emphasizes that:

> Indonesia, as well as having oil, has been competitive in a range of other export crops similar to those of Africa, like cocoa, tea, coffee, and palm oil. It invested in them heavily to achieve higher productivity and lower costs. Then, unlike Nigeria, Indonesia invested not only in import-substitution but also in agriculture, education, infrastructure and health.[45]

South Korea embarked upon the building of the industrial capacity destroyed during World War II and the Korean War (1950-53). We must also consider the assistance rendered by the US, which for geo-political considerations, was eager to integrate non-Communist countries into the capitalist system of world trade.

Commenting on the lessons that African nations ought to learn from the experiences of South Korea and Taiwan, Wolfgang Hillebrand made several observations. He concluded that behind the success of these Asian Tigers were development policies that considered the following factors:

- The world market was accepted as a strategic reference point for a number of firms in South Korea and Taiwan (thereby enhancing their external orientation and competitiveness).
- Both visible and invisible infrastructure was developed.
- Foreign technology was imported..
- There was a combination of import-substitution and export promotion.

This shows that the Asian nations are quite innovative.

Part of the reasons for the successes of South Korea and Taiwan could be attributed to several factors: (1) they were blessed with pro-industrial ruling elites; and (2) those countries enjoy both cultural and geographical proximity to Japan that served as a model.[46]

The Newly Industrializing Economies (NIEs) expanded their share of world trade from 2.5 percent in 1960 to 4.6 percent in 1987. The exports of industrial goods from Taiwan and Korea in 1988 accounted for nearly $60 billion each. This exceeded the exports of finished goods from the whole of Latin America. Wolfang Hillebrand predicted that, based on the spectacular performance of the NICs, so far:

> It would come as no surprise either if at the start of the 1990s Taiwan (20 million inhabitants) and Korea (42 million inhabitants) were to export more industrial goods than the United Kingdom, the home of the Industrial Revolution.[47]

Economic policies and strategies will make a difference as to which African countries are likely to benefit the most from the European Single Market. This is particularly true of Mauritius. Mauritius established an export promotion zone as a way of boosting its economy. A key factor in the success of the Export Promotion Zone (EPZ) is that about 60 percent of the investment come from local sources, mainly the sugar barons in the country. The other factor is attributable to the ethnic tolerance of the island which has encouraged local entrepreneurs to stay and invest at home, rather than save their money in Swiss banks.[48]

One of the many challenges facing the Black Africa's giant, Nigeria, is severe economic recession and how to allay the fears that foreign investors harbor that the country will be politically unstable. Nigeria is the fifth largest crude petroleum producer in the OPEC, making it the eighth in the world.

Prospects for survival

Theoretically, this study adopts a critical approach to the issue of the EU and its global ramifications. The author's pessimistic assessment of the prospects for Africa of European unification is also based on empirical evidence. For example, a study published by the ECOWAS concluded that most African economies will suffer when the EU becomes a Single Market. The following are the highlights of the Report: (1) even though the 1980s were years of impressive economic growth in Europe, European imports from ACP countries declined, despite the so-called preferential access to the EU; (2) Lome preferences did not result in any qualitative change in the structure of EU-ACP trade; (3) development and investment capital is being deflated to newly liberated Eastern Europe which, like Africa, has abandoned central planning; (4) Nigeria stands to gain the most from her petroleum exports, but most ACP nations would lose out to other developing countries that would be in a position to export manufactured and semi-manufactured goods to the EU.

Environmental regulations in Europe have already affected Africa's fate in the Single Market. The directive on the use of plastic material adopted in 1990 states that after 1 January 1993, suppliers will no longer be allowed to market, use or bring into contact with food items any plastic material that does not satisfy the requirements set forth in the directive. The directive states that the material "must be accompanied by a technical dossier including all the necessary toxicological and technological data, in order to prove that its use does not involve risks for human health, especially in the long term". [49]

There is a need for effective counter-bloc strategies to be able to deal with the European challenge. As at now, it is early to think of Africa as negotiating with United Europe as a single bloc.

Policy initiative at the firm, national and continental, if not global, level will be important. One of the most important strategies for Africa is better marketing, which implies access to large number of services, information systems such as goods exchanges (computer, postal, and maritime etc), and efficient links with the importing firms in the EU countries.

In evaluating the external effects of "1992" on Africa, Walton Brown noted that Africa is not predestined to remain marginal, weak and dependent just as Europe, the US and Japan are not predestined to become dominant powers. According to Brown, "the destinies of nations are clearly determined by the decisions made by leadership and the ability of nations to define, pursue, and achieve goals".[50]

European unity may even be a catalyst for Africa integration. As Europe turns inward, a political vacuum may be created in Africa, which Africans may have to fill themselves. To Africa, Europe provides a lesson that unity strengthens individual country economies.

The starting point for an effective policy response to the EU market will be an understanding of the political, ideological, and global context of EU integration.

Guy Arnold has asked the question: "Why are African leaders always obliged to consult with the World Bank, the IMF, the Paris Club, the EU through Lome or their main donors before they can actually implement anything?".[51] The answer, provided by Arnold himself is that it is because African leaders are not "independent".[52] Robert Mugabe, President of Zimbabwe, referred to the G-7 as the "Seven Divine Kings of the World".[53]

Internal politics within the European Union would also make a difference. When EU leaders gathered in Brussels to discuss how to use their newly created power (the Maastricht Treaty), they found demonstrators in the street protesting proposed cutback in wages that the Belgium government argues, were necessary if Belgium was to qualify for the treaty's monetary union.[54] Unemployment soared from 8.75 percent in 1991 to 11.5 percent in 1993. Unions paralyzed French airports to protest a plan to cut 4,000 jobs at the government-owned Air France, and to sell the money-losing airline to private investors.[55] The "go-slow" economy in Europe has short and long term effects on Africa. In the short term, it is likely to result in protectionism. In the long term, there is likely to be xenophobia in Europe.

The contradictions in EU's policy towards Africa need to be removed. For example, Lome IV protected the Lome banana: at the same time, it also protects banana from Greece, Spain, and Portugal who have domestic suppliers. The EU has committed substantial structural adjustment finance to support the weaker, less competitive, ACP economies. Nonetheless, it is difficult to see how far limited short-term finance can compensate for long-term displacement of the export economy (hence the economic development potential) of the ACP countries which are affected by the banana regime.

External forces work against Africa's interests in so far as the Single Market is concerned. If external markets, such as the EU are closed to African exporters-because of tariffs and other non-tariff barriers-then the internal trade and market reforms that are taking place in Africa will not have any meaning for the continent. Africa's trade liberalization will have to have an external catalyst: the opening-up of foreign markets.

One major paradox in international politics has been noted by William Zartman. Zartman observed that:

> In the 1960s it was Africa that was proclaiming unity, to cover the weakness of separate independencies, in the 1990s it is Europe that is constructing unity, to combine the strengths of separate development.[56]

Notes

1 See David Aaronsin, "Why Africa Stays Poor: And Why it Doesn't Have to", *The Humanist*, March/April 1993.

2 Basil Davidson, *The Blackman's Burden: The Curse of the Nation State*, New York, New York Times Books, 1992.

3 See Dirk Vandewalle, "At the Periphery" North Africa, the European Community and the End of the Cold War", *The Maghreb Review*, Vol. 17, Nos. 1-2, 1992.

4 UN Economic Commission for Africa, *African Charter for Popular Participation in Development and Transformation*, Arusha 1990, p. 2.

5 Julius Ihonvbere, and Terisa Turner, "Africa in the Post-Containment Era: Constraints, Pressures and Prospects for the 21st Century", *The Round Table*, No. 328, 1993.

6 Gavin Williams, "Africa in Retrospect and Prospect", in *Africa South of the Sahara*, London, Europa Publications, 1994, p. 3.

7 Eboe Hutchful, "Eastern Europe: Consequences for Africa", *Review of African Political Economy*, No. 50, 1991, p. 52.

8 Aaronson, *op cit*, reference 1.

9 See Fantu Cheru, *The Silent Revolution in Africa:Debt, Development and Democracy*, London: Zed Books, 1989.

10 *Financial Times*, Sept. 1, 1993.

11 "United We Stand, Divided We Trade", *South*, May 1991, p. 6.

12 World Bank, *Sub-Saharan Africa: From Crisis to Sustainable Growth*, Washington, D.C., 1989.

13 *The Baltimore Sun*, May 30, 1993.

14 *Ibid.*

15 *Ibid.*

16 Adebayo Adedeji, "African and the International Community in the 1990s", Statement Before the European Parliament Committee on Development and Co-operation", Brussels, 27 February 1990, p. 2.

17 Cited in Special studies on Africa published in *Financial Times*, Sept. 1, 1993.

18 Desmond Colbourne, "Writing Off Africa", *South Africa International*, October 1992, p. 95.

19 *Africa Recovery*, (UN) No. 2, August 1990, p. 2.

20 Arrghiri Emmanuel, *Unequal Exchange and the Imperialism of Trade*, New York: Monthly Review, 1972.

21 *Ibid.*, p. 11.

22 David Gould, *Bureaucratic Corruption and Underdevelopment in the Third World: The Case of Zaire*, New York, Pergammon, 1980.

23 *Development and Cooperation*, No. 1, 1993, p. 12.

24 Volkmar Kohler, "EC Donor Coordination- A Shocking Balance", *Development and Cooperation*, No. 1 1993, p. 12.

25 See *ACP-EEC Courier*, No. 118, November-December 1989, p. 2.

26 World Bank, *European Community Protection Against Manufactured Import from Developing Countries: A Case Study in the Political Economy of Protection*, World Bank Staff Working Paper No. 432., October 1980, p. 14.

27 "Towards Africa's Economic Integration", *West Africa*, July 1992, p. 34.

28 The OAU, "Addis Ababa Declaration of African Ministers Responsible for Trade and Development Preparatory to UNCTAD VII, E/ECA/Trade/70, 18 March 1987.

29 Edward Mayo, "Beyond 1992: The Effects of the Singe European Market on the World's Poor", The World Development, London, June 1989, p. 18.

30 *EEC-ACP Courier*, No. 143, January-February 1994, p. 7.

31 "Eurobeef Swamps West Africa", *Africa Business*, July 1993.

32 *Ibid.*

33 *IMF Annual Report*, (1990).

34 *New African*, January 1993, p. 15.

35 Michael Davenport, "Africa and the Unimportance of Being Preferred", *Journal of Common Market Studies*, vol. 30, No. 2, June 1992, p. 241.

36 *Ibid.*

37 *Ibid.*

38 Mary Alexander, "Threat to Developing Countries From EC Integration: 1992 and all That Trade", *West Africa*, 29 June 1992, p. 1092.

39 Carol Cosgrove, "The Impact of 1992 on EC-ACP Trade", in I. William Zartman (ed) *Europe and Africa: The New Phase*, Boulder, Colorado: Lynne Rienner, 1993, p. 66.

40 *EEC-ACP Courier*, July-August, 1993, p. 6.

41 ACP-EEC Joint Assembly, Working Documents, 5 September 1989, p. 7.

42 *Ibid.*

43 Quoted in interview given in *EEC-ACP Courier*, No. 118, November-December, 1989, p. 4.

44 Baffour Ankomah, "Who Isn't Afraid of 1992", *New African*, October 1989, p. 25.

45 David Vick, "Looking to Asia for Development Advice", *African Business*, February 1992, p. 50.

46 *Ibid.*, p. 16.

47 Wolfang Hillebrand, "Lessons From Experience: Can Korea and Taiwan Serve as Models", *Development and Cooperation*, no. 2, 1990, p. 15.

48 Colleen Lowe Morna, "Africa's First Tiger?", *Africa Report*, November-December, 1991, p. 44.

49 "ECOWAS Report Warns Fortress Europe Will Hurt African Economies", *African Business*, November 1992, p. 5.

50 Walton L. Brown, "The 1992 European Community and Africa", *TransAfrica Forum*, Fall 1992, p. 12.

51 Guy Arnold, "Why is Africa Being Squeezed", *New African*, April 1992, p. 20.

52 *Ibid.*

53 Quoted in *Ibid.*

54 "Recession Dogs EC as Unity pact Takes Effect", *Washington Post*, November 1, 1993.

55 *Ibid.*

56 Zartman, I. William (ed.), *Europe and Africa: The New Phase*, Boulder, Colorado, Lynne Rienner, p. 1.

9 Confronting the European challenge: The task ahead

The fate of developing nations and how they fit into the EU unification plan appears to have been relegated to the sidelines in the most critical decisions taken at the European political arena. Mary Alexander has even charged that "[EU] Community officials have refused to be drawn into seriously analyzing the detrimental trade effects [of the Single Market], focussing instead on the benefits exporters to the EC [EU] will gain from increased growth".[1] There is lack of critical debate on the implications of European unity for Africa. This is not surprising, since the European Single Act (1987), that ushered in the Single Market, virtually ignores the external ramifications of the Single Market.

African nations would have to work out a strategy to ensure that the existing or emerging *hegemonic blocs* do not exclude them, and that their interests are addressed.

The liberalizing effect of the Single Market will bestow some benefits to third parties via exports to the EU. However, the extent of benefits will depend partly on the structure of individual countries. The luckiest ones will be those that possess more flexible production capacities to take advantage of an enlarged European market and the new opportunities that accompany it. In general, the most fortunate would be nations:

- That possess competitive supply capabilities.
- With manufacturing capabilities to take advantage of increased demand for consumer goods in the EU.

- That are already established in the EU.

In reality, then, the Single Market offers new opportunities for African nations as well, though particularly of course, for the more advanced, competitive ones.

Africa's burden

Africa's strategy for confronting the "European challenge" need to address, among other things, how Africa could maximize the benefits of "1992", sustain its market access to Europe, and minimize the risks associated with European unification. While such issues cannot be isolated from their overall global contexts, it is assumed that the initiatives that African leaders and business people take would determine how well they can compete in Europe. Mauritius, for example, has taken the opportunity of the Lome Convention to exploit its trade provisions, and not only supplied about one-third of the total quotas under the Lome sugar protocol, but successfully maintained a booming trade in canned tuna on the basis of a derogation from the rules of origin. The tiny island country in Africa has established a very competitive textile industry.

Quite often, African countries have complained about their shrinking market access at the EU. The erosion of Africa's margin of preference in the EU market is effective, if the prevailing margin was a major factor for existing trading patterns. In some cases, preference margins are not important, because African countries are already competitive in certain sectors (the case of Mauritius and textiles), or even with preferences, African exporters are still not competitive. In the latter case, since African countries generally gain no further concessions when they are faced with zero tariffs, the major way by which they could benefit from the single market is to address the fundamental issues of competitiveness.

The EU market has already become a tougher place, where less competitive developing countries face competition not only from the EU, American, and Japanese companies, but those from the NICs. The "Four Tigers" (Hong Kong, South Korea, Taiwan and Singapore) sold $24 billion of manufactured goods to the EU in 1987, as compared to only $6 billion for Latin America, and a mere $0.6 billion for Mexico.[2] Successful diversification of African exports to the EU would require increased financing from multilateral and regional institutions. Developed countries would also need to provide increased market access.

Unfortunately for Africa, it is a "catch 22" situation. Africa can only be competitive at the EU market place, if it is able to diversify its products to include more manufactured items. For Africa, "the Lome experience", however, has shown that the level of protectionism in Europe is most severe with processed and manufactured items. The Lome Convention, which should have been Africa's springboard to the EU market, so far, has discouraged processing for two reasons. In the first place, there are restrictive clauses that prevent African nations from getting access to the EU manufactured sectors. Also, by stabilizing export earnings of primary commodity exports, the STABEX scheme, that is part of the Lome Convention, acts as a disincentive for African nations to process their exports. Paradoxically, then, the Euro-African scheme makes it more difficult for Africa to advance beyond the raw material-based development, as it makes them "comfortable" with their status in an unequal international division of labor.

The more African nations are competitive as exporters and as location for investment, the more likely they are to benefit from "1992". Three interrelated efforts must be undertaken: aggressive export promotion, quality management and control, and export diversification to include manufactured items.

Speaking on the subject of competitivity at Conference in Nairobi, Kenya, in February 1987, L.D.M. Mackenzie (speaking on behalf of the EU), for example, noted that "competitivity" means that the [African] product must: (1) be competitive in price; (2) conform to the quality standards in Europe; (3) cater for the taste of specific markets (and there are many in Europe); (4) meet health and safety regulations; (5) must be available on regular basis (and adapt to shifts in the direction or structure of the market).[3] Commenting on the access of ACP products under the Lome Conventions, Mackenzie further observed that:

> It is not the fault of the Lome Convention or its provision if ACP industry, despite favorable wage rates, suffers from high unit costs of production, or if the product is subject

to a heavy export tax or if an unsound exchange rate policy overvalues the product in the foreign market. It is not the fault of the Convention if in penetrating a market the supply suddenly stops or the deliveries arrive late. The customer will rightly look elsewhere.[4]

How will "1992" affect Africa's export strategies?

With non-EU suppliers struggling to beat global competition, it is important for African exporters to realize that their export strategies might have to be altered, in order to take account of the emerging changes related to "1992". There would be changes in taste, laws, distribution channels, competition, etc.

In the past, many export strategies meant targeting a single European country. Now, one might want to alter the strategy, to reach several EU countries. For example, instead of exporting to one agent in one country, the exporters might ship to three or more countries - taking advantage of the distribution channels established by centralized sales and distribution centers in Europe. Under the "1992" program, border checks are to be eliminated. This will, all things being equal, reduce transportation costs;

Harmonization of standards also means reduced cost for many African exporters. In the past, products had to be tested and certified to meet different member states' standards. Harmonization of product labelling has already affected some products exported to the EU.

Africa will need more aggressive export strategies in order to maintain export competitiveness in sectors in which Africa possesses a comparative advantage. Improvements are needed in product development, market identification, and distribution networks.

That Africa needs alternative market outlets, in addition to commodity diversification, cannot be overemphasized. The structure of African exports to the EU is such that over 80 percent is covered by primary commodities. Unfortunately, as Kenneth Dadzie (the Secretary-General for UNCTAD) noted, exports of primary commodities would face difficulties in the 1990s due to depressed markets abroad.[5] Since African economies are so much dependent on receipts from such commodities, the need to diversify, or adapt production to changing European market situations, is not always accorded a top priority. As the OAU rightly pointed out, "the paradox in Africa's performance is shown by the fact that whilst its exports earnings had been declining, it's volume of exports continue to increase".[6]

The elimination of technical barriers to trade is subject to GATT code on standards. For this reason, the EU must, whereby possible, align harmonization of its standards with international ones. Assuming that this would be the trend in the future, there is a challenge for African nations to adapt to international standards, and seek new markets for their products. There is also an urgent need for the African countries to actively participate in international negotiations, and the creation of international standards.

Action plan

In the first place, planning at the national and regional levels must consider trade and services as important sectors in the development planing process. Second, partnership with EU-based firms is likely to offer African firms an edge, by providing a link to the Single market. Third, obstacles to intra-African trade also need to be removed. They include transportation and communication problems, paucity of trade information, lack of industrial complementarity, limited competitiveness in relation to the rest of the world, and trade financing problems.

Africa also needs the scientific and technological base to process its products for both exports and internal markets. The challenge of Africa countries is not only to "industrialize" and find markets for their new products, but must also adapt to the challenges from competitors on their traditional strong markets. For example, faced with the unreliable future in rubber because of the development of synthetics, the level of industrial activity in the importing country, and change of use, Malaysia is diversifying her economy by focussing on alternate crops, including cocoa. Malaysia is already strong in the EU market, and is expected to be a dominant world supplier of cocoa at the turn of the century.[7] This provides a serious competitive challenge for African cocoa exporters, such as Ghana, Cote d'Ivoire, and Nigeria. While it is difficult to make a definitive assessment of the external impact of the "1992" program, a timely adjustment to trade, investment, and alternative market strategies is a critical policy issue for Africa. The ability of African countries to effectively respond to "1992" is important, if they are to benefit from the Single Market. This involves meeting new European technical standards, adjusting exports to changing conditions in Europe, and projecting the future of export prices and revenue, as a result of changes in the EU market.

Lobbying the European Commission would be an important strategy that must be kept on going. EU officials may be naturally more responsive to recommendations that are from large economic groups, than they would to those from small individual companies. For example, in case of a trade dispute between an African country (exporter) and an EU firm, an inquiry from the Head of an African Association of Industries, for example, would definitely attract more attention than a mere complaint from a single exporter from Africa.

Teaming up with European industrial groups that share similar concerns as those from Africa would also help. For example, if an EU directive entails production, certification or market access problems, it would be most helpful to contact the European trade association covering the particular product. In other words, a joint approach with EU firms may be necessary.[8]

Intensive collaboration and increased solidarity among African countries is also needed, as African nations negotiate with the EU in areas where Africa's interests may be at stake. The EU has been a tough negotiator, not only for developing countries, but even for developed countries. As a result, the EFTA countries, for example, are strengthening their decision making process and collective negotiating capacity for an European Economic Space (EES) involving the EU.[9] This conforms to the doctrine of collective self-reliance. The question is: Is "self-reliance" possible in Africa in the face of united Europe? Unfortunately, the experience with self-reliance has been paradoxical. Let's look at the case of African Development Bank (ADB), which has nearly $500 million in delinquent loans. The Congo, an oil-producing country, is $62 million behind in loan payments to the ADB.[10]

Counter-bloc strategies

As a continent, Africa has tried to overcome its limitations as a dependent region, by adopting several strategies. These have included (1) international non-alignment, (2) continental diplomatic interdependence, (3) regional integration, and (4) collective advocacy at international conferences.[11] African leaders must realize that it is only in collectivities that the continent can escape the dependence quagmire, and be able to negotiate with united Europe. At present, the mercantalist potential and the international economic influence of most African states is limited, unless they act as a group.

Regional integration as collective self-reliance

Regional Integration has been embraced in Africa as a collective bargaining strategy in dealing with international actors. It can be considered as Africa's answer to the world of increasing polarization. As Table 9.1 shows, a significant part of international trade is being conducted within existing regional integration schemes, such as the European Union, the Central American Common Market, and ASEAN.

Table 9.1
Regional trading schemes: Intra-regional exports & world exports

	Founded	1960	1970	1975	1980	1985	1990
ANZCERTA	1983	5.7	6.1	6.2	6.4	7.0	7.6
		(2.4)	(2.1)	(1.7)	(1.4)	(1.6)	(1.5)
EU	1957	34.5	51.0	50.0	54.0	54.5	60.4
		(24.9)	(39.0)	(35.9)	(34.9)	(35.6)	(41.4)
EFTA	1960	21.1	28.0	35.2	32.6	31.2	28.2
		(14.9)	(14.9)	(6.3)	(6.1)	(6.3)	(6.8)
Canada-	1989	28.5	32.8	30.6	26.5	38.0	34.0
US FTA		(21.9)	(20.5)	(16.8)	(15.1)	(16.7)	(15.8)
ASEAN	1967	4.4	20.7	15.9	16.9	18.4	18.6
		(2.6)	(2.1)	(2.6)	(3.7)	(3.9)	(4.3)
ANDEAN	1969	0.7	2.0	3.7	3.8	3.4	4.6
PACT		(2.9)	(1.6)	(1.6)	(1.6)	(1.2)	(0.9)
CACM	1961	7.0	25.7	23.3	24.1	14.7	14.8
		(0.4)	(0.4)	(0.3)	(0.2)	(0.2)	(0.1)
LAFTA/	1960/80	7.9	9.9	13.6	13.7	8.3	10.6
LAIA		(6.0)	(4.4)	(3.5)	(4.2)	(4.7)	(8.4)
ECOWAS	1975	—	3.0	4.2	3.6	5.8	6.0
		—	(1.0)	(1.4)	(1.7)	(1.1)	(0.6)
PTA	1987	—	8.4	9.4	8.9	7.0	8.5
		(1.1)	(0.5)	(0.4)	(0.3)	(0.2)	

Source: Jaime de Melo, Arvind Panagariya, "The New Regionalism", *Finance and Development* (IMF), December 1992, p. 39.

The benefits of an African economic integration are numerous. Official trade among countries in sub-Saharan Africa amounts to a mere $4 billion - just 6 percent of total African trade estimated to be $65 billion - and has stagnated or declined for most nations since 1970s, when most of the regional integration schemes were formed.[12]

At the political level, Africa's integration could be seen as African nations' collective strategic response to post cold war geo-political re-alignments.[13] As the world shrinks into hemispheric blocs, an effective African regional bloc will serve as a political shock absorber.

African integration is also needed because multilateral initiatives have failed, or are slow to usher in global trade liberalization. The justification for inter-state cooperation in Africa also arises from historical as well as day-to-day realities. The growth in informal trade appears to have re-established the extensive trade in goods and the migration of people that were the reality of economic and social life before Africa's colonization.

What are the prospects for African unity, as Europe moves further on the ladder of unity? Afro-pessimists argue that the prospects for an effective African integration are slim. Part of such pessimism is based on looking at African integration through Euro-centric paradigms. The need for regional integration in Africa goes beyond the mere necessity to augment intra-African trade. Africa needs the integration of the Two "Ms"—(African) Minds and Markets.

The adoption of the Pan-African [Abuja] Treaty is Africa's response to the world of emerging trading blocs, not the least of which is the EU that "threatens to isolate Africa from world markets".[14] However, there are a catalogue of problems that militate against African unity.

In the first place, there is the previously strong extra-regional trade ties (eg. the Commonwealth preference schemes, Franco-African Community). Also, there are diverse interests among the constituent groups: Anglophone versus Francophone; South African versus the frontline states, and Arab North vs. Sub-saharan Africa.

As a bloc, Africa could enhance her bargaining power, for example in negotiation for better prices for Africa's commodities. It is quite absurd that the African Economic Community will not kick off until 1934, at a time when other regional blocs in the world, including the European bloc are operational! African leaders can not hide behind political and technical excuses. If the demise of the East African Community (EAC) was because it covered a relatively small area (Tanzania, Kenya, and Uganda) as some analysts imply, then ECOWAS (that covers sixteen nations) should be doing better than it is doing.[15]

EU's initiatives and responsibilities

For most African countries, adjusting to a more demanding post-"1992" European standards would be financially costly and time-consuming. Therefore, technical aid - particularly from the EU in assisting African countries in adapting to 1992-related changes would be necessary. Such assistance could be in the form of transfer of technology, so African countries could adapt to the new EU standards and to safeguard their interests. This could help dispel the fear that "1992" implies a shift in EU's focus to Europe, to the detriment of Euro-African relations. As the Vice President of the European Commission, Manuel Marin, declared in a speech marking the signature of the Lome IV, the EU's relations with the ACP countries is of "paramount political importance to the Community".[16] Africa's declining commodity prices, structural adjustment difficulties, and debilitating debt burdens are all detrimental to EU's interests to the extent that they limit the capacity of Africa as potential market for European industry.

The EU must resist overly protectionist measures in connection with the creation of the Single Market which could be planned as a compensation to EU firms for abolishing quotas, tariffs and taxes. The EU must also make sure that official aid flows to Eastern Europe will be additional, and not at the cost of aid budgets to Africa.

The EU will be preoccupied with the debate over widening and deepening the integration arena. According to J.E. Spence, the Community would become inward looking, as it becomes "absolved in solving the problems arising from the process of closer union".[17]

The former EU's Director-General for Development, Dieter Frisch, noted that "in so far as the effects of the Single Market are not simply mechanical, but can be controlled, the Community will have to differentiate between strong, fully competitive non-member countries and weaker trading partners". Consequently, Africa's survival in Europe will partly depend on the kind of redistributive policies that the EU would pursue.

In this regard, the EU should demonstrate a political commitment to assist the African nations. The EU must:

(1) Not only maintain, but also improve existing special provisions to aid African countries through the Lome Convention, the Agreements with the Mediterranean countries, and the Generalized System of Preferences;

(2) Assist African countries to get acquainted with new developments of the Single Market, so that they can adopt more easily and become more competitive. This could be done through the media of seminars, technical assistance, and trade promotion, etc). For example, the EC Commission, together with the Paris-based Aproma, which promotes tropical foods for the ACP countries, sponsored a four-day seminar in Brussels between importers from three Central European countries-Poland, Czechoslovakia, and Hungary and the ACP countries. The aim of the seminar was to develop Central European market for coffee, tea, and tropical fruits.

(3) Encourage private investment in Africa. This could be done through the provision of insurance scheme on the lines of the US Overseas Private Investment Company.

(4) Use its aid facilities to compensate African countries for the losses they sustained as a result of the concessions that the EU granted to other competing developing nations at the Uruguay Round of GATT negotiations. This could help reduce the impact of lateral preferential erosion among the ACP countries.

(5) Improve the access of manufactured items from Africa into the EU.

In addition to the above initiatives, the EU must also help eradicate the negative publicity in Africa about a Fortress Europe. The EU should not solve immigration problem by "isolationism, cutting itself off behind a closed-door policy".[18] To the African traveller, new EU immigration policies are the vivid reminder of a fortress Europe. The European Parliamentary Committee Against Racism and Xenophobia has got a lot of work to do in its efforts to extinguish the fire of racism and xenophobia in the context of European political and economic unification.

In December 1993, two neo-Nazi skinheads accused of fire-bombing murders of three Turks were given maximum prison sentences - a verdict that was considered as a heavy blow to counter against right-wing violence in Germany.[19]

Criticizing current EU immigration policies, Franz Nuscheler, Director of the Institute for Development and Peace (INEF) in Germany, argues that instead of the "militarization" of refugee policy, developed nations must "fight the causes of flight, not the refugees".[20] Nuscheler emphasizes that fighting 'the immigration bing' is not the sole responsibility of one nation or a group of countries. Nuscher's argument, which this author also shares, include the following recommendations for nations. Nations must pursue:

-An active peace policy through "humanitarian interventionism".

-A socially acceptable policy on the debt crisis, whose management by the IMF through structural adjustment policies, has increased mass *immiseration*.

-An international environmental policy, with tries to prevent further environmental degradation, and the feared mass movement of "environmental refugees".

-An international equalization of burdens and benefits that would create a just and equitable world order.

A new development policy is needed

Some writers have hailed the present structure of Euro-African relation as a "model" for equitable North-South relations, while others have condemned it as a tool to split the Third World in their alliance for more equitable global order.[21] After two decades of "partnership", African countries still remain skeptical about the prospects of development via incorporation into the EU-ACP framework. As a result, Sam Olofin even questioned whether the co-existence of Intra-African links (exemplified in ECOWAS) and Euro-African links (the case of Lome Convention) is "complementary" or "conflicting?".[22]

What future has Euro-African relations? Is the new European market a Manna or a Menace for Africa? The uncertainty remains as to whether EU-African development cooperation gains as a result of the gigantic

European unity drive. Given the dramatic changes that are taking place in Europe, as well as the increasing liberalization of the global economies, it is time to question whether Euro-Africa cooperation in the twenty-first century will be a new wine in an old bottle, or an old wine in a new bottle. S.K.B. Asante, for example, has charged that the Lome regime "updates and institutionalizes, albeit in a comprehensive generous language, the traditional post-colonial dependency structures, charting no new path for Africa, breaking no fundamentally new ground, and offering no new perspectives".[23]

Even though the principle of non-reciprocity is enshrined in the Lome Convention and most of the Mediterranean Agreements, the EU has warned that "if certain developing countries become more competitive, it is quite natural to expect a fuller participation of these countries in the multilateral trading system".[24] It is possible, then, that the access of LDCs to the EU market in the fields of services and capital may be based on reciprocity in the future.

Africa is now submerged in a new world order. The Cold War is over, or has been neutralized for now. New democratic regimes, such as Mandela's South Africa, are emerging in Africa which need external help. The traditional EU-African relations of the STABEX-type has produced both positive and negative results, but it has reached a stalemate. Therefore, a more effective way has to be found to correct the imbalances in Euro-African relations. Africa urgently needs a new 'development model'.

The EU has supported a preferential rules of origin for developing countries that have concluded regional trade agreements. By supporting 'cumulative origin rules', the EU encourages cross-border production within LDC integration schemes, such as ACP, ASEAN, and the Andean Pact. The Lome IV also supports multilateral projects, whereby 1250 MECU was allocated for regional integration (see Table 9.2).

Table 9.2
EU assistance to ACP in support of regional integration in ACP in million ecus

Lome 1	304	304
Lome 11	632	632
Lome III	1,000	1,000
Lome IV	1,250	1,250

Source: EU

In addition to the Lome scheme, the EU must consider other complementary policies that are likely to help lift the African continent up from below. These must include cancellation of Africa's debt. Also, unfair subsidies in advanced nations must be removed. The EU must actively promote development and democracy building in Africa.

Other observers have suggested that it is time for a Marshall Plan for Africa. The argument goes that now that the Cold War has ended, Europe should "look South".[25] The call for an African Marshall Plan, along the lines that is unofficially being extended to Eastern Europe, has not received an audience in Europe. In the first place, the end of the Cold War has already devalued the geo-strategic importance of Africa. Second, the failure of development aid in Africa has made Afro-skeptics to be critical of an "African Marshall Plan".

What is needed for Africa is a "troika" development model that would be based on fair trade, more aid, and debt forgiveness. For example, Ghana's ability to sustain reforms over the past decade was due, in part, to the fact that annual gross aid flows (averaging 8 percent of GDP were) available almost from the moment reforms began in Ghana.

Some observations

In evaluating the potential implications of 1992 on Africa, two major issues are important: (1) the potential effects on Euro - African ties - economic, political and social, and (2) the effect on Africa's own regional and continental unification.

The first set of effects of the EU integration have pull-in and push-out implications. The national economic crisis in Europe, stemming in part, from the sudden demise of the Cold war, may delay European integration, and may also contribute to the inward-looking tendencies of the EU.

The EU plan to complete its internal market is, indeed, a challenge to Africa. The challenge involves Africa's ability to maximize the benefits that it may bring and to overcome the protectionism that it may entail.

There is a positive catalytic impact of European unification, to the extent that the Lome Conventions have brought a common Community approach to matters of trade. In Africa, too, it has also triggered a region-wide recognition of individual country vulnerability. This recognition has led to renewed interest in regional cooperation in Africa. The slow but steady increase in EU's internal trade, from 53 percent of total trade in 1984 to 58 percent in 1987, emphasizes the increasing independence of the EU from external markets and sources for goods. EU's 1992 liberalization and harmonization of rules may further this trend.

As the preceding chapters have suggested, the grave risks and upsets for Africa - as a result of 1992 - would not only be in the fields of trade relations, but also in financial, investments, and human relations.[26]

In addition to potential losses in trade, aid and investments, Europe's political attention has been diverted elsewhere. Eastern European countries are abandoning communism and adopting capitalist, Western-style democratic systems. The major implication for Africa, is that Western Europe would be tempted to participate in the reconstruction of these economies, while closing their own ranks with the formation of a single market.[27]

As a result of a thaw in East-West relations, military policies of advanced nations have been refocussed on contingencies in the developing world. Africa could even be a dumping ground for cheap "disarmed" weapons. The pitfalls of peace are scattered every where. In Western Europe, for example, the cost of German reunification is rising. This has already put a constraint on Europe's ability to help African nations. In the Middle East, too, the cost of the "Saddam war" has put some strains on international aid flows from the Gulf region. What is worse for Africa, the PLO's accord with Israel will help divert international financing to Middle East reconstruction.

There is a non-economic impact of 1992 on Africa. Current efforts of European integration - in the face of the disintegration of Eastern Europe - could be positive in the sense that it could act as a catalyst for Africa's own efforts at continental, and sub-continental integration. This line of argument goes beyond merely viewing "1992" in terms of whether Europe will be "partnership" or "protectionist", or trade-creating/trade-diverting.

Already, European unification efforts have awakened the consciousness of African leaders about African cooperation. Speaking about the sluggish efforts at integration in West Africa, former Nigerian leader, Olesegun Obasanjo, saw current European unification attempts as a pressure to "rekindle our flickering West African flames from the European torch".[28] A Symposium on "Africa and Europe 1992", held in Rabat, Morocco, in October 1989, called on African countries to reinforce their regional economic integration efforts.[29] Efforts seem to have been doubled in the search for African integration. European unification should also spur African countries to look at human resource development and technical capacity - building more seriously.

In *The Impact of Europe in 1992 on West Africa*, Olesegun Obasanjo, former Nigerian Head of State foresees some catalytic effect of "1992" on Africa. According to Obasanjo:

> Beyond the immediate gain that we hope to be able to reap from 1992, we also look to the European example of inspiration in our efforts to build a thriving economic community in West Africa.[30]

The EU efforts have had a positive catalytic effect on Africa. African leaders saw the ease with which resources were mobilized for the Eastern bloc, in sharp contrast to the "go-slow" in resource mobilization to Africa, particularly the stalling of the UN Program for African Economic Recovery (1985-91) because of lack of funds. As Oluyemi Adeniji has noted, "Africa rightly drew the conclusion that, if it is to have any chance in global economic cooperation, regional integration is a sine qua non".[31] Consequently, at the annual summit of the OAU in 1991, African leaders signed the African Economic Community Treaty.

Europe can also learn a lesson from Africa. The route to Maastricht is going to be a tortious one for strategists of European unity. One of the major obstacles to the implementation of the Maastricht Treaty is the fear about the encroachment on national sovereignties—the extent to which EU nations would sacrifice national sovereignty on the alter of regional unity. Perhaps, here, Kwame Nkrumah's proposals on pan-African Unity offers an important model for Europe. Quite unique in constitutional history, Ghana's constitution written by Nkrumah's government, specified that Ghana's sovereignty could be sacrificed in furtherance of pan-African unity!

From the perspective of dependency theory, there is incompatibility between African regionalism as exemplified in the *Lagos Plan of Action* (the Lagos Plan) drawn by African leaders in 1980, and Africa's association with the EU.[32] The Lagos Plan perceives "disengagement" from the global economic system as a *sine qua non* for Africa's economic development, and as an alternative to the World Bank's prescription for interdependence, as exemplified in World Bank's *Agenda for Action*.[33] Which ever option Africa chooses, there are bound to be problems. The EU is bound to increase its imports from Africa at the expense of the minimal intra-African trade. African countries might find it cheaper to import from the EU what is produced locally in Africa at higher cost. In both ways, the trade-creating and trade-diverting effects of Euro-African trade are likely to discriminate against Africa.

In addition to being an alternative strategy for Africa's development, closer economic and political cooperation in Africa could also be seen as a 'demonstration effect' of European unity. The EU — on which the Economic Community of West African States (ECOWAS) was modelled — has metamorphosed into a new phenomenon whose impact on the world economy is being assessed in every capital in the world.[34]

At the OAU meeting in Cairo in 1993, President Jerry Rawlings of Ghana emphasized that the absence of effective integration has made Africa vulnerable, since stronger nations are in a position "to define democracy for us".[35]

The EU gains geo-politically as it becomes a political entity. Its responsibility for the global economy has grown accordingly.[36] Thus, European integration in 1992 has the potential to accelerate the political imbalance in Euro-South relations. For example, the Lome Convention links a group of developed countries (including all the former colonial powers) on one hand, and the weakest and most economically dependent of their former colonies in Africa, Caribbean and the Pacific, on the other. The challenge that African countries face, as a result of 1992, hinges on their dependent status in the Euro-African division of labor. Lacking an effective continental mechanism for Africa's own interdependence, Africa's "cruel choice", at the present time, at least, would be to be part of the Euro-South system, while simultaneously negotiating for the kinds of deals which would enable the African continent to exercise greater control over the process of their development.

Suggestions

(1) It is essential that African nations monitor the activities and trends in the EU '1992' program, and also update information on them. The private sector in Africa must be informed of all policy issues affecting future foreign trade with the EU. There must be an improvement of local business environments.
(2) The service sector in Africa must be developed. Services would be one of the major booming sectors in EU after unification. The deplorable conditions of African airlines is a testimony to Africa's lack of preparation for the Single Market.
(3) Communication with the EU, its financial institutions, trade associations and political institutions is vital. The African Development Bank has appointed a Resident Director to Europe. The objectives of the Resident Directorship include the establishment of lines of communication with European business groups, by organizing business opportunities,

such as seminars, where subjects for discussion would include issues related to Africa's interests and how they would be affected by EU unification.

(4) There is the need for the formation of Associations of African Professional Groups (eg an Association of African Lawyers) to monitor immigration and refugee policies of the EU and its member countries, and how they impact directly and indirectly on African students, residents, and travellers in Europe.

(5) There is also the need for more research on EU affairs by African scholars. This author recalls that when he was in Brussels, some African diplomatic missions in Brussels ironically relied on the European Commission for information pertaining to the effect of "1992" on Africa. During a Conference on the theme of "1992" in Accra, Ghana, some African participants approached the EU mission in Ghana for last-minute information about the subject. Africans must conduct their own independent research on the effects of the Single market on Africa.

(6) Africa should establish an 'European Challenge Assessment Center'. This center should: (a) analyze the EU program; (b) examine African nations interest and stake in the "1992" process; (c) disseminate information about "1992" to African countries, scholars, businessmen and policy-makers. Such a Center must be funded by African governments and philanthropists.

(7) Obtaining influential positions in the EU will also be important. According to Walton L. Brown:

> The emergence of EC [EU] 92 will create a situation in which the existing neo-colonial ties between African and its former colonists will be beneficial only to the degree that the former colonial nations are able to obtain influential positions in the European Community.[37]

(8) At the firm level, certain initiatives need to be taken, if Africa is to survive global competition. In relation to the EU single market, African firms must:

-Identify relevant proposals that relate to issues of interest to Africa;

-Evaluate their business implications;

-Develop strategies and business plans;
-Implement plans at appropriate times;
-Train their employees in foreign languages;
-Have sales agents in the rest of Europe;
-Establish plants in Europe;
-Conduct market research about the Single market.

(9)Private sector development will be a key factor. Since in most cases, private companies in Africa are too small that it is often difficult for foreign companies to deal with them.

(10) Africa must also initiate their own audio-visual revolution. Gross disinterest about African peoples and their cultures in European capitals translates into poor reporting, in addition to inadequate Western market for educational and media materials on Africa. In the same way that African business persons must fight to win at the economic arena, the African media must fight against gross racial and social stereotypes about the peoples and cultures of Africa.

Global networking and coordination

Africa must pursue policies of empowerment in Europe to fight against EU's policies that seem overtly racist and anti-African. The black experience in the United States provides a useful model. For the past 30 years, key African-American students, faculty, church leaders, labor groups and liberal movement mobilized forces against apartheid, that created, perhaps, one of the most remarkable changes in US foreign policies.

African leaders must also recognize that an appeal to the guilty conscience of their former colonizers in Europe, or to Europe's massive wealth, has not and will not work. As a former member of the Select Committee of European Legislators put it:

> Africa has the ability to present thousands of its people dying on television and we've seen this time and time in Europe. But the threat that exists from the 27,000 nuclear warheads in the former Soviet bloc tends to concentrate the minds of the European decision-makers far more.[38]

Africa must adopt a "Twenty-first Century Resolution". By this resolution, Governments and private firms in Africa must pledge not to procrastinate in addressing the challenges of market access in the EU. Procrastination has already led to a big loss to Africa. According to Baffour Ankomah, though "we [Africans] had ten years to prepare for the decision of the International Civil Aviation Organization (to implement new aircraft standards), we did not react until 18 months after the entry into force of the measure".[39]

There must be more action beyond mere rhetoric. K.B. Asante, the Secretary for Education in Ghana, noted at a symposium on 'Europe 1992, Implications for Africa' that although African nations daily condemn colonialism and imperialism, little has been done to uproot the structures planted by these forces.[40]

Africa needs to develop a more aggressive approach at international negotiations, particularly as it concerns the improvement of the terms of access of major commodities in the markets of industrialized nations. For example, SADC has a substantial share in world exports in a number of strategic materials, hence the bargaining power to seek better deals with international actors. Sad to relate, while Southern African countries have control over significant amount of diamond, this precious commodity is still tightly regulated by world monopoly, the Central Selling Organization (CSO), which is controlled by de Beers Corporation, an associate company of the foremost South African-based TNC, the Anglo-American Corporation.[41]

African nations cannot stand unprepared for the 21st century. Developing enabling policies to be able to survival in the global system must be given a top consideration.

Notes

1 Mary Alexander, "Threats to Developing Countries From EC Integration", *West Africa*, 29 June 1992, p. 1091.

2 Pierre Defraigne, Director of North-South Affairs, European Commission, "EC and Mexico's Respective Contributions", Seminar "Mexico and EC 1992", Mexico City, 18-19 October 1989, p. 4.

3 L.D.M. Mackenzie, "Export From ACP Countries to EEC Under Lome III Regulations", CDI Conference, Nairobi, February 1987, pp. 4-5.

4 *Ibid.* p. 5.

5 See *Financial Times*, June 7, 1990.

6 OAU, "Addis Ababa Declaration of African Ministers Responsible for Trade and Development Preparatory to UNCTAD VII".

7 *Ibid.*, p. 6.

8 For a review of this strategy, see *Business America*, February 24, 1992, p. 28.

9 See for example, Xavier Pintado, *et al* (eds.) *Economic Aspects of the European Economic Space*, European Free Trade Association, Economic Affairs Department, Occasional Paper # 25, November 1988.

10 *Baltimore Sun*, (US), 30 May, 1993.

11 Ali Mazrui, "Beyond Dependency in the Black World: Five Strategies for Decolonization", in Agibou Yansane (ed.), *Decolonization and Dependency: Problems of Development in African Societies*, Eawstport, CT: Greenwood Press, 1980, p. 94.

12 See The World Bank, *Sub-Saharan Africa: From Crisis to Sustainable Growth*, Washington, D.C, 1989, p. 158.

13 See Charles Kwarteng, "Africa and the Changing Global Arena", Dept. of Political Science & Int. Studies, Morgan State University, Baltimore, MD, USA, (1992) unpublished paper.

14 S.K.B. Asante, "New Hope for Africa: Pan-African Economic Community", *Development and Cooperation*, No. 4, 1992.

15 John Ravenhill, "Regional Integration and Development in Africa: Lessons from the East African Community", *Journal of Commonwealth and Comparative Politics*, November 1979.

16 Manuel Marin, Vice President of the European Commission, Speech on the Occasion of the Signature of the Fourth Lome Convention, Lome, Togo, 15 Dec., 1989.

17 J.E. Spence, "A Post-Apartheid South Africa and the International Community", *Journal of Commonwealth and Comparative Politics*, Vol. 31, No. 1, March 1993, p. 93.

18 Reff Bjerregaard, "Populations Movements in the 1990s:Challenge for Policy-makers", *Development*, No. 1, 1993.

19 "Two Neo-Nazis Get Maximum Sentences", *Washington Post*, December 9, 1993.

20 Franz Nuscheler, "Fight the Causes of Flight, Not the Refugees", *Development and Cooperation*, No. 4, 1993, p. 4.

21 For such alternative view points, see Otto Schmuch, "Half Time in Lome IV Negotiations", *Development and Cooperation*, No. 5, 1989.

22 Sam Olofin, "ECOWAS and the Lome Convention: An Experiment in Complementary or Conflicting Customs Union Arrangement?", *Journal of Common Market Studies*, September 1977.

23 S.K.B. Asante, "Lome II: Another Machinery for Updating Dependency", *Development and Cooperation*, No. 3, 1981.

24 Dieter Frisch, Director-General for Development, EC Commission,"1992 and the Developing Countries", Address Delivered in Bonn, 25 October, 1988, p. 13.

25 See Winrich Kuhne "Looking south After the End of the Cold War", In I. William Zartman (ed.), *Europe and Africa: The New Phase*, Boulder, Colorado, Lynne Rienner, 1990, p. 20.

26 Francis Wurtz, Joint ACP-EEC Rapporteur in the Effects of the Single Market, Interview in the *EEC-ACP Courier, No.* 118, November/December 1989.

27 See Dieter Brauer, "Europe at a Crossroads: What Effects on the Third World?", *Development and Cooperation*, No. 3 1993, p. 4.

28 Olesegun Obasanjo, "Leverage Against 1992", *West Africa*, 8-14 May 1989, p. 718.

29 Agence France Press, 26 October, 1989.

30 Olesegun Obasanjo, Hans d'Orville (ed.) *The Impact of Europe in 1992 on West Africa*, New York: Crane Russak, 1990, p. 4.

31 Oluyemi Adeniji, "Regionalism in Africa", *Security Dialogue*, Vol. 24, No. 2, 1993, p. 213.

32 On the conflicting issue of interdependence and the problems of reducing dependency between Africa and Europe, see Charles Kwarteng, "Opportunities and Challenges of Regional Economic Cooperation Among the ECOWAS States of West Africa", Ph.D. dissertation, University of Pittsburgh, Pittsburgh, 1989, esp. chap. 5.

33 World Bank, *An Accelerated Development for Sub-Saharan Africa: An Agenda for Action*, Washington, D.C., 1981.

34 The ECOWAS is the largest regional organization in the world in terms of the size of its members which is 16. The countries involved are Benin, Burkina Faso, Cape Verde, the Gambia, Ghana, Guinea, Guinea-Bissau, the Ivory Coast, Liberia, Mali, Mauritania, Niger, Nigeria, Senegal, Sierra Leone, Togo.

35 See Excepts of his Speech delivered at the OAU Summit in Cairo, Egypt cited in *Africa Analysis*, 6 August 1993.

36 Lorenz Schomerus, "Partners in Progress", *Development and Cooperation*, No. 2, 1990, p. 4.

37 Walton L. Brown. "The 1992 European Community and Africa", *TransAfrica Forum*, Fall 1992, p. 5.

38 Quoted in Robert Swain, "The european Communities and South Africa: New Threats, New Opportunities", *South Africa International*, July 1992, p. 12.

39 Baffour Ankomah, "Who Isn't Afraid of 1992?", *New African*, February 1989, p. 25.

40 *Ghanaian Times*, 30 August, 1989.

41 Gerhard Dedorath, Paul Mensah-Quainoo, Afriwile Mwake Jungu, *Study on SADDC Trade Existing Pattern and Potential for Growth*, MB Consulting, Maseru, Lesotho, November 1988, p. 166.

Selected Bibliography

Books

Amin, Samir. *Unequal Development* (Hassocks, Sussez: Haverster Press, 1976).

Cecchini, Paolo, *The European Challenge: The Benefits of a Single Market* (Brussels, 1988).

Center for Economic Research on Africa, Montclair State College, *Europe 1992, Africa and the US*. Upper Montclair, NJ: 1990.

Cheru, Fantu. *The Silent Revolution in Africa: Debt, Development and Democracy*. London. Zed Books, 1989.

Chikeka, Charles O. *Africa and the European Economic Community*. Lewiston, New York: E. Mellen Press, 1993.

Chipman, John. *French Power in Africa*. (Oxford, Basil Blackwell, 1989).

Davidson, Basil. *The Black Man's Burden: The Curse of the Nation State*. New York: Times Book, 1992.

Emmanuel, Arghiri. *Unequal Exchange and the Imperialism of Trade*. New York: Monthly Review, 1972.

Gould, David. *Bureaucratic Corruption and Underdevelopment in the Third World: The Case of Zaire*. New York, Pergammon, 1980.

Koehane, Nye, Joseph. *Power and interdependence*, Boston: Little, Brown, Co. 1977.

Nkrumah, Kwame. *Africa Must Unite*. New York: Heinmann, 1963.

Obasanjo, Olesegun, *The Impact of Europe in 1992 on West Africa*
Crane Russak, 1990.

Tovias, Alfred. *Foreign Economic Relations of the European Community: The Impact of Spain and Portugal.* Lynne Rienner Publishers, Boulder, Colorado, 1990.

Viner, Jacob. *The Customs Union Issue*. New York: Carnegie Endowment for International Peace, 1950.

Welch, Claude, *Dream of Unity: Pan-Africanism and Political Unification in West Africa.* Ithaca, NY: Cornell Univ. Press, 1966.

White, Gilliam M., *GATT Laws and Community Law: Some Comparisons Illustrated By Recent Trade Disputes*. London: Sweet and Maxwell, 1990.

Zartman, I. William, *Europe and Africa: The New Phase*
Boulder, Colorado: Lynne Rienner, 1993.

Official documents

ACP-EEC Joint Assembly, Resolution on the Fourth Convention of Lome, Adopted in Versailles, 29 September, 1989.

Adedeji, Adebayo, (Executive Secretary of UN ECA), "Africa and the International Community in the 1990s", Statement Before the European Parliament Committee on Development Cooperation", Brussels 27 February 1990.

—"Africa: The Crisis of Development and the Challenge of a New Economic Order", Address Delivered at the 4th Meeting of the Conference of Ministers at the 19th Session of the ECA, Kinshasa, Zaire, 28 Feb - 3 March 1977.

Defraigne, Pierre, Director of North-South Affairs, EC Commission, "EC and Mexico's Perspective Contributions", (Seminar on 'Mexico and EC 1992'), Mexico;, 18-19 October 1989.

Delors, Jacques (EC Commission President), "Presenting the Commission's Program for 1990", Address to the European Parliament, Strasbourg, France, 17 January 1990.

EC, "The European Community and the Developing Countries", Brussels, June 1989.

IIth General Report on the Activities of the European Communities, 1993.
—Comite pour l'Etude de l'Union Economique et Monetaire, *Rapport Sur l'Union Economique et Monetaire dans la Communaute Europeene* (Delors' Committee), Brussels, April 1989.
—"Europe 1992" Europe World Partner"., Brussels, 19 October 1988.
—The European Community and its Eastern Neighbors, Brussels, Jan. 1991.
—*The Community and its Eastern Neighbors*, Brussels 1991.
—*The European Community: 1992 and Beyond*. Brussels, 1991.
—*Southern Africa and the European Community*, Brussels, 1990.
—Treaty On European Union (The Maastricht Treaty).
Economic Intelligence Unit, "External Relations and the Uruguay Round", *European Trends*, (London), No. 3, 1989.
Guillaumount, Patrick, Guillaumont, Sylviane, "The Implications of European Monetary Union for African Countries", *Journal of Common Market Studies*, Vol. XXVIII, No. 2, December 1989.
—"Horizontal Mergers and Competition Policy in the European Community", *European Economy*, No. 40, May 1989.
Frisch, Dieter, Director-General for Development, EC Commission, "1992 and the Developing Countries", Address Given in Bonn, 25 October 1988.
—"The Lome Convention: Practical Aspects Past Experience and Future Prospects", Address to the Committee on Developing Countries, Berlin, November 30, 1984.
Mackenzie, L.D.M., "Export From ACP Countries to EEC Under Lome III Regulations", CDI Conference, Nairobi, February 1987.
IMF, *Annual Report* (1990).
Marin, Manuel. Vice-President of the EC Commission, Speech on the Occasion of the Signature of the Fourth Lome Convention, Lome Togo, 15 December 1989.
Musto, Stefan A. "The Common Agricultural Policy of the European Community and its Consequences for Less Developed Countries", *Document Interne*, (C), No. 15, 1990.
OAU, "Addis Ababa Declaration of African Ministers Responsible for trade and Development Preparatory to UNCTAD VIII, E/ECA/Trade/ 70, 18 March 1987.

—African Common Position on Africa's External Debt Conditions, EAHG/2 (III), Addis Ababa.

—"Africa's Alternative Framework to Structural Adjustment Programmes for Socio-Economic Recovery and Transformation (AAF-SAP), CM. 15/6/Rev. 3.

OECD, *Development Co-Operation in the 1990s*, Paris, December 1989.

Tovias, Alfred. *The European Communities' Single Market: The Challenge of 1992 for Sub-Saharan Africa* (Washington: DC The World Bank, 1992).

UNCTAD, "Evaluation of the Draft Final Results of the Uruguay Round by African Countries, Working Paper, December 1993.

United States International Trade Commission, "The Effect of Greater Economic Integration Within the European Community on the United States", USITC Publication 2204, July 1989.

World Bank, *Africa and the European Community after 1992*. Washington, D.C. 1993.

—*European Community Protection Against Manufactured Imports From Developing Countries: A Case Study in the political Economy of Protection*, Staff Working Paper # 432, October 1980.

Monographs

Sapir, Andre. *Does 1992 Come Before or After 1990? On Regional Versus Multilateral Integration*. London: Center for Economic Policy Studies, Discussion Paper # 313, May 1989.

Gisele, Vigual, Reboud, Louis, "La Protection de l'article 115: Trente Ans d'applications et Perspectives Pour 1992", *Les Cashiers du CUREI*, Grenoble, France 1988.

Henderson, David. *1992: The External Dimension*, Group of 30, Occasional Papers No. 25, 1989.

Murphy Anna. *The European Community and the International Trading System*, Center for European Policy Studies, Bruxelles Belgium, 1990.

Pintado, Xavier, *et al*. "Economic Aspects of the European Economic Space", European Free Trade Association, Economic Affairs Dept. Occasional Paper No. 25, November 1988.

Robe, Jean-Philippe "Contravailing Duties, State Protectionism and the Challenge of the Uruguay Round", EIU Working Paper, No. 89/372.

World Bank, *European Community Protection Against Manufactured Imports from Developing Countries: A Case Study in the Political Economy of Protection*, World Bank Staff Working Paper No. 432, October 1980.

Articles

Aaronson, David, "Why Africa Stays Poor: And Why it Doesn't Have To", *The Humanist* March/April 1993.

Adedeji, Adebayo, "The European Integration Process: Lessons for Africa", *EEC-ACP Courier*, No. 125, January-February 1991.

Adeniji, Oluyemi, "Regionalism in Africa", *Security Dialogue*, Vol. 24 (2) 1993.

Alexander, Mary. "Threats to Developing Countries From EC Integration", *West Africa*, 29 June 1992.

Ankomah, Baffour, "Who isn't Afraid of 1992?", *New African*, February 1989.

Ardent, Sven W., Willet, Thomas D., "EC 92: From a North American Perspective", *Economic Journal*, vol 101, November 1991.

Asante, S.K.B. "New Hope for Africa: Pan-African economic Community", *Development and Cooperation*, No. 4, 1992.

— "Lome II: Another Machinery for updating Dependency?", *Development and Cooperation*, 3, 1981.

Baynham, Simon, "Geopolitics, Glasnost and Africa's Second Liberation: Political and Security Implications for the Continent", *Africa Insight*, Vol. 21, No. 4, 1991.

Bjerregaard, Ritt. "Population Movements in the 1990s" Challenges for Policy Makers", *Development*, No. 1 1993.

Blanc, H. "Schengen: le Chemin de la Libre Circulation en Europe", *Revue du Marche Commun*, No. 351, October 1991.

Brauer, Dieter, "Europe at a Crossroads: What Effect on the Third World?", *Development and Cooperation*, No. 3, 1993.

—"Political Conditionality in Practice", *Development and Cooperation*, No. 2, 1992.

Bressand, Albert, "Beyond Interdependence: 1992 as a Global Challenge", *International Affairs*, Vol. 66 January 1990.

Brittain, Victoria. "Africa, the Lost Continent", *New Statesman & Society*, 8 April 1994.

Brown, Walton, L. "The 1992 European Community and Africa", *TransAfrican Forum*, Fall 1992.

Cahen, Alfred, "Consequences of the EC Enlargements for Political Cooperation", *The Jerusalem Journal of International Relations*, Vol. 10, No. 3, 1988.

Cantwell, John. "Foreign Multinational and Industrial Development in Africa", Dept. of Economics, University of Reading, 1989.

Cawthorn, Robert E. "Are US Multinationals Ready for the US of Europe", *Vital Speeches*, Vol. XL No. 2, August 15, 1989.

Clarke, Hilary "Fortress Europe Confronts Third-World Asylum-Seekers", *Gemini*, 5, September 1989.

Claus, Burghard., "The Lion's Share for Francophone Countries: The Development Policy of France", *Development and Cooperation*, No. 6, 1992.

Colbourne, Desmond, "Writing Off Africa", *South Africa International*, October 1992.

Cooper, Lor, Treinen, Marie. "The New Europe: Europe in Evolution in the 1990s", *Business America*, February 24, 1992.

Davenport, Michael, "Africa and the Unimportance of Being Preferred", *Journal of Common Market Studies*, vol. 30, No. 2, June 1992.

—"The External Policy of the Community and its Effects upon the manufactured Goods of the Developing Countries", Paper prepared for Meeting Convened by the Netherlands Economic Institute and the Ministry of Foreign Affairs on 'Europe 1992 and Developing Countries', The Hague, 6-7 October 1989.

Dhasi, Antar, "The Emerging World Trading System: Some Implications for LDCs", *Development*, No. 1 1993.

Dischamps, Jean Claude, "The European Community, International Trade, and World Unity", *California Management Review*, Winter 1993.

Downes, Ruth, Bachtler, John. "Foreign Investment in Central and Eastern Europe", *European Business and Economic Development*, Vol. 1, Part 1, July 1992.

Emerson, Michael, "1992 and After: The Bicycle Theory Rides Again", *The Political Quarterly*, Vol. 59, July-September 1988.

Evans, Richard. "Contesting the Euro-Vision", *Geographical Magazine*, January 1993.

Faber, Gerrit. "The Economics of Stabex", *Journal of World Trade Law*, vol. 18, No. 1, 1988.

Faini, Richardo, de Melo, Jaime, Takacs, Wendy, "The Effect of EC-92 on the Multifibre Agreement", *European Economic Review*, vol. 36, April 1992.

Farley, Jonathan, "The Mediterranean-Southern Threats to Northern Shores?", *The World Today*, February 1994.

Fieleke, Norman S., "One Trading World, or Many: The Issue of Regional Trading Blocs", *New England Economic Review*, May/June 1992.

Garson, Jean-Pierre, "International Migration: Facts, Figures, Policies", *OECD Observer*, o. 176 June/July 1992.

Ghosh, Bimah, "1992: Third World in the Margin", *European Affairs*, Fall 1989.

Goldstein, Walter, "EC After Maastritch", *Foreign Affairs*, Winter 1992/93.

Guess, John, "The Effect of Relaxed East-West Tension on the Third World", *Urban Profile*, Spring 1990.

Guillaumont, Patrick, Guillaumont, Sylviane, "The Implications of European Monetary Union for African Countries", *Journal of Common Market Studies*, Vol. XXVIII, No 2, December 1989.

Haarh, Jens Henrik. "The Same Old Game? The EC in the International Political Economy: 1985-1991", *Cooperation and Conflict*. Vol. 28 (1).

Haslach, Robert D. "The Bright Lights of Eastern Europe", *Europe*, March 1992.

Heiba, Farouk I. Khalil, Mohammed A. "Marketing Strategies in Europe 1992: New Challenges to American Executives", Paper presented at the Academy of International Business, Northeast Conference, Baltimore, MD, 1-3 June 1992.

Hillebrand, Wolfang, "Lessons From Experience: Can Korea and Taiwan Serve as Models", *Development and Cooperation*, No. 2, 1990.

Hine, Robert C. "Regionalism and the Integration of the World Economy", *Journal of Common Market Studies*, June 1992 .
Issacs, Mark D. "Forcing a United Europe", *News American*, November 16, 1992.
Holland, Martin, "The European Community and South Africa" In Search of a Policy for the 1990s", *International Affairs*, Vol. 64, No.3, Summer 1987.
Hutchful, Eboe, "Eastern Europe: Consequences for Africa", *Review of African Political Economy*, No. 50, 1991, p. 52.
Ikein, Augustine. "Soviet Bloc Reforms and the Western Neo-Marshall Plan for Changing Eastern Europe and Implications for Developing Countries", Paper Presented at the First North American Research Conference on the Changes in Europe", Baltimore, 1-3 March 1992.
Indorf, H.H. "Political Dimensions of Interregional Cooperation: The Case of ASEAN and the EEC", *The Round Table*, No. 286, April 1983.
Isaacs Mark D. "Forcing a United Europe", *New American*, November 16, 1992.
James, Canute, "The Banana War", *African World*, November-December 1993.
Kaps, Carola. "Free Market for Africa's Farmers", *Development and Cooperation*, 5, 1987.
Katseli, Loulca T., "The Political Economy of European Integration: From Euro-sclerosis to Euro-Corporatism", *International Spectator*, Vol 24, No. 3/4, July-December, 1989.
Koekkoek, Ad., "1992 and the Developing Countries: Fortress Europe or Outward Orientation?", Ministry of Foreign Affairs, Directorate-General for International Co-operation, the Netherlands, December 1989.
Kohler, Volkmar, "EC Donor Coordination—A Shocking Balance", *Development and Cooperation*, No. 1, 1993.
Kwarteng, Charles, "Africa and the European Challenge after 1992", *International Social Science Journal*, vol. 137, August 1993.
——"Confronting the European Single Market of 1992: Challenges for the ACP and ASEAN Countries", *Journal of Developing Societies*, Vol. VIII (1992).

—"Africa and the Changing Global Arena", *TransAfrica Forum*, Spring 1996.
—"External Influences on Africa's Economic Decolonization", *TransAfrica Forum*, Winter 1989.
Lopez-Claros, Augusto, "The European Community: On the Road to Integration", *Journal of Social, Political and Economic Studies*, Fall 1987.
Mackenzie, L.D.M. "Export From ACP Countries to EEC Under Lome III Regulations", CDI Conference, Nairobi, February, 1987.
Maganza;, Glorgio, La Convention de Lome", *Commentaire Megret*, vol. 13, 1990.
Marin, Manuel (Vice-President of the EC Commission) "Lome IV—the Scope of a New Convention", *EEC-ACP Courier*, No. 120, March-April 1990.
Martin, Guy "Africa and the Ideology of EuroAfrica: Neo-Colonialism or Pan-Africanism?", *Journal of Modern African Studies*, Vol. 20, No. 2, 1992.
—"The Historical, Political and Economic Bases of France's African Policy", *Journal of Modern African Studies*, Vol. 23, No. 2, 1985.
Matsis, Demetrak, "Guestworker Policies and Apartheid: Does One Resemble the Other?", *Marquette Law Review*, Spring/Summer, V. 74, 1991.
Mattews, A., McAleese, Dermont, "LDC Primary Exports to the EC: Prospects Post-1992", Paper Prepared for Experts for Expert Meeting convened by the Netherlands Economic Institute and Organized by the Dutch Ministry of Foreign Affairs on 'Europe and Developing Countries', The Hague, 6-7 October 1989.
Mayo, Edward, "Beyond 1992: The Effects of the European Single Market on the World's Poor", The World Development Movement, London, June 1989.
Mazrui, Ali. "Eastern European Revolutions: African Origins?, *TransAfrican Forum*, Vol. 7, #2, Summer 1990.
McQueen, Malten, Stevens, Christopher, "Trade Preferences and Lome IV: Non Traditional ACP Exports to the EC", *Development Policy Review*, Vol 7, 1989.

Misser, Francois, "European Single Currency Won't Kill CFA Zone", *African Business*, June 1992.

Morna, Colleen Lowe. "Africa's First Tiger", *Africa Report*, November-December, 1991.

Musto, Stefan A. "The Common Agricultural Policy of the European Community and Its Consequences for Less Developed Countries", *Document Interne*, No. 15 1990.

Neven, Damien, Roller, Lars-Hendrik, "European Integration and Trade Flows", *European Economic Review*, Vol. 35, August 1991.

Nuscheler, Franz, "Fight the Causes of Flight, Not the Refugees", *Development and Cooperation*, No. 4, 1993.

Nye, Joseph. "Patterns and Catalyst in Regional Integration", *International Organization* 19 Autumn 1965.

Nyerere, Joseph. "More Poor for the Poor: A third World View on North-South Relations", *Development and Co-Operation*, 4, 1985.

Ohaegbulan, F. Ogboaja. "Africa and the Demise of the Soviet Bloc", *Journal of the Third World Spectrum*, Spring 1994.

—"Containment in Africa: From Truman to Reagan", *TransAfrica Forum*, Fall 1988.

Ola-Davies, George. "French Nationality Changes", *West Africa*, 31 May 1993.

Olofin, Sam. "ECOWAS and the Lome Convention: An Experiment in Complementary or Conflicting Customs Union Arrangement?", *Journal of Common Market Studies*, 16, Sept. 1977.

Randolph, Alan, Smith, Deborah. "Harmonization of the European Market: Implications for European Businesses", *European Business and Economic Development*, vol. 1, Part 1, July 1992.

Ravenhill, John, "Regional Integration and Development in Africa: Lessons from the East African Community", *Journal of Commonwealth and Comparative Politics*, November 1979.

Richards, Howard, "Developing Relations Between the EC and the Association of Southeast Asian Nations", *European Research*, February 1991.

Rist, Roy C., "Migration and Marginality: Guestworker in Germany and France", *Daedulus*, Spring 1979.

Rocher, Joseph, "GATT—The Non-Agricultural Round: The South on a Rozor-Edge", *ACP-EEC Courier*, No. 139, May-June 1993.

Samboma, J. Lahai. "Africa Must Renegotiate GATT", *New African*, April 1994.

Samuels, Micheal A. "The Decline of Multilateralism—Can We Prevent it?", *World Today*, January 1990.

Santos, dos Theotonio, "The Structure of Dependence", *American Economic Review*, Vol. 6, No. 2 May 1970.

Sassen, Jane, "Out of Africa", *International Management*, May 1992.

Sawada Margarete, "Completion of the EC Internal Market and Japanese Business Strategies", *Business Research*, No. 773, Tokyo, 1988.

Scarborough, Jack, "Global Vulnerabilities: Opportunities in International Niche Markets in an Environment of Economic Growth in Developing Countries", Paper presented at Academy of International Business Annual Conference, Baltimore, June 1-2, 1992.

Schultz, Siegfried, "Third World Foreign Debt Crisis: Which Way Out?", *Development and Cooperation*, 2, 1985.

Shaw, Timothy, Grieve, Malcolm J., "Dependence as an Approach to Understanding Continuing Inequalities in Africa", *Journal of Developing Areas*, 13, 3, 1979.

Schneidman Witney W. "Africa's Transition to Pluralism: Economic and Investment Implications", *CSIS Africa Notes*, No. 142, November 1992.

Spence, J.E. "A Post-Apartheid South Africa and the International Community", *Journal of Commonwealth and Comparative Politics,* Vol. 31 No. 1 (March 1993).

Stewart, Terrence, Edozien, Margaret, "Yowarda Truly Global Marketing Strategy" A Need to Consider Trade an investment Opportunities in West Africa", *North Carolina Journal of Investment Law and Commercial Regulations*, Vol. 17, Winter 1992.

Swain, Robert, "The European Communities and South Africa: New Threats, New Opportunities", *South Africa International*, July 1992, p. 12.

Tovias, Alfred, "Migration and the Deepening of the European Community", Paper Presented at the Third ECSA Conference, Washington, D.C., May 27-29 1993.

—"The Impact of Liberalizing Government Procurement Policies of Individual EC Countries of Trade With Non-Members", *Weltwirstschaftliches Archiv*. vol 126 # 4 December 1990.

—— "Western Europe's Ongoing Economic Integration and Its Status in the World", *Jerusalem Journal of International Relations*, Vol. II, No. 3, 1989.

Tagaras, Harissis, "Recent Developments in Community Anti-Dumping Law", *European Community Review*, No. 7, 1990.

van de Walle, Nicolas. "Is the Bundesbank Running Africa?", *The International Economy*, January/February 1994 .

Vandewalle, Dirk. "At the Periphery: North Africa, the European Community, and the End of the Cold War", *The Maghreb Review*, Vol 17, Nos. 1-2, 1992.

Verster, Jenny, "Will the Third World Lose to Eastern Europe?", *Development and Cooperation*, Vol. No. 1, 1990.

Vial, Catherine, "The European Community and Environmental Policy and Regulations", *Europe Now*, (US Dept of Commerce), September 1991.

Vigand, Vladimir, "Africa, the EEC and the CMEA", *Development Policy Review*, Vol. 6. 1988.

Viner, Jacob. *The Customs Union Issue* (The Carnegie Endowment, 1951).

Wallerstein, Immanuel, "Dependence in an Interdependent World: Limited Possibilities for Transformation Within the World Capitalist Economy", *African Studies Review*, 1974.

Wang, Jugi, "An Analysis of Three Economic Rims", *Beijing Review*, Vol. 32 May 20, 1989.

Williams, Gavin. "Africa in Retrospect and Prospect", *Africa, South of the Sahara*. London: Europa Publications, 1994.

Yannaopulas, G.W. "Mediterranean Labor in an Era of Slow Economic Growth", *World Today*, 35, December 1979.